Stepping Out of
the Brain Drain

Stepping Out of the Brain Drain

Applying Catholic Social Teaching in a New Era of Migration

Michele R. Pistone
and John J. Hoeffner

LEXINGTON BOOKS

A division of
ROWMAN & LITTLEFIELD PUBLISHERS, INC.
Lanham • Boulder • New York • Toronto • Plymouth, UK

LEXINGTON BOOKS

A division of Rowman & Littlefield Publishers, Inc.
A wholly owned subsidiary of The Rowman & Littlefield Publishing Group, Inc.
4501 Forbes Boulevard, Suite 200
Lanham, MD 20706

Estover Road
Plymouth PL6 7PY
United Kingdom

British Library Cataloguing in Publication Information Available

Library of Congress Cataloging-in-Publication Data

Pistone, Michele R.
  Stepping out of the brain drain : applying Catholic social teaching in a new era of
migration / Michele R. Pistone and John J. Hoeffner.
    p. cm.
  ISBN-13: 978-0-7391-1505-3 (pbk. : alk. paper)
  ISBN-10: 0-7391-1505-7 (pbk. : alk. paper)
  ISBN-13: 978-0-7391-1504-6 (cloth : alk. paper)
  ISBN-10: 0-7391-1504-9 (cloth : alk. paper)
  1. Emigration and immigration—Religious aspects—Catholic Church. 2. Brain drain.
  3. Catholic Church—Doctrines. I. Hoeffner, John J. II. Title.
  BX1795.E44P57 2007
  261.8'36—dc22   2006038196

Printed in the United States of America

∞™ The paper used in this publication meets the minimum requirements of American
National Standard for Information Sciences—Permanence of Paper for Printed Library
Materials, ANSI/NISO Z39.48–1992.

We dedicate this work to our mothers,

Rachael Scala-Pistone & Patricia M. Hoeffner,

and to our daughter, Julia,

who helps us to see

what our mothers see in us

Contents

Acknowledgments

Many people contributed to this project and we are indebted to them all. Special thanks go to Donald Kerwin, the Executive Director of the Catholic Legal Immigration Network, Inc., and to Professor Michael Scaperlanda, of the University of Oklahoma Law School, each of whom provided insightful and thought-provoking comments on earlier drafts of this work. We also thank Professor Charles Keely of Georgetown University and Sister Mary Louise Sullivan, MSC, former President of Cabrini College. At an early stage of the project, both Professor Keely and Sister Sullivan took particular interest in the ideas presented here and encouraged us to pursue the work.

Many professors at Villanova Law School also provided helpful comments on earlier drafts, including Michelle Anderson, Les Book, Marisa Cianciarulo, Associate Dean John Gotanda, Beth Lyon, John Murphy, and Richard Redding. We thank them all. We also thank Robert Miller, whose knowledge of Latin, *inter alia*, proved particularly helpful in resolving some knotty problems we encountered.

Our work also benefited from the thoughts and perspectives of the participants at several conferences, including the first two conferences for the *Journal of Catholic Social Thought*; an informative conference hosted by Amy Uelman at Fordham University School of Law entitled "Strangers No Longer: Immigration Law and Policy in Light of Religious Values"; and an immigration law professors' workshop at the University of Maryland School of Law organized by Professor Isabel Medina, at which Professor Lenni Benson led a thoughtful discussion on an early draft of the manuscript.

We are indebted, too, to many Villanova law students who helped along the way, including Evan Foster, Rachel Gallegos, Sara Havas, Kristen Kelly, Jared McCutcheon, Hee John Oh, Casey Stehlin, Jessica Roscoe Webb, and

Michael Wynn. Several librarians at Villanova also deserve thanks, especially Naz Pantaloni, Darren Poley, and Mary Cornelius. And, as always, Pat Brown's organizational skills saved the day again and again—we are grateful that she is in our lives.

Finally, thanks are due to Dean Mark Sargent for his continued support and his commitment to bringing the Catholic intellectual tradition to bear on the development of law and public policy, and to Dr. Barbara Wall, Special Assistant to the President on Mission, whose leadership in the study of Catholic social thought at Villanova University inspired us to pursue this project.

Michele R. Pistone
John J. Hoeffner
Villanova, PA

Foreword

The Catholic Church supports the right to emigrate. And although it recognizes the right of the receiving country to control its borders by limiting immigration, it "rejects such control when it is exerted merely for the purpose of acquiring additional wealth. More powerful economic nations, which have the ability to protect and feed their residents, have a stronger obligation to accommodate migration flows."[1]

The Church, in its social teaching, has, however, taken a dim view of what is commonly referred to as "brain drain" migration where highly educated or trained persons migrate from less developed countries to more developed countries. The Church's position—its reluctance to embrace this type of transnational migration—seems to be based on two assumptions. First, the highly skilled emigrant is abandoning her country of origin, which might be in desperate need of her services to aid in its own development, and emigrates merely out of a selfish desire to advance her own position in the world with very little if any thought given to those she leaves behind. Second, the receiving country exploits its economic advantage to gain the services and talents of the immigrant at the expense of the sending country, which in some sense has a greater claim to her labor.

Armed with data from the past few decades, Pistone and Hoeffner convincingly demonstrate that the economic, social, and psychological situation surrounding STEP OUT migration (their term designed to replace the "brain drain" nomenclature) is far more fluid than the Church had previously assumed. This is partly due, as the authors point out, to technological advances that have made it easier for people to move back and forth between sending and receiving countries (i.e., the shift from boats to jet airplanes) and communicate between sending and receiving countries (i.e., from cable to telephone to e-mail to Skype). With these lowered transactions costs, there is often a dynamic interchange between the emigrant and her country of origin. Far from abandoning the sending country, the emigrant is often involved in knowledge transfers, monetary transfers, and technology transfers, all to the development and aid of the sending country.

I read an earlier draft of this book with a very skeptical eye. My gut reaction when I started reading was that the authors had it wrong and that, in the absence of dire hardship or similar exceptional circumstances, we should discourage the transnational migration of highly skilled people from less developed countries to more developed countries. But, as I continued to read, Pistone and Hoeffner persuaded me that STEP OUT migration can be and often is a good consistent with the human values proposed by the Catholic Church in its social teaching, and that the Church ought to embrace it as it embraces other forms of migration.

In researching and writing this book, *Stepping Out of the Brain Drain: Applying Catholic Social Teaching in a New Era of Migration*, Pistone and Hoeffner serve as living examples of the lay person's important role of thinking with the mind of the Church as the Church engages the temporal order. Vatican II said, "[S]ince they are tightly bound up in all types of temporal affairs, it is [the laity's] special task to order and to throw light upon these affairs in such a way that they may come into being and then continually increase according to Christ to the praise of the Creator and the Redeemer."[2]

Much of the laity's work involves bringing the Church's human and personalist values to the world, proposing that the world set aside the seemingly endless quest for power and dominion, which can only come at the expense of other persons, and, instead, see the dignity and value in each and every human being and the importance of community in the development and flourishing of the person. But, every once in a while, the laity, in full humility, must shed light upon these temporal affairs by suggesting that the Church, in its use of secular tools (i.e., economics) to assess temporal affairs, has missed something vital and that its specific proposal about the temporal order (frowning upon STEP OUT migration) is inconsistent with its own deepest convictions about the human person in community. This is one of those occasions.

The Church sees a sacred dimension to time, space, and history. A person is born into a particular family, society, and country. Those communities, each in their own way, have a duty to assist the child in realizing her full human potential. As the child grows into an adult, she then has a corresponding duty to work for the common good and development of her family, the society, and her country. In this reciprocal way, the inviolate dignity of the person and the common good of the community are served. Where human development and flourishing are impossible within a given community, the Church teaches that the person has a right to leave—to emigrate. But, emigration is the second best option.

The best option is the creation of an environment where emigration would be unnecessary. The brightest and most educated persons in a country are the ones most likely to possess the talents and skills needed to create the economic and political systems necessary for human development and flourishing. If they leave their homeland to seek their own selfish ends, they have abandoned their community, violating their duty to work toward the creation of just societal structures where all who are left behind—who can't migrate to a better life—have a real chance at development.

Based upon outmoded and probably inadequate data, the Church seemed to assume that transnational migration of highly educated and skilled labor from less developed to more developed countries was a one-way street to the detriment of the sending country and to the benefit of the emigrant and her new home. Pistone and Hoeffner "shed light" on the subject, demonstrating that such emigration/immigration is often a dynamic two-way street, and that the country of origins benefits far more than originally assumed.

It is my hope that Catholic social teaching will incorporate the insights provided in this volume. While continuing to caution against emigration for purely selfish and greedy reasons, the Church's social doctrine ought to reflect the nuanced view that emigration might, in some circumstances, aid in the sending country's development. It is also my hope that this volume will serve to attract policymakers and others to the richness of Catholic social teaching, which has much valuable insight to offer a world grappling with many complex issues, including the transnational migration of millions of people.

Michael A. Scaperlanda
Gene and Elaine Edwards Family Chair in Law
Professor of Law
University of Oklahoma College of Law

NOTES

1. United States Conference of Catholic Bishops and Conferencia del Episcopado Mexicano, *Strangers No Longer: Together on the Journey of Hope: A Pastoral Letter Concerning Migration from the Catholic Bishops of Mexico and the United States* (U.S. Conference of Catholic Bishops & Conferencia del Episcopado Mexicano, 2003), par. 36.

2. Second Vatican Council, *Lumen Gentium* (1964), par. 31.

Preface

The Roman Catholic Church is generally supportive of immigration. The one major exception to this general rule—and the focus of this book—concerns immigration to developed countries by skilled and educated persons from developing countries. With regard to this exception, our book ultimately concludes that the Church's current policy is an anachronism, dependent on economic assumptions largely rebutted by events. We accordingly recommend adoption of a new policy—one that is more open to such immigration—as more consonant with current economic reality, as well as more consistent with the larger world of Catholic social teaching. (The definition and meaning of "Catholic social teaching" is discussed throughout this work; for now, we might simply draw a distinction between, in the words of Pope John Paul II, teachings concerning "a purely otherworldly salvation," and Catholic social teaching's focus on "specific human situations, both individual and communal, national and international.").[1]

Because the authors of this work are two Catholic laypersons, our subject matter necessarily implicates the larger issue of lay participation in the life of the Catholic Church. The contention that lay Catholics need to take on a greater role in their Church has been argued with increasing frequency and fervor in recent years.[2] There is, however, ample opposition to increasing the laicization of the Church and, in many respects, positions could not be more polarized. Thus, while some assert that the Church can be saved from catastrophe only by expanding opportunities for meaningful lay input, others regard such an expansion as more likely to cause, rather than to prevent, a crisis in the Church.[3]

The scope of this larger debate far exceeds issues of Catholic social teaching. Yet Catholic social teaching is part of that larger debate, as was pointedly illustrated to us by the response to an early query to a publisher about this work: "I do not like people who pretend to teach the Pope how to do his job."

We think that a view such as the publisher's is a mistake when made in reference to the present work and writings like it. The focus in this work is on (1) expounding current social teaching and (2) identifying various factual changes that have occurred in the world over the last forty years which have had the combined effect of undermining a small portion of the social teaching. Both Pope John Paul II and Pope John XXIII not only expressly commended the first activity,[4] but they also recognized the general importance of the second.[5] Indeed, in *Mater et Magistra*, Pope John XXIII urged all people of goodwill to undertake the "difficult, though lofty task" of applying the principles of Catholic social teaching to "the various situations of time or place."[6]

This work represents, if not precisely such an application, certainly a good faith attempt at one. Moreover, there are substantial reasons for regarding works such as ours here not as attempting to do the work of the pope but, to the contrary, as "making" work—albeit of a welcome nature—for him. As the Second Vatican Council indicated, the Church is obligated to identify and correct "deficiencies" in church teaching.[7] Given the scope and fact-dependent nature of much of Catholic social teaching, the often difficult and uncertain nature of many fact-finding tasks, and the complications arising from the turbulence of a dynamically changing world in which even previously well established facts sometimes may be found in flux, the obligation articulated by the Council seems an awesome one, indeed. One might even say that the task is impossible to do in a timely manner, absent assistance from the many lay people who by occupation or avocation find themselves on the front lines of social, political, economic and/or technological changes which may have consequences for the continued viability or relevance of particular Catholic social teachings.

In light of this, and without suggesting that our own conclusions are free from possible error, it seems that lay input of the type offered here should be encouraged rather than discouraged. The Church need not ever accept anyone's conclusions but its own, but it is for the good of the Church's social teaching that the chance of identifying changes in circumstance that make established teaching no longer responsive to the world *as it is* is maximized. It is our hope that the instant work might serve as a kind of model in this regard, in that it represents a relatively exhaustive treatment of a relatively specific social teaching formed at a time substantially different than our own, with the significance of some of the most important differences linked to the necessity for change in ways that might not be obvious to the casual observer. These are exactly the circumstances, we think, in which lay input is most likely to prove of value.

While we thus believe that this work is highly relevant for Roman Catholics and members of other faith communities in dialogue with the Catholic Church,[8] it additionally is our hope that members of the general community, and especially advocates of human rights, also might find it informative. A familiarity with Catholic social teaching can benefit members of the broader community in at least two ways. First, theorists of modern liberal democracy agree that political discourse benefits from the tumult of a multitude of voices.[9] Among the benefits is a greater likelihood that new ideas will be heard and that all ideas will be forced to address hard questions.[10] Catholic social teaching is a legitimate participant in this process; as Professor Stephen Carter has noted, political discourse should welcome "arguments from religious tradition . . . as it welcomes every useful, thoughtful voice, not because their epistemological suppositions are universally shared, but because even those with very different epistemologies might learn—or teach."[11] This is especially true because, as Professor Michael Scaperlanda explains, with its reliance on natural law reasoning, Catholic social teaching is "objectively available to all of us independent of our own faith (or non-faith) traditions."[12] A knowledge of Catholic social teaching, or any other serious body of thought,[13] gives one access to a fuller spectrum of ideas, and makes one better positioned generally to advance those ideas that are right, and challenge those ideas that are wrong, all to—our system assumes—the larger society's long-term benefit. To the extent a mutual engagement between the larger community and Catholic social teaching is lacking, so too will this societal benefit be lacking.[14]

Second, an increased awareness of Catholic social teaching also could enable the general community to gain a better understanding of the political discourse that already takes place. Catholics have constituted 26 percent of the U.S. electorate in recent national elections, and "represent probably the largest swing constituency in the nation."[15] Not surprisingly, politicians of all political stripes make efforts to connect with this constituency; indeed, they have done so in the United States—with some notable exceptions—for over 150 years.[16] Recent efforts sometimes include subtle and nuanced appeals rooted in the language of Catholic social teaching.[17] An informed electorate that understands the language of Catholic social teaching will better comprehend the nature of those appeals and their implications. On the other hand, those members of the electorate who are not conversant in the particular language of the social teachings invariably will miss the full meaning of what is being communicated with such appeals, however attentively such persons may listen.

Apart from the general benefits noted above, human rights advocates in particular can gain an additional advantage through an understanding of the

Church's social teachings. Among international organizations, "the Catholic Church [is] one of the most visible non-governmental actors in the struggle for human rights."[18] Moreover, the Church, along with other faith communities, may often be the most effective ally of advocates seeking to promote a human rights agenda. As one commentator has noted,

> Neither governments nor international agencies, such as the United Nations, are especially effective advocates of human rights. Either their own self-interest, or pressing diplomatic reasons, severely limit[] governmental moral leverage on human rights questions. Transnational, nongovernmental advocates of human rights . . . lack, generally, adequate resources to organize, nurture, or protect local, indigenous human rights advocacy in places as diverse as Lithuania or Bolivia. The churches are uniquely on the spot to monitor human rights abuses and sustain human rights advocacy. The Church has local, grass roots listening posts, and often the churches are the only possible sources of information across national boundaries.[19]

Accordingly, the Catholic Church can provide invaluable assistance to human rights advocates in helping to advance the human rights agenda. And because Catholic social teaching lies "[a]t the base of [the Church's] action" on behalf of human rights,[20] to the extent that human rights advocates can utilize the language and framework of Catholic social teaching to appeal to the Catholic community, the more effective such advocates will be in persuading the Church to assist in their work.[21]

Gaining such assistance is a particularly desirable goal with respect to advocacy on behalf of migrants, because the Catholic Church's voice is particularly credible on matters involving migration policy both within the United States and abroad. This credibility has been earned through extensive experience. On a daily basis, the American Catholic Church's network of affiliated social service institutions at the grassroots level offers immigrants everything from food and shelter to education and legal services.[22] As an example of the extent of the Church's commitment, "[s]ince the passage of the Refugee Act of 1980, the Office of Migration and Refugee Services of the U.S. Catholic Conference has resettled some 650,000 refugees—nearly 32 percent of the total number—and more than any other agency."[23] The Catholic Church's history in the United States as an "immigrant church" further reinforces its credibility on matters related to immigrants.[24] Similar efforts by the Church abroad deepen this credibility still more.[25]

In sum, with all due modesty, there is ample reason for Catholics and non-Catholics alike to read this book. The most important reason, however, has not yet been mentioned. We believe that, in general, the migration of skilled and educated persons from developing to developed countries tends to benefit more than harm than world's poorest populations. Given the amount of poverty in the world, where so many people live at barely subsistence levels,[26] the "benefits" we speak of are measured most crucially in terms of lives saved and tragedies averted. It is our hope that we have presented our argument persuasively, because the more support that is generated on behalf of policies that allow the migration of skilled citizens from developing countries, the more likely it is that the poor in those countries will receive some measure of respite from their very difficult lives that are far too often marked most of all by unremitting want.

NOTES

1. Pope John Paul II, *Centesimus Annus* (1991), sec. 5. Unless otherwise indicated, all quotations of papal encyclicals in this work have been drawn from *Catholic Social Thought: The Documentary Heritage* (Maryknoll: Orbis Books, 1992), the well-known collection edited by David J. O'Brien and Thomas A. Shannon. Their book also includes the Second Vatican Council's *Gaudium et Spes*, the Synod of Bishops' *Justice in the World*, and the U.S. bishops' pastoral letters, *The Challenge of Peace* and *Economic Justice for All*. O'Brien and Shannon's book has been the source for our references to all these works. Unless otherwise indicated, all quotations of papal or Vatican documents other than encyclicals are to versions found on the Vatican's official website, http://www.vatican.va, which also, of course, remains a comprehensive source for the encyclicals as well.

2. See Peter Steinfels, *A People Adrift: The Crisis of the Roman Catholic Church in America* (New York: Simon & Schuster, 2003), 11–12, 102, 307, 358; Gerald V. Bradley, "Lay Leadership," *Fellowship of Catholic Scholars Quarterly* 24:2 (Spring 2001): 1.

3. See generally Steinfels, *A People Adrift*, passim (arguing that greater lay involvement is both necessary and inevitable, but presenting concerns others have about the consequences of a decrease in clerical leadership). See also David Gibson, *The Coming Catholic Church: How the Faithful Are Shaping a New American Catholicism* (San Francisco: HarperSanFrancisco, 2003), 343–45 (arguing that numerous structural changes that would substantially increase lay involvement in the Church are needed to prevent institutional decline); George Weigel, *The Courage to Be Catholic: Crisis, Reform, and the Future of the Church, passim* (New York: Basic Books, 2002) (arguing that a culture of dissent has created an internal schism in the Church, and that greater adherence to Church teaching is required to resolve the current crisis). Proponents of each view might find support in the example of a popular but conflict-ridden parish in Washington, D.C., in which lay involvement is extensive. See Jim Naughton, *Catholics in Crisis, passim* (Reading: Addison-Wesley, 1996) (portraying Holy Trinity parish in Washington, D.C.'s Georgetown section). Interestingly, the movement toward greater lay leadership is not a novel development in the American Church, but harkens back to the Church's pioneer roots, which often saw lay-initiated parishes developed without clergy and governed, in substantial part, by powerful boards of lay trustees. F. Michael Perko, *Catholic & American: A Popular History* (Huntington: Our Sunday Visitor, 1989), 58, 116, 137, 140.

4. Pope John Paul II, *Centesimus Annus*, sec. 56 (thanking "all those who have devoted themselves to studying, expounding and making better known Christian social teaching"); Pope John XXIII, *Mater et Magistra* (1961), par. 224 (noting that "the laity have much to contribute through their work and effort, that this teaching of the Catholic Church regarding the social question be more and more widely diffused").

5. See Pope John Paul II, *Sollicitudo Rei Socialis* (1987), sec. 3 (noting that the Church's "teaching in the social sphere . . . is ever *new*, because it is subject to the necessary and opportune adaptations suggested by the changes in historical conditions and by the unceasing flow of the events which are the setting of the life of people and society"; Pope John XXIII, *Pacem in Terris* (1963), sec. 155 (noting that the "pronounced dynamism" of modern society makes concrete applications of Catholic social teaching never "definitive").

6. Pope John XXIII, *Mater et Magistra*, sec. 221.

7. See *Second Vatican Council, Decree on Ecumenism, Unitatis Redintegratio* (1964): sec. 6, available at http://www.vatican.va. See also Michele R. Pistone, "The Devil in the Details: How Specific Should Catholic Social Teaching Be?," *Journal of Catholic Social Thought* (2004): 507, 517 (noting that the Church might more fully satisfy its obligation to fix "deficiencies" by soliciting continued "input from experts in the subject matter of the more concrete social teachings").

8. "Catholics and Protestants are in serious dialogue with one another on social issues and social theory; the literature is substantial. There also have been less extensive Catholic-Jewish dialogues on issues facing society." Charles E. Curran, *Catholic Social Teaching, 1891–Present: A Historical, Theological, and Ethical Analysis* (Washington, D.C.: Georgetown University Press, 2002), 250.

9. Thomas I. Emerson, *The System of Freedom of Expression* (New York, Random House, 1970), 6–7. As Professor Emerson noted, "An individual who seeks knowledge and truth must hear all sides of the question, consider all alternatives, test his judgment by exposing it to opposition, and make full use of different minds." Moreover, "The reasons which make open discussion essential for an intelligent individual judgment likewise make it imperative for rational social judgment." Emerson, *The System of Freedom of Expression*, 6–7.

10. Emerson, *The System of Freedom of Expression*, 7. Indeed, as Michael Novak has noted, the same dynamic of open discussion that can strengthen and sharpen ideas in the larger society also must be at play in the development of Catholic social teaching, if it is to fulfill the hopes its supporters have for it. Michael Novak, *Catholic Social Thought & Liberal Institutions: Freedom with Justice* (New Brunswick: Transaction, 1989), 244 ("The competition of ideas is as necessary to Catholic social thought as it is to the free society."); Michael Novak, *The Catholic Ethic and the Spirit of Capitalism* (New York: Free Press, 1993), 154 (stating that all treatments of Catholic social teaching "deserve to be submitted to rigorous criticism in the lively and active 'public square' of civil society").

11. Stephen L. Carter, *The Culture of Disbelief: How American Law and Politics Trivialize Religious Devotion* (New York: Basic, 1993), 232.

12. Michael Scaperlanda, "Immigration Justice: Beyond Liberal Egalitarian and Communitarian Perspectives," *Review of Social Economy* 57 (1999): 523, 533. *See*

Pope John Paul II. Address to the Members of the Pro Pontifice Foundation (September 12, 1999) (stating that the mission of Catholic social teaching "can be shared by anyone who wishes to place the human person and the common good at the center of every social project"); Bishop Dr. Walter Kasper, "The Theological Foundation of Human Rights," *The Catholic Lawyer* 34 (1991): 253, 261 (noting that, in the "ascending natural law" tradition, "the foundation of human dignity is derived from human nature itself," and that this foundation "enables the Church to address itself beyond the confines of Christendom, listening to the voice of conscience of all people of goodwill, and to work together with them"). "While biblical references and religiously based exhortations have always been included in Roman Catholic social teaching, they usually have functioned, as they did for Thomas [Aquinas], as authoritative support for conclusions derived more centrally from natural law appeals to what seems reasonable and fair." Lisa Sowle Cahill, "The Catholic Tradition: Religion, Morality, and the Common Good," *Journal of Law & Religion* 5, no. 1 (1987): 75, 92–93. *See also* Curran, *Catholic Social Teaching, 1891–Present,* 45 (noting post-Vatican II "documents do not consider the Scriptures in and for their own sake; they use the Scriptures to give support to moral teachings").

13. Even most commentators from outside the Church agree that Catholic social teaching represents a serious attempt to grapple with complex social questions. See, e.g., Adrian Hastings et al., *The Oxford Companion to Christian Thought* (Oxford: Oxford University Press, 2000), 675, 676 ("Official Roman Catholic social teaching presents, cumulatively, an impressive body of doctrine").

14. The loss will be especially keenly felt in areas like human rights and immigration, which "are different [than many problems] because they do not admit of single-state solutions." Philip Bobbitt, *The Shield of Achilles: War, Peace, and the Course of History* (London: Novello, 2002), 697. Rather, "[o]nly coordinated action within the society of states can treat these particular problems effectively and with an attention to their interconnection." Philip Bobbitt, *The Shield of Achilles,* 697. Since successfully implementing solutions in these areas will require real agreement across the society of states, the quality of being open to new perspectives is a *sine qua non* for those aiming to develop such solutions. Indeed, a "World Migration Organization" has been proposed to identify problems and to facilitate the dialogue necessary to reach the required multi-state solutions. See Jagdish Bhagwati, "A Champion for Migrating Peoples." *A Stream of Windows: Unsettling Reflections on Trade, Immigration, and Democracy* (Cambridge: MIT Press, 1998): 315, 315–17.

15. Adam Clymer, "Bush Aggressively Courts Catholic Voters for 2004," *New York Times,* June 1, 2001, A14. *See* Mark J. Rozell, "'The Catholic Vote'? No Such Thing." *Pittsburgh Post-Gazette,* August 8, 2004, J1 (noting "that the Catholic vote in the United States is deeply divided").

16. See George J. Marlin, *The American Catholic Voter: Two Hundred Years of Political Impact* (Chicago: St. Augustine's Press, 2004).

17. *See* Appendix A for examples of and comments upon this phenomenon.

18. David Hollenbach, *Claims in Conflict: Retrieving and Renewing the Catholic Human Rights Tradition* (New York: Paulist Press, 1979), 1.

19. John A. Coleman, "Catholic Human Rights Theory: Four Challenges to an Intellectual Tradition," *The Journal of Law and Religion* 2 (1984): 343, 344. See also

Patricia W. Fagen, *Bibliography of Human Rights*, 17 (1980) (stating advocacy for human rights "can occur only where there exists some institutional umbrella that can protect human rights advocates and offer both political and material support for human rights activities. . . . Almost everywhere, the churches play the most critical role. Religious groups, when internally strong, are the least vulnerable institutions.").

20. Hollenbach, *Claims in Conflict*, 1.

21. It also has been suggested that study of the social teaching of the Catholic Church and other churches is important because "the churches offer a narrative framework within which human rights can become coherent and be embraced as something more than a collection of abstract rules." Martin Shupack, "The Churches and Human Rights: Catholic and Protestant Human Rights Views as Reflected in Church Statements," *Harvard Journal of Human Rights* 6 (1993): 127, 153, 154–55, 157. Such a narrative, Shupack contends, can "strengthen respect for human rights and increase the opprobrium attached to their violation." Shupack, 153. Absent such a narrative, Shupack fears for the permanence of any human rights regime. Shupack, 154–55 (lamenting that "in the liberal democracies the rhetoric of rights is becoming less compelling because it cannot anchor itself in a greater moral and intellectual framework that can provide meaning and bring conviction"). See also Hollenbach, *Claims in Conflict*, 1 (arguing that "Catholic thought may prove an important resource for all participants" in the human rights debate because the "theoretical sophistication with which the tradition has addressed a wide array of human rights issues has given it both conceptual strength and practical suppleness"); Scaperlanda, "Immigration Justice," 532–33 (arguing Catholic social teaching provides "a stronger foundation for a just immigration policy" than the liberal egalitarian and communitarian perspectives).

22. See chapter 4 and Appendix B.

23. Terry Coonan, "There Are No Strangers Among Us: Catholic Social Teaching and U.S. Immigration Law" *The Catholic Lawyer* 40 (2000): 105, 161 n.187.

24. See chapter 4.

25. In addition to its work on behalf of migrants to the United States, the Catholic Church is also one of the largest agencies providing hands-on assistance to refugees and migrants worldwide and advocating globally on behalf of migrant rights. It has a presence in almost every country, and its positions influence many intergovernmental agencies. For instance, Catholic Relief Services, just one of the U.S. Catholic bishops' overseas projects, reached more than 62 million people in 91 countries in 2001 alone. Catholic Relief Services, Annual Report 2 (2002).

26. Indeed, a recent report by the U.N. Food and Agriculture Organization estimates that 815 million people suffer from malnourishment in developing countries. Food and Agriculture Organization, United Nations, "The State of Food Insecurity in the World: Monitoring Progress Towards the World Food Summit and Millennium Development Goals," 6 (2004). Moreover, "[h]alf the human race — 3 billion people — still lives on less than $2 a day. More than 1 billion do not have safe water to drink. Two billion lack adequate sanitation. Another 2 billion have no electricity." Colin L. Powell, "Aid for the Enterprising." *Washington Post*, June 10, 2002, A21.

Part One

DEFINITIONS

Chapter One

The Scope of This Book

Migration by skilled and educated professionals, especially those migrating from developing to developed countries, has garnered international attention since the 1950s. By one account, more than 1,800 works were written on the topic—popularly called "brain drain"—during the four decades between 1954 and 1995.[1] Since 1995, interest in "brain drain" has grown, and is now greater than at any time in the last thirty years.[2] In one way or another, the "brain drain" phenomenon touches almost every country in the world—as a sending country, a receiving country, or both. "Brain drain" occurs, for example, from Ghana to Nigeria, from China to Thailand, from South Korea to the United States, from the countries of Eastern Europe to those of Western Europe, from Algeria to France, from Russia to Israel, from Latin American countries to Spain, from India to Canada, and from Canada to the United States.

This work focuses on the migration of skilled and educated persons from developing to developed countries and, to that extent, is about both "brain drain" the term and "brain drain" the phenomenon. It has two central goals. The first aims at expediting the replacement, in the scholarly and popular literature, of the imprecise and decidedly biased term "brain drain" with an alternative and more appropriate terminology. As detailed below, it increasingly has been recognized that "brain drain" misleadingly describes the phenomenon of migration by skilled and educated individuals from developing to developed countries. While a sound nomenclature might not be a prerequisite to sound thinking, it is surely a good place to start; accordingly, we propose, in chapter 2, the replacement of "brain drain" with a new term—"STEP OUT" migration—with STEP OUT being an acronym for Scientific, Technical, and Educated Professionals Out of Underdeveloped Territories.

From others' prior attempts at developing a new terminology, we know that
technical and dry language, such as "outflow of trained personnel from developing to developed countries," cannot overcome the ingrained advantage
of the seriously flawed, but well-known and vivid, "brain drain" metaphor.
Among other advantages, STEP OUT migration provides an easily remem-
bered alternative metaphor, one that neutrally and appropriately suggests a
movement away from a home base, while avoiding the pejorative connota-
tions of "brain drain."

Our second and much larger aim is to explore and assess Catholic social
teaching's position on the phenomenon that we call STEP OUT migration.
As discussed in chapter 3, Catholic social teaching refers to the collective
body of the Roman Catholic Church's teachings on social and political issues. For four decades, Catholic social teaching, especially as articulated
by the U. S. Catholic bishops, has asserted that developed countries should
discourage immigration by skilled and educated individuals from lesser-
developed countries, and that the individuals themselves should migrate
with reluctance and only upon the utmost necessity. The basis for Catholic
opposition to "brain drain" immigration has three elements: first, the sending country is unfairly hurt by the emigration of skilled or educated individuals; second, the choice to emigrate rather than to remain in one's home
country and help it to develop is often a selfish or greedy act; and third, a
developed country that allows such individuals to immigrate also is selfish
or greedy because it is enriching itself at the expense of poorer nations. A
mix of economic and ethical considerations informs each of these elements—indeed, inevitably so, as "immigration is par excellence an issue
that is at the crossroads of economics and ethics."[3]

Since the U.S. Catholic bishops' policy against "brain drain" immigration
was first formulated, however, both the economic and ethical foundations
for the policy have been undermined in several important respects. In the
economic sphere, this is partly due to an increased understanding of the nature of economic development and of migration—that is to say, certain aspects of these realities are now better understood. Probably even more important than the new understandings of "old" reality, however, are new
changes in reality itself, in particular, the changes engendered by the ongo-
ing revolutions in technology and globalization. These new realities, deeply
felt but not yet fully understood, have huge implications for migration policy in general, and for the economic and ethical foundations of Catholic social teaching's position on "brain drain," or STEP OUT migration, in particular.

To give one example of the latter type, one ethics-based ground for
Catholic social teaching's opposition to STEP OUT migration is the belief

THE CHURCH AND STEP OUT MIGRATION

The Church is decidedly unenthusiastic about, and even actively discouraging of, STEP OUT migration. Illustrating the concerns of the Church, the Sacred Congregation for Bishops stated in 1969 that

> [e]ven though they have a right of emigrating, citizens are held to remember that they have the right and the duty . . . to contribute according to their ability to the true progress of their own community. Especially in underdeveloped areas where all resources must be put to urgent use, those men gravely endanger the public good, who, particularly possessing mental powers or wealth, are enticed by greed and temptation to emigrate. They deprive their community of the material and spiritual aid it needs.

Seven years later, the U.S. bishops repeated the sentiment of the Sacred Congregation for Bishops by denouncing U.S. immigration policies that facilitated STEP OUT migration:

> [T]he special preference afforded by the United States to highly skilled persons should be restricted. Our immigration policy should not encourage a flow of educated persons needed for development in other countries. . . . It does not make good sense to direct foreign aid to developing countries and at the same time receive reverse foreign aid in the form of professional persons whose talents are badly needed in the same countries.

Source: *People on the Move: A Compendium of Church Documents on the Pastoral Concern for Migrants and Refugees* (Washington, D.C.: United States Catholic Conference, 1988), 65, 85.

that, by emigrating, skilled and educated persons render themselves unable to contribute to their homelands, a serious indictment according to Catholic social teaching because the teaching stresses the individual's duty to make this kind of a contribution. However, while it is true that such a failure to contribute may amount to a failure of duty, it is no longer true that migration so isolates STEP OUT migrants from their homelands that they are, in most cases, unable to make such a contribution. Massive technological change is largely responsible for this development. Moreover, in our globalized economy, many of the most important contributions that migrants can make are possible *only because* they have migrated. The ethical implications of these new developments have not yet been completely absorbed by Catholic social teaching.

These new developments will be fully discussed in Parts IV and V. Parts II and III will lay the foundation for this discussion by exploring the content of Catholic social teaching in general, as well as the historical development and content of the teaching's specific application to immigration issues. In the latter discussion, it will be noted that the Church's strictures against STEP OUT migration represent a great exception in a social teaching that is otherwise extremely encouraging to migrants. After Parts IV and V examine how developments in technology and globalization have coalesced to create a new environment that facilitates contributions by STEP OUT migrants to their home countries, and thereby facilitates the ability of migrants to fulfill the duty imposed by Catholic social teaching, Part VI will show that recent developments in Catholic social teaching have increasingly recognized the seriousness of the deprivation that can befall individuals when they are unable to productively deploy their talents within a society. In other words, Parts IV, V, and VI collectively will demonstrate that as world developments have made it easier for STEP OUT migrants to fulfill duties imposed on them by Catholic social teaching, developments in Catholic social teaching itself have made it easier to justify migration away from societies that, intentionally or not, deny their own people the opportunity to freely and fully exercise their talents.

This combination of events, along with many other factors discussed in this book, make it imperative that a reassessment of the Church's opposition to STEP OUT migration be undertaken. We conclude that such a reappraisal cannot help but determine that the current policy should be amended. Part VII outlines a recommended new policy, which would provide greater opportunities for poor countries to develop, while enhancing opportunities for STEP OUT migrants to assist in that development. Those who feel most keenly the individual and national dislocations that can result from STEP OUT migration should be the greatest advocates of such a change for, as Pope John Paul II recognized, in the end successful development is the only remedy that can work in limiting the "push" factors that are the cause of every substantial migration.[4]

NOTES

1. Anne Marie Gaillard and Jacques Gaillard, *International Migration of the Highly Qualified: A Bibliographic and Conceptual Itinerary* (Staten Island: Center for Migration Studies, 1998), 9, 11. Indeed, many more than 1,800 works were written on the topic during this time period; the bibliography establishing the cited number excluded, *inter alia*, "writings devoted exclusively to the legal aspects of migration," and many psychological and anthropological studies.

2. Jagdish Bhagwati, "Borders Beyond Control," *Foreign Affairs* 98, no. 99 (January/February 2003): 82; B. Lindsay Lowell, "Skilled Migration Abroad or Human

Capital Flight?" *Migration Information Source* (Migration Policy Institute, June 1, 2003), at http://www.migrationinformation.org/Feature/display.cfm?ID=135.

3. Jagdish Bhagwati, "Sanctuary," *A Stream of Windows: Unsettling Reflections on Trade, Immigration, and Democracy* (Cambridge: MIT Press, 1998): 343, 344.

4. See Pope John Paul II, "The Church and Illegal Immigrants: Message of Pope John Paul II for World Migration Day" (July 25, 1995), *The Pope Speaks* (January/February 1996): 8, 9, 41 (stating that to achieve "long-lasting results" in curbing the flow of immigration it will be necessary to "eliminate underdevelopment [and] [t]he present economic and social imbalance").

Chapter Two

STEP OUT Migration:
A New Term for Brain Drain

Before addressing the Catholic social teaching issues that constitute the bulk of this book, it is necessary briefly to discuss the preliminary matter of the terminology that we will employ. As noted previously, the phenomenon of migration by skilled and educated persons is most commonly referred to as "brain drain," a phrase we believe should be replaced by a new term, STEP OUT migration. In this chapter, we detail the origins of the "brain drain" phrase, its shortcomings, the shortcomings and failures of prior alternative terms, and the advantages of the new term proposed here.

"Brain drain" apparently originated in 1957, in Ayn Rand's novel, *Atlas Shrugged*.[1] The first academic use of the term occurred in 1962, in a report by the British Royal Society detailing the migration of British scientists and engineers to the United States.[2] The term quickly became popular, especially among opponents of the migration of educated persons from rich to poor countries, who recognized "brain drain" as a catchy and rhetorically effective label. Indeed, the term even found favor in official U.S. government publications[3] and in non-English speaking nations, where it sometimes was translated literally (the German "*Gehirnenttrug*"), and sometimes approximately. Illustrating the tenor of the times, in the latter cases the translation "quite often increase[ed] the original pejorative meaning of brain drain," e.g., "*hémorragie de la matiére grise*."[4]

In the forty-plus years since its introduction into the migration lexicon, "brain drain" has done some traveling of its own. The meaning of the term has broadened well beyond its original use describing a particular period in the history of a specific type of migration from Great Britain to the United States, so that it now can additionally refer to non-scientifically trained persons as well as highly trained scientists, or to students who are not yet highly trained in any subject, or to any combination of these groups.[5] Indeed, one writer has suggested that the meaning of the phrase appropriately may shift depending upon the state of development of the sending country.[6] Certainly, "brain drain" has been "used to describe the migration of trained manpower in general and from developing to developed countries in particular."[7]

One of the problems with the term is that it has gained its additional meanings without shedding previously acquired ones. Thus, while "brain drain" has been used "particularly in connection with the migration of skilled manpower from developing to developed countries,"[8] it is still used in other contexts. During the "new economy" euphoria of recent years, for example, many publications in the decidedly developed country of Canada lamented the "brain drain" caused by the movement of educated Canadians to the United States;[9] similar articles have recently been written concerning the "brain drain" from Western Europe to the United States.[10] Earlier, articles discussed the "brain drain" from Ghana to Nigeria.[11] Other writings have noted Israel's unique gain from the demise of the Soviet Union,[12] while Arab countries may suffer from a "female brain drain."[13] Even within the United States, some areas are said to be victims of "brain drain."[14]

As the meanings of the term have multiplied, to a certain extent its scholarly utility has correspondingly declined. Imprecision, however, has never been the main objection to the "brain drain" term. Rather, as explained by the prominent international economist, Harry Johnson,[15] the principal objection has long been that "brain drain" "is obviously a loaded phrase, involving implicit definitions of economic and social welfare and implicit assertions about facts. This is so because the term 'drain' conveys a strong implication of serious loss."[16] Scholars who dispute the factual support for this implication naturally regard "brain drain" as an inappropriately "pejorative description of one aspect of a process that has been going on throughout human history," especially if they also believe that that process "has contributed a great deal to both the rise in human living standards—economic development—and the improvement in the quality of human life—cultural and social progress."[17] Interestingly, "brain drain" also has been attacked by those who share the pejorative view of STEP OUT migration, on the ground that it disparages emigrants not deemed part of the "brain drain."[18]

In response to one or the other of these objections, alternatives to the term "brain drain" often have been employed. "Transfer of talent" is a substitute term preferred by some,[19] but it suffers from vagueness and carries at least as negative an implication toward other emigrants as "brain drain." "Reverse transfer of technology" is a popular alternative, especially in United Nations documents,[20] but it too is a loaded term which additionally is vague as well as misleading to those not initiated into the jargon, as it is grounded on the unintuitive understanding that skilled migrants constitute "technology."[21] A third alternative, "outflow of trained personnel"—also common in U.N. documents[22]—is better, but still vague as to how wide a net it is casting, that is, whether it is limited to the old meaning of scientific and technical personnel, or whether it is concerned about some or all other kinds of trained personnel as well. In all events, as the United Nation's return to the use of "brain drain" in more recent documents indicates,[23] neither of the alternative terms championed by the U.N. have proven capable of replacing "brain drain" even in the official vernacular.

As for other terms employed in lieu of "brain drain," "highly skilled migrants" is sometimes used today, but it too is vague—in fact, it has been defined to include even secondary school graduates,[24] a far cry from the original "brain drain" conception of migration by elite scientists and engineers. "Outflow of trained personnel" and "highly skilled migrants" certainly are less precise than still another alternative, "PTK immigration," meaning Professional, Technical, and Kindred categories of immigrants. The clunky PTK term, however, clearly belongs more to the past than to the future. Indeed, it is today something of an anachronism, being based upon a now discarded U.S. government statistical category.[25] Moreover, even in its prime, scholars and researchers rarely used the PTK acronym, making PTK's utility dubious even among persons generally familiar with the migration literature.[26] In sum, if we are searching for a practical alternative to the popular if loaded "brain drain," PTK certainly has proved its inadequacy to the task, as "brain drain" has been utilized thousands of times while PTK, in thirty years, has only occasionally been employed in the migration context.

Given the inadequacies of all the alternatives,[27] we propose and will utilize in this work a new term—"STEP OUT" migration. STEP OUT migrants are *Scientific, Technical, and Educated Professionals Out of Underdeveloped Territories*. The term is appropriate when the intent is to describe a broad spectrum of skilled immigrants spanning every sector of society, including the scientific, technological, cultural, political, educational, and corporate business fields. The inclusion of "professionals" will exclude in most cases students and high school graduates. The "OUT" provides a shorthand way of communicating that the STEP migrants under consideration are from developing countries. Concomitantly, as the previous sentence demonstrates, omission of the "OUT" provides a shorthand way of referring to the larger universe of all skilled and educated migrants.

The STEP OUT terminology is thus more precise, more complete, more flexible, more standardized, and less fraught with bias than any of the alternatives. It also is less classist than the alternatives "brain drain" and "transfer of talent," as it casts no aspersions on those migrants who fall outside its scope.[28] Finally, the new term is also, we hope, more memorable than any of the other alternatives to "brain drain." "Brain drain" is so well entrenched in large part because, despite its well-recognized flaws, it is undeniably catchy and easy to remember. Any term that presumes to challenge "brain drain" must at least make an effort to compete with the vividness of the images the famous term inspires. Whatever other virtues they may have, we think "reverse transfer of technology," "outflow of trained personnel," "highly skilled migrants," and

"PTK immigration" all self-evidently fall more than a little short in this regard. STEP OUT migration, however, may prove memorable because the spelling of the acronym creates a phrase whose meaning is suggestive of the movement that is the migrant's lot. It is our hope that the phrase does prove useful and that "STEP OUT migration" can become a favored term because, as noted, it is superior to "brain drain" in clarity, inviting of debate where "brain drain" prejudges, and free of inadvertent insult as "brain drain" is not. It is true that "[e]very field of thought has its carefully developed vocabulary, its code words, that facilitate serious discussion."[29] But "brain drain"—used by experts and non-experts alike—stands as an impediment to serious discussion. This is most unfortunate, for the important migration topic discussed here deserves serious discussion, and thus warrants a memorable terminology that—rhyme or no rhyme—does not require an explanatory apology.

WHY WE USE THE TERM "UNDERDEVELOPED"

We recognize that some might regard our use of the word "underdeveloped" as arrogating upon ourselves the determination as to what level of development is appropriate, and then unfairly tagging economies operating at a different level with a rhetorical badge of inferiority. To the extent that this charge implies that we claim to know the precise level of economic development that is optimal for a society, we reject the charge, and believe nothing in this work supports it, including our use of "underdeveloped." On the other hand, we have little trouble concluding that some levels of development are better than others; not all levels are equally desirable. Regarding the relative living standards of the developed countries we speak of in this work and the underdeveloped ones, for example, there is equality only in the sense of Anatole France's famous statement mocking "the majestic egalitarianism of the law, which forbids rich and poor alike to sleep under bridges, to beg in the streets, and to steal bread." Thus, it is true that in developed and underdeveloped countries alike, citizens are free to suffer from malnutrition, to die in childbirth, and to go without childhood vaccines, but we have no qualms about expressing a preference for societies in which these tragedies happen rarely rather than with regularity. In this sense, we believe it is appropriate to aspire to a world in which all countries are "developed," and similarly to point out with clarity that some countries are still below, that is, under, that standard. In making this value judgment, we are comforted by persuasive social science demonstrating that, by comfortable margins, people all over the world aspire to better material standards of living more than they aspire to anything else. In sum, we think use of the word "underdeveloped" is not the, or even a, problem; rather, the problem—which deserves the attention of us all—is the underlying and lamentable reality that the word accurately describes.

Indeed, the need for a more appropriate popular terminology is especially acute at this time, for several reasons. First, there is currently more interest in the issue of skilled and educated migration than there has been in a generation. In modern times, "brain drain" first arose as an important issue within and among nations in the 1960s,[30] but, relatively speaking, interest in the phenomenon faded after about a decade of it being in the spotlight.[31] Today, however, "[t]he brain drain of the 1960s is striking again with enhanced vigor,"[32] and "[n]ot since the 1970s has concern about 'brain drain' been as prominent" as it is now.[33] Given all of "brain drain's" advantages, including the power of habit and inertia in the use of language, one might reasonably fear that if an alternative term fails to make any inroads on "brain drain's" dominance during the current period of high interest, its roots will have been planted so deeply that a satisfactory terminology will never be able to emerge. "Brain drain," like kudzu,[34] will then be with us forever (or at least a very long time), a bad idea whose continued spreading is as inevitable as it is lamented.

The second reason that a change of terminology is now more important than ever is that it is now clearer than ever that the factual reality implied by "brain drain" is a misleading one. The widely held assumption of forty years ago was that the "brain drain" phenomenon was, on the whole, undeniably and permanently harmful to the developing world.[35] Were this assumption true, the use of "brain drain" would be much less objectionable, akin to calling someone who today claims to cure disease through the use of blue light a "quack."[36] After all, if it walks like a duck and talks like a duck, who can object if it gets called a duck?[37]

The best evidence available, however, is that STEP OUT migration neither walks nor talks like a "brain drain."[38] The fact that the term at one time was generally regarded as fitting the facts is no defense for using it now, any more than one could today justify routinely calling surgeons "butchers" because they at one time killed more patients than they saved. Surgery is different now, and so is the scholarly understanding of STEP OUT migration. This assertion, of course, anticipates the arguments that are to follow, and so it is to those arguments, broadly speaking, that this work will now turn.

NOTES

1. Anne Marie Gaillard and Jacques Gaillard, *International Migration of the Highly Qualified: A Bibliographic and Conceptual Itinerary* (Staten Island: Center for Migration Studies, 1998), 22

2. Gaillard and Gaillard, *International Migration of the Highly Qualified*; J. d'Oliveira e Sousa, "The Brain Drain Issue in International Negotiations," *The Impact of*

International Migration on Developing Countries, ed. Reginald Appleyard (Paris: Development Centre of the Organisation for Economic Co-operation and Development, 1989): 197, 197; D. Chongo Mundende, "The Brain Drain and Developing Countries," *The Impact of International Migration on Developing Countries*, ed. Reginald Appleyard: 183.

3. See, e.g., *The Brain Drain into the United States of Scientists, Engineers, and Physicians, A Staff Study of the Committee of Government Operations* (U.S. Government Printing Office, 1967), cited in Hla Myint, "The Underdeveloped Countries: A Less Alarmist View," in *The Brain Drain*, ed. Walter Adams (New York: Macmillan, 1968): 233, 233 n.1.

4. Peter Vas-Zoltan, *The Brain Drain: An Anomaly of International Relations* (Leyden: A. W. Sijthoff, 1976), 13. "Hémorragie de la matiére grise" translates from the French to a "hemorrhage of grey matter."

5. Gaillard and Gaillard, *International Migration of the Highly Qualified*, 23.

6. See Hla Myint, "The Underdeveloped Countries: A Less Alarmist View," in *The Brain Drain*, ed. Walter Adams: 233, 233 (suggesting the meaning of the term broadens when used to describe migration from developing to developed countries).

7. D. Chongo Mundende, "The Brain Drain and Developing Countries," 183.

8. J. d'Oliveira e Sousa, "The Brain Drain Issue in International Negotiations," 197.

9. Daniel Schwanen, *Putting the Brain Drain in Context: Canada and the Global Competition for Scientists and Engineers* (C.D. Howe Institute, 2000) (explaining that "Canada cannot afford to be complacent about the number of highly educated individuals leaving for the United States"); Alan Toulin, "Canada Bleeding MDs, Nurses to U.S.—Canada Study Finds Medical Professionals Leaving in Startling Numbers," *National Post*, May 25, 2000 (reporting on study that found increasing trend of migration by professional doctors and nurses); see also Michael O'Reilly, "Research Institute Tries to Ease Brain Drain by Bringing Researchers Back to Canada," *Canadian Medication Association Journal* 152 (1995): 1,109, 1,109–11 (noting concern in Canada over the emigration of Canadian scientists and physicians to the United States, and describing efforts to encourage repatriation).

10. See, e.g., Jeff Chu, "How to Plug Europe's Brain Drain," *Time Europe* (January 11, 2004), at http://www.time.com/time/europe/magazine/article/0,13005,901040119-574849-1,00.html; Margret Steffen, "Brain Drain Hurting Germany," *Deutsche Welle* (February 9, 2004), *at* http://www.dw-world.de/english/0,3367,1450_A_1107052_1_A,00.html.

11. Akin Adebayo, "Ghanaian Migration to Nigeria: Causes and Consequences," *Migration Today* 13 (1985): 29, *passim*.

12. Neal Sandler, "The Challengers—The Brains Keep Draining In: Thanks to Émigré Scientists, Israel Is Charging Ahead in High Tech," *Business Week*, June 15, 1990, at 160 (noting that the influx of Jewish scientists and engineers from the Soviet Union has helped Israel to become a leading hub for technology development). But see David Nordell, "Soviet Brain Drain May Overwhelm Israel," *New Scientist* (March 3, 1990) (noting a concern that Israel would not be able to absorb all of the immigrants from the Soviet Union).

13. See Mona L. Russell, "The Female Brain Drain, the State, and Development in Egypt," *Journal of Developing Societies* 8 (1992): 122, *passim*.

14. See, e.g., David Kohl, "Farming's Brain Drain—Where It Will Be, What You Can Do," *ABA Banking Journal*, May 20, 2002: 20; Jeffery L. Sheler, "Now, A Brain Drain from the Frost Belt," *U.S. News and World Report*, September 21, 1981, 87–89. See also "Gays in the Military: Don't Ask, Don't Tell," *CNN Saturday Night* (CNN cable, July 20, 2003, 1:35 a.m.) (during report, caption stated "critics say [don't ask, don't tell] policy leads to military 'brain drain'").

15. See Jagdish Bhagwati, *A Stream of Windows: Unsettling Reflections on Trade, Immigration, and Democracy* (Cambridge: MIT Press, 1998), 36 (recalling Professor Johnson as a "great international economist").

16. Harry G. Johnson, "The Economics of the 'Brain Drain': The Canadian Case," *Minerva* 3 (1965): 299; see also Vas-Zoltan, *The Brain Drain*, 13 (quoting statement by Brinley Thomas that "[b]rain drain is a loaded journalistic term, and it is unfortunate that it was ever used in scientific discussion"); "Brain Drain: A Study of the Persistent Issue of International Scientific Mobility," *Congressional Research Service for the House Subcommittee on National Security and Scientific Developments, 93d Congress*, 11 and n.37 (U.S. Government Printing Office, 1974) (quoting scholarly assertions that "brain drain" was "loaded and pejorative" because it "lead[s] those who use it to think automatically of a loss of vital resources without compensation" and of the phenomenon itself as "*ipso facto* a bad thing").

17. Johnson, "The Economics of the 'Brain Drain,'" 300.

18. See Mundende, "The Brain Drain and Developing Countries," 183.

19. Mundende, "The Brain Drain and Developing Countries," 183.

20. d'Oliveira e Sousa, "The Brain Drain Issue in International Negotiations," 197. The U.N. documents are mainly products of UNCTAD, the United Nations Conference on Trade and Development. See, e.g., UNCTAD, "Case Studies in Reverse Transfer of Technology (Brain Drain): A Survey of Problems and Policies in India" (UNCTAD Secretariat, Geneva, 1978); UNCTAD, "Case Studies in Reverse Transfer of Technology (Brain Drain): A Survey of Problems and Policies in Sri Lanka" (UNCTAD Secretariat, Geneva, 1978); UNCTAD, "Reverse Transfer of Technology: Economic Effects of the Outflow of Trained Personnel from Developing Countries," No. TD/B/AC.11 (Inter-governmental Group on Transfer of Technology, Trade and Development Board, Geneva, 1975); UNCTAD, "Developmental Aspects of the Reverse Transfer of Technology," No. TD/B/C.6/41 (1978); UNCTAD "Report of the Group of Governmental Experts on Reverse Transfer of Technology," Nos. TD/B/C.6/28 and ID/B/C.6/AC.4/10 (Geneva Meeting, 1978); UNCTAD, "Technology: Development Aspects of the Reverse Transfer of Technology," No. TD/239 (UNCTAD Secretariat 1979); UNCTAD, "The Reverse Transfer of Technology: A Survey of Its Main Features, Causes and Policy Implications," No. TD/B/C.6/47 (New York, 1979). See also United Nations, "Reverse Transfer of Technology, Report of the General Secretary," No. A/34/593 (New York 1979).

21. d'Oliveira e Sousa, "The Brain Drain Issue in International Negotiations," 197.

22. See, e.g., United Nations, "Outflow of Trained Personnel from Developing to Developed Countries, Report of the Secretary General of the United Nations to the

Committee on Science and Technology for Development," No. E/C.8/21 (New York 1974); United Nations, "The 'Brain Drain' Problem: Outflow of Trained Personnel from Developing to Developed Countries," No. E/1978/92 (New York 1978); United Nations Statistical Office, "Improvement of Statistics on the Outflow of Trained Personnel from Developing to Developed Countries: A Technical Report," No. ST/ESA/STAT/SER.F/30 (New York 1980).

23. See, e.g., UNESCO-ROSTE, "Brain Drain Issues in Europe, Cases of Russia and Ukraine, Technical Report" No. 18 (Venice 1994); UNESCO-ROSTE, "Brain Drain from Russia and Ways of Regulations" (Moscow, January 10, 1994); UNESCO-ROSTE, "Brain Drain Issues in Europe, Report of the Round Table, Brain Drain Issues: A Look from Italy," (Venice, October 6, 1992); UNESCO-ROSTE, "Report of the Task Force Meeting" (Venice, November 27–29, 1991).

24. B. Lindsay Lowell, "Skilled Migration Abroad or Human Capital Flight?" *Migration Information Source* (Washington, D.C.: Migration Policy Institute, June 1, 2003), at http://www.migrationinformation.org/Feature/display.cfm?ID=135. It is, of course, perfectly legitimate to define ordinary high school graduates as highly skilled migrants, as Professor Lowell's article clearly did. The problem arises only with the fact that others have used "highly skilled" to refer to professionals and college-level graduates only. See, e.g., Robyn Iredale, "The Internationalization of Professionals and the Assessment of Skills: Australia, Canada and the U.S.," *Georgetown Immigration Law Journal* 16 (2002): 797, 797, 812 (using "highly skilled migrants" to refer to "highly skilled professionals" authorized entry under certain immigration laws of Australia, Canada and the United States). These differing usages at best create inefficiencies and at worst confusion. Without a shared vocabulary, however, such problems are inevitable.

25. In 1980, the U.S. Census Bureau replaced its PTK classification with a category called "Managerial and Professional Specialty Occupations."

26. A Lexis search of all law reviews for "PTK" reveals no references to PTK in the migration context, only references to a federation of Swedish trade unions (Privattjanstemannakartellen) and the Hungarian Civil Code (Polgarl Torvenykonyv). Additionally, the comprehensive bibliography of articles on the International Migration of the Highly Qualified lists hundreds of articles that include "brain drain" in the title, but not one that includes PTK in the title. Gaillard and Gaillard, *International Migration of the Highly Qualified.* Finally, a search of the following six social science databases for the acronym "PTK" yielded only two articles that employed PTK in the migration context: Expanded Academic Index; Social Science Citation Index; Sociological Abstracts, ABI Index; PAIS; and EconLit. The few references to PTK in the migration context include the following: Jagdish N. Bhagwati, "The Brain Drain Tax Proposal and the Issues," in *Taxing the Brain Drain I: A Proposal*, eds. Jagdish N. Bhagwati and Martin Partington (Amsterdam: North-Holland Publishing, 1976): 1, 4; Jagdish N. Bhagwati, "The International Brain Drain and Taxation," in *The Brain Drain and Taxation II: Theory and Empirical Analysis*, ed. Jagdish N. Bhagwati (Amsterdam: North-Holland Publishing, 1976): 3, 5; Edwin P. Reubens, "Some Dimensions of Professional Immigration into Developed Countries from Less Developed Countries, 1960–1973,"

in *The Brain Drain and Taxation II: Theory and Empirical Analysis*, ed. Jagdish N. Bhagwati: 217 ("PTK" term employed throughout article); Charles W. Stahl, "Overview: Economic Perspectives," *The Impact of International Migration on Developing Countries*, ed. Reginald Appleyard: 361, 364–66 (using "PTK" and "PTKs").

27. We have assessed in this section the terms most frequently or prominently used in discussions of "brain drain." Other terms exist, but they tend to be variations on the terms discussed here and, accordingly, suffer from the same flaws. See, e.g., Howard W. French, "Insular Japan Needs, but Resists, Immigration," *New York Times*, July 24, 2003, A1 (mentioning "'high end' migration").

28. Mundende, "The Brain Drain and Developing Countries," 183.

29. Peter Steinfels, A *People Adrift: The Crisis of the Roman Catholic Church in America* (New York: Simon & Schuster, 2003), 227

30. Gaillard and Gaillard, *International Migration of the Highly Qualified*, 17 ("International migration of highly qualified manpower first appeared as a theme of attention in the early 1960s"). Incidentally, although the term "brain drain" is of relatively recent vintage, the phenomenon meant to be captured by the term is not new. Indeed, it is almost as old as recorded history itself. For example, when ancient Athens and Alexandria were at the height of their powers, their most prominent scientists and thinkers "c[a]me from somewhere else." Stevan Dedijer, "'Early' Migration," in *The Brain Drain*, ed. Walter Adams: 9, 13–16. Nor is the apparent intractability of the issue new. After Europe's first university was founded in Bologna, for example, not even a constantly escalating series of edicts against the recruitment of Bolognese faculty by more recently established universities— culminating in a statute levying the death penalty against both successfully recruited faculty and their recruiters—could stem the migration of Bologna's university personnel to universities in other cities. Stevan Dedijer, "'Early' Migration," in *The Brain Drain*, ed. Walter Adams: 22–23. See generally Congressional Research Service for the House Subcommittee on National Security Policy and Scientific Developments, 93d Congress, "Brain Drain: A Study of the Persistent Issue of International Scientific Mobility" (U.S. Government Printing Office, 1974) 18–29 (providing an interesting overview of more than twenty-three centuries of "brain drain").

31. See, e.g., Mundende, "The Brain Drain and Developing Countries," at 183. ("During the 1960s and early 1970s the movement of highly skilled workers received a great deal of attention from scholars of international migration . . ., [but] the brain drain issue . . . received less attention" afterward); Vas-Zoltan, *The Brain Drain*, 8, 101 (stating that "[f]rom 1960 onwards, there was a flood of monographs, studies, articles and daily news items" that "for ten years or so [made the "brain drain"] phenomenon . . . the topical problem for international public opinion," but noting that interest declined after 1971); Herbert G. Grubel, "A Sober View of the Brain Drain," *Minerva* 11 (1973): 147 (reviewing *Education and Emigration*, by R.G. Myers, Grubel states that interest in "brain drain" peaked from 1965 to 1969, and then progressively decreased until 1972, when articles on the subject "disappeared almost altogether").

32. Jagdish Bhagwati, "Borders Beyond Control," *Foreign Affairs* 82 (January/February 2003): 98, 99. Professor Bhagwati is an authoritative source for assessing relative interest in the migration of skilled and educated persons. He has been writing about the issue since at least 1967, V.M. Dandekar, "India," in *The Brain Drain*, ed. Walter Adams (1968): 203, 204 (referring to an article by Professor Bhagwati that appeared in an April 1967 issue of *Seminar*, a monthly journal published in New Delhi, India) and, in the forty years since, "brain drain" has remained one of his enduring scholarly concerns. See, e.g., *Taxing the Brain Drain I: A Proposal*, eds. Jagdish N. Bhagwati and Martin Partington; *The Brain Drain and Taxation II: Theory and Empirical Analysis*, ed. Jagdish N. Bhagwati; Jagdish Bhagwati, "The Brain Drain," *International Social Science Journal* 28 (1976): 691; Jagdish Bhagwati and Milind Rao, "Foreign Students in Science and Engineering Ph.D. Programs: An Alien Invasion or Brain Gain?" in *Foreign Temporary Workers in America: Policies That Benefit the U.S. Economy*, ed. B. Lindsay Lowell (Westport: Quorum Books, 1999): 239; Jagdish Bhagwati, "International Migration of the Highly Skilled: Economics, Ethics and Taxes," *Third World Quarterly* 1 (1979): 17; Jagdish Bhagwati and Milind Rao, "The U.S. Brain Gain—At the Expense of Blacks?" *Challenge* (March/April 1996): 50; Jagdish Bhagwati, "Borders Beyond Control," *Foreign Affairs* 82 (January/February 2003): 98.

33. B. Lindsay Lowell, "Skilled Migration Abroad or Human Capital Flight?" *Migration Information Source* (June 1, 2003), at http://www.migrationinformation.org/Feature/display.cfm?ID=135.

34. Introduced from China and Japan, kudzu is an extremely fast-growing vine that, "in the absence of support, becomes a coarse, rampant ground cover." Louise Bush-Brown and James Bush-Brown, *America's Garden Book*, rev. ed., ed. Howard S. Irwin, (New York: Macmillan, 1996), 296. In the near-perfect growing conditions of the American southeast, this "vicious pest" has proven nearly impossible to eradicate, as it is "extremely difficult to control by mechanical means," and may not be eliminated chemically unless it is treated over the course of several years "while in full leaf and actively growing." Bush-Brown and Bush-Brown, *America's Garden Book*, 783.

35. See, e.g., N.K. Onuoha Chukunta, "Human Rights and the Brain Drain," *International Migration* 15 (1977): 281, 281 (noting that ever since the term "brain drain" was coined, "private foundations, and national governments" have been aligned with "public international organizations . . . to remedy a situation that they consider injurious to national development," i.e., "brain drain"). The author adds that "there is hardly any of these [international] organizations—universal or regional—that has not condemned the phenomenon."

36. In the nineteenth century, blue light was alleged to cure a variety of diseases. See Paul Collins, *Banvard's Folly: Thirteen Tales of Renowned Obscurity, Famous Anonymity, and Rotten Luck* (New York: Picador, 2001), 214–15, 221, 225 (detailing the phenomenon as well as the life of blue light's main proponent, Philadelphia lawyer and Civil War era Brigadier General A.J. Pleasonton). Before the theory was discredited, many people sought a "blue light cure," some going so far as to build entire rooms with blue windows. Collins, *Banvard's Folly*, 221, 225. See also A.J. Pleasonton, *The Influence of the Blue Ray of the Sunlight and of the Blue Colour of the Sky*, 2nd ed. (Philadelphia: Claxton, Remsen and Haffelfinger, 1877).

37. As Professor Dana Wilbanks has noted, "the metaphorical discourse about immigration and refugee policy" depends upon a "complex interrelation" between values and perceived facts. Dana W. Wilbanks, *Re-Creating America: The Ethics of U.S. Immigration and Refugee Policy in a Christian Perspective* (Nashville: Abingdon Press in cooperation with the Churches' Center for Theology and Public Policy, 1996), 22.

38. See chapters 11–14 (detailing evidence that STEP OUT migration can be beneficial to sending countries); See also Gaillard and Gaillard, *International Migration of the Highly Qualified*, 28 (noting changing views of former opponents of brain drain, including developing countries themselves, who now increasingly view as helpful "what appeared as a brain drain"); World Bank, *Global Economic Prospects 2006: Economic Implications of Remittances and Migration* (Washington, D.C.: World Bank, 2006), 68 (noting that China, Cuba, India, the Philippines, Sri Lanka, and Vietnam all have programs that encourage skilled migration, thereby indicating that these countries perceive the benefits of the phenomenon).

Chapter Three

Catholic Social Teaching

"Catholic social teaching" is a term with several meanings. The broadest definition encompasses the entire body of theories and principles on social, political, and economic life that have been developed throughout the Church's nearly 2000-year history.[1] That is not the common definition, however, and is *not* the definition that we adopt for this book.

Rather, we use the term "Catholic social teaching" to refer to that body of Church teaching about social, political, and economic issues dating from 1891 to the present. This narrower understanding is by far the more common meaning of Catholic social teaching and it is almost always what is meant by the phrase "modern Catholic social teaching."[2] In the remainder of this work we will use the term "Catholic social teaching" exclusively in the latter, narrower, sense.

Modern Catholic social teaching is generally thought to date from 1891 because that was the year of publication of "the Magna Carta of Catholic social teaching,"[3] Pope Leo XIII's encyclical letter, *Rerum Novarum* (On the Condition of Labor).[4] Commenting on the enormous transformations and changes in economic, political, and social life taking place at the end of the 19th century, *Rerum Novarum* dealt with the plight of the worker in the industrial age.[5] Pope John Paul II described the effect of *Rerum Novarum* as giving "the church 'citizenship status,' as it were, amid the changing realities of public life."[6]

While there is no definitive list of all documents that have been published since *Rerum Novarum* that fall within the category of Catholic social teaching, there is general agreement that the core of the social teaching includes many encyclicals, which are "papal letter[s] circulated throughout the whole of the Catholic church, and in more recent days, a letter addressed beyond the church to all people of goodwill;"[7] certain other statements by sitting Popes, such as important speeches concerning social issues; certain documents issued by the

Second Vatican Council; and pastoral letters and statements authorized by international, regional, or national congregations of bishops.[8]

Examples of pertinent encyclicals, other than *Rerum Novarum*, include *Quadragesimo Anno* (After Forty Years), published in 1931;[9] *Mater et Magistra* (Mother and Teacher), published in 1961;[10] *Pacem in Terris* (Peace on Earth), published in 1963;[11] *Populorum Progressio* (On the Development of Peoples), published in 1967;[12] *Laborem Exercens* (On Human Work), published in 1981;[13] *Sollicitudo Rei Socialis* (On Social Concern), published in 1987;[14] and *Centesimus Annus* (One Hundred Years), published in 1991.[15] Other pertinent papal statements include the Christmas radio address of Pope Pius XII, delivered in 1941, *The Apostolic Constitution, Exsul Familia*, published in 1952, and Pope Paul VI's apostolic letter, *Octogesima Adveniens* (A Call to Action), published in 1971.[16] Contributions of the Second Vatican Council to the social teaching include *Gaudium et Spes* (the Pastoral Constitution On the Church in the Modern World)[17] and *Dignitatis Humanae* (the Declaration on Religious Liberty), each of which was published in 1965.[18] Additionally, relevant bishops' pastoral statements include those by the U.S. Conference of Catholic Bishops or its predecessor organizations in the United States,[19] especially (for purposes of the instant work) documents focused on immigration, such as *The Pastoral Concern of the Church for People on the Move*,[20] *Together, a New People*,[21] *One Family Under God*,[22] *Welcoming the Stranger Among Us: Unity in Diversity*,[23] and *Strangers No Longer: Together on the Journey of Hope*, the last of which was co-authored by the U.S. and Mexican bishops.[24] Finally, statements by the Sacred Congregation for Bishops in the Vatican, especially *Instruction on the Pastoral Care of People Who Migrate*,[25] and its successor document, *The Love of Christ towards Migrants*,[26] by the Pontifical Council for the Pastoral Care of Migrants and Itinerant People, also may appropriately be considered authoritative Church documents on the subject of migration.

NOTES

1. Kenneth R. Himes, *Responses to 101 Questions on Catholic Social Teaching* (New York: Paulist Press, 2001): 5.

2. While most scholars refer to Pope Leo XII's *Rerum Novarum* as the beginning of modern Catholic social teaching (Charles E. Curran, *Catholic Social Teaching, 1891–Present: A Historical, Theological, and Ethical Analysis* (Washington, D.C.: Georgetown University Press, 2002), 1, 6), that position is not universally held. See Michael J. Schuck, *That They Be One: The Social Teaching of the Papal Encyclicals, 1740–1989* (Washington, D.C.: Georgetown University Press, 1991), ix–x. Professor Schuck argues that the seventy-seven encyclicals predating Pope Leo XII should not

be overlooked and would "move the discussion [regarding modern Catholic social teaching] back to its true origin," i.e., 1740. Of course, even those who recognize the 1891 starting date for modern Catholic social teaching understand that a long trail of intellectual forerunners paved the way for today's teaching. See Michael Novak, *Catholic Social Thought & Liberal Institutions: Freedom with Justice*, 2nd edition (New Brunswick: Transaction Publishers, 1989), 61–80 (characterizing the nineteenth-century German thinkers Wilhelm von Ketteler and Heinrich Pesch as architects of Catholic social thought, and discussing the importance of their work); Terry Coonan, "There Are No Strangers Among Us: Catholic Social Teaching and U.S. Immigration Law," *The Catholic Lawyer* 40 (2000): 105, 113 n.21 (noting the contributions of Thomas Aquinas and earlier writers to Catholic social teaching).

3. Robert A. Sirico, *Catholicism's Developing Social Teaching* (Grand Rapids: Acton Institute for the Study of Religion and Liberty, 1992), 5. See also Patricia A. Lamoureux, "Immigration Reconsidered in the Context of an Ethic of Solidarity," in *Made in God's Image: The Catholic Vision of Human Dignity*, eds. Regis Duffy and Angelus Gambatese (1999): 105, 131 n.3 (calling *Rerum Novarum* "a kind of 'magna carta' for modern Catholic social thought").

4. Pope Leo XIII, *Rerum Novarum*. As noted in our preface, David O'Brien and Thomas Shannon have organized a collection of many of the major social encyclicals, as well as several other important church documents. See *Catholic Social Thought: The Documentary Heritage*, eds. David J. O'Brien and Thomas A. Shannon (Maryknoll: Orbis Books, 1992). Except where otherwise indicated, all references to papal encyclicals in this work are to translations provided by O'Brien and Shannon. English translations of the papal encyclicals also are available on the Vatican's website, http://www.vatican.va. Latin scholars will note that the English title given *Rerum Novarum* in our text—On the Condition of Labor—is not a literal translation of *Rerum Novarum* (which means "of new things"), but rather a particularized statement of what "new things" are discussed in the encyclical. Sometimes this particularized statement is alternatively given as "On the Condition of the Working Classes," "On the Condition of the Workers," or "The Rights and Duties of Capital and Labor." Compare, e.g., Pope John Paul II, *Centesimus Annus* (1991): sec. 4 (referring to Pope Leo XIII's discussion of the "condition of the workers") with Pope Leo XIII, *Rerum Novarum* (1891), at http://www.vatican.va (providing the English language title, *Rights and Duties of Capital and Labor*, but stating at note 1 that "[t]he title sometimes given to this encyclical, *On the Condition of the Working Classes*, is . . . perfectly justified"), and Robert A. Sirico, at 29 n.1 (asserting that the more appropriate title is *The Rights and Duties of Capital and Labor*). See also Michael Evans, *An Analysis of U.N. Refugee Policy in Light of Roman Catholic Social Teaching and the Phenomena Creating Refugees* (Ann Arbor: University Microfilms International, 1991), 74 n.5 (noting various translations of *Rerum Novarum*'s title).

5. In many respects, *Rerum Novarum* remains relevant regarding the plight of the worker even today, in the midst of the information age. See, e.g., Kathleen Brady, "Religious Organizations and Mandatory Collective Bargaining: Freedom From and Freedom For," *Villanova Law Review* 49 (2003): 77, 106, 111; David Gregory,

"Br(e)aking the Exploitation of Labor?: Tensions Regarding the Welfare Workforce," *Fordham Urban Law Journal* 25 (1997): 1, 31.

6. Pope John Paul II, *Centesimus Annus*, sec. 5.

7. Sirico, *Catholicism's Developing Social Teaching*, 6.

8. Sirico, *Catholicism's Developing Social Teaching*, 29 n.2 (listing social encyclicals and other important papal addresses); Curran, *Catholic Social Teaching, 1891–Present*, 7 (listing major documents of Catholic social teaching, including social encyclicals and bishops' pastoral letters); Thomas Massaro, *Living Justice: Catholic Social Teaching in Action* (Franklin: Sheed & Ward, 2000), 59 (stating that "the sources of official Catholic social teaching [are] papal encyclicals, statements of Vatican offices and commissions, church councils, and episcopal conferences of bishops"); Himes, *Responses to 101 Questions on Catholic Social Teaching*, 7–9 (listing papal encyclicals, certain other papal addresses, and various documents by Church councils and episcopal conferences). However, not every such document is thought to contribute to the body of work that is considered Catholic social teaching. Papal and magisterial documents, including several encyclicals, which comment on matters other than the social conditions of the times are not considered to comprise the church's social teachings. See, e.g., Pope John Paul II, *Ecclesia de Eucharistia* (2003) (discussing the meaning of the Eucharist).

9. Pope Pius XI, *Quadragesimo Anno* (1931).

10. Pope John XXIII, *Mater et Magistra* (1961).

11. Pope John XXIII, *Pacem in Terris* (1963).

12. Pope Paul VI, *Populorum Progressio* (1967).

13. Pope John Paul II, *Laborem Exercens* (1981).

14. Pope John Paul II, *Sollicitudo Rei Socialis* (1987).

15. Pope John Paul II, *Centesimus Annus* (1991).

16. Pope Pius XII, *Christmas Radio Message*, Dec. 24, 1941, AAS 34 (1942): 10–21; Pope Pius XII, "The Apostolic Constitution, Exsul Familia" (Washington, D.C.: Catholic University of America, 1952), reprinted in *Exsul Familia: The Church's Magna Charta for Migrants*, ed. Rev. Giulivo Tessarolo (Staten Island: St. Charles Seminary, 1962); Pope Paul VI, *Octogesima Adveniens* (1971).

17. Second Vatican Council, *Gaudium et Spes* (1965).

18. Second Vatican Council, *Dignitatis Humanae* (1965).

19. The most widely read (and probably most controversial) of the U.S. bishops' pastoral letters is *Economic Justice for All*. National Conference of Catholic Bishops, *Economic Justice for All: Pastoral Letter on Catholic Social Teaching and the U.S. Economy* (U.S. Catholic Conference, 1986). The U.S. Conference of Catholic Bishops is the successor organization to a number of organizations, e.g., the National Catholic War Council (which was established during World War I), the National Catholic Welfare Council, the National Catholic Welfare Conference, the National Conference of Bishops, and the U.S. Catholic Conference. The most recent name was adopted in 2001, as the National Conference of Catholic Bishops and the U.S. Catholic Conference combined to form the U.S. Conference of Catholic Bishops.

20. National Conference of Catholic Bishops, *The Pastoral Concern of the Church for People on the Move* (U.S. Catholic Conference, 1976). This publication referenced

and was accompanied by a document prepared by the National Conference of Catholic Bishops' Ad Hoc Committee on Migration and Tourism, entitled *The Church and the Immigrant Today*.

21. National Conference of Catholic Bishops, *Together a New People: Pastoral Statement on Migrants and Refugees* (U.S. Catholic Conference, 1987).

22. U.S. Bishops' Committee on Migration, *One Family Under God* (U.S. Catholic Conference, 1995).

23. National Conference of Catholic Bishops, *Welcoming the Stranger Among Us: Unity in Diversity* (U.S. Catholic Conference, 2000).

24. United States Conference of Catholic Bishops and Conferencia del Episcopado Mexicano, *Strangers No Longer: Together on the Journey of Hope: A Pastoral Letter Concerning Migration from the Catholic Bishops of Mexico and the United States* (U.S. Conference of Catholic Bishops & Conferencia del Episcopado Mexicano, 2003).

25. Sacred Congregation for Bishops, "Instruction on the Pastoral Care of People Who Migrate" (U.S. Catholic Conference, 1969), reprinted in *People on the Move: A Compendium of Church Documents on the Pastoral Concern for Migrants and Refugees* (U.S. Catholic Conference, 1988).

26. Pontifical Council for the Pastoral Care of Migrants and Itinerant People, *Erga migrantes caritas Christi (The Love of Christ toward Migrants)* (Vatican City: 2004), at Presentation, available at www.vatican.va (noting intent "to update the pastoral care of migration, thirty-five years after the publication of Pope Paul VI's Motu Proprio *Pastoralis migratorum cura* and the Congregation for Bishops' related Instruction"). The Pontifical Council for the Pastoral Care of Migrants and Itinerant People notes at the conclusion of *Erga migrantes caritas Christi* that the document was approved by Pope John Paul II on May 1, 2004.

Part Two

CATHOLIC SOCIAL
THOUGHT AND IMMIGRATION

Chapter Four

The Openness of the
Tradition and the Exception

Long before the modern era of Catholic social teaching, the Roman Catholic Church expressed concern for immigrants and refugees.[1] The roots of such concern are deeply ingrained in the faith; indeed, some of the most vivid images found in the scriptures arise from stories concerning migration, exile, travel, and flight.[2] Such images—always sympathetic to the traveler—inspire the social teachings of the Catholic Church on the level of general orientation: "broad theory, basic vision, and fundamental values."[3] Of course, the social teachings grant Scripture "a lesser role with regard to specific considerations that require heavy emphasis on human and scientific reasoning and a reading of the signs of the times."[4] Still, in the case of migration, the more specific social teachings are, in fact, largely sympathetic to refugees and migrants, and thus are in accord with the general orientation of the Scriptures. This can plainly be seen by reviewing the Church's responses to the three most basic questions concerning immigration policy: (1) who can migrate? (2) where can individuals migrate? and (3) how should migrants be treated in the receiving country? Such a review follows below. In general—with one important exception—it will demonstrate that the Catholic Church's position on migration is extremely welcoming.

WHO CAN MIGRATE?

Ideally, for one aiming at maximum simplicity, the debate about the right to emigrate would not, in order to be meaningful, require a separate discussion about the right to immigrate. The two would be recognized as two sides of the same coin; in this ideally simple universe, if one had the right to *emigrate*, that is, leave one's country, *of course* one must also have the right to *immigrate*, that is, enter another country. Unfortunately, however, emigration and immigration are treated as analytically distinct—at least some of the time—by almost everyone who has considered the matter, including the Catholic Church. In truth, there are valid reasons for this; simply because one has the right to emigrate *from* somewhere does not mean one must have the right to immigrate *to* everywhere. On the other hand, this separating of the two issues could risk turning a theoretically broad right into a potentially empty right; for example, it could mean that while one has the right to emigrate from everywhere, one has no right to immigrate to anywhere.

All this serves as a warning to the reader not to conflate the two issues in the discussions that follow. The reader should recognize that—in Catholic social teaching and elsewhere—a broad, even absolute, right to emigrate does not necessarily imply a concomitantly broad right to immigrate.[5] Emigration rights are worth considering in isolation, however, both because the right to emigrate is usually a practical prerequisite to the right to immigrate, and because a broad right to emigrate is always of some value as long as the right to immigrate is not denied by every country.

With these cautionary words of explanation as a preface, we now turn to Catholic social teaching's treatment of the right to emigrate. Catholic social teaching implicitly divides emigrants into three groups: (1) refugees, (2) migrants, and (3) skilled and educated emigrants, and bestows different rights to migrate on each group.

As for refugees, Catholic social teaching endows them with an extremely strong right to migrate.[6] As the U.S. and Mexican bishops explain in a 2003 pastoral letter, "The right to asylum must never be denied when people's lives are truly threatened in their homeland."[7] A refugee's fundamental right to migrate also exists in U.S. and international law. As signatories to the United Nations Refugee Convention[8] or its Protocol,[9] most countries, including the United States, are obligated not to deport someone who, "owing to well-founded fear of being persecuted for reasons of race, religion, nationality, membership in a particular social group, or political opinion," is outside of the country of the individual's nationality and is "unable or, owing to such fear, unwilling to avail" himself or herself of the protection of the home country.[10] The Church's teachings would extend the refugee's right to migrate to individuals who fall outside the scope of a Convention refugee or refugee under U.S. law. For example, Catholic social teaching considers the term refugee appropriately to include not only people who fear persecution on account of one of the five grounds protected by the Convention, but also individuals who are compelled to leave their home country for such reasons as natural disaster, famine, severe economic deprivation, or war.[11]

THE LAWS GOVERNING REFUGEE PROTECTION IN THE UNITED STATES

U.S. law offers fewer persons refugee status than recommended by the Church. Rather than offer protection to broad categories of persons, such as the seriously economically deprived, U.S. law offers relief only to persons who are specifically targeted for certain types of persecution. For such persons, there are two forms of relief available—withholding of removal and asylum protection. Both of these forms of protection derive from U.S. obligations under two related international treaties—the Convention Relating to the Status of Refugees, signed on July 28, 1951, 189 U.N.T.S. 150, and its Protocol Relating to the Status of Refugees, signed January 31, 1967, 19 U.S.T. 6223, T.I.A.S. 6577. These treaties obligate the United States not to return victims of persecution to their home countries, an obligation known in international law as *non-refoulment*.

The United States' *non-refoulment* obligations pursuant to the Refugee Convention and Refugee Protocol were incorporated into U.S. law through the Refugee Act of 1980. Under U.S. law, an individual who establishes that it is more likely than not that his or her life or freedom would be threatened on account of his or her race, religion, nationality, membership in a particular social group, or political opinion if returned to his or her home country is entitled to "withholding of removal," a *non-refoulment* protection from deportation. If someone is granted withholding of removal, then the United States government is prohibited from removing the individual to the country in which the individual fears persecution. Individuals who are granted withholding of removal do not receive benefits or rights under U.S. laws other than the right not to be removed.

The Refugee Act also authorizes the Attorney General to grant asylum protection to qualified refugees who are present in the United States or who arrive at its borders or airports. An asylee is a person who is outside of his or her country of nationality and who is unwilling or unable to return to his or her home country because he or she suffered past persecution or has a well-founded fear of future persecution on account of race, religion, nationality, membership in a particular social group, or political opinion if returned to the home country. The Supreme Court stated in *INS v. Cardoza-Fonseca*, 480 U.S. 421, 431 n.7 (1987) that the well-founded fear of persecution standard for asylum protection could be established if an applicant proved that there was a one in ten chance of persecution.

Although the standard for obtaining asylum protection is easier to establish than the standard for withholding of removal, asylum protection offers recipients more rights than withholding. Thus, unlike individuals who are granted withholding of removal, asylum seekers can apply for asylum for their spouses

(*continued*)

and minor children, and are eligible for work permits. One year after being granted asylum protection, asylees also become eligible to adjust their immigration status to become U.S. permanent residents. One other difference between asylum and withholding of deportation is that certain bars that disqualify an individual from receiving asylum—such as the filing deadline that requires that the asylum application be filed within one year of the individual's last arrival in the United States—do not disqualify someone from receiving withholding of removal.

Sources: Refugee Act of 1980, Pub. L. No. 96-212, 94 Stat. 102; INA secs. 101(a)(42), 208, 209(b), 241(b)(3), and 8 U.S.C. §§ 1101(a)(42), 1158, 1159(b), 1231(b)(3).

With respect to the migration rights of individuals who are not fleeing dire circumstances—usually referred to by Church teachings as "migrants"—Catholic social teaching also adopts a strong position of welcome.[12] Pope John Paul II stated flatly that "[m]an has the right to leave his native land for various motives—and also the right to return—in order to seek better conditions of life in another country."[13] The most common non-emergency motive is economic opportunity; indeed, "the Church's first formal reflections on immigration evolved on behalf of persons immigrating specifically for reasons of economic want."[14] The right to migrate for economic reasons stems from the right to support one's self and the duty to sustain one's family.[15]

Finally, Catholic social teaching's liberal view of the right to emigrate also extends—in a technical sense—to educated and skilled persons, but, in contrast to the teaching's enthusiastic backing for the emigration rights of refugees and migrants generally, Church support for the practical exercise of the right by skilled and educated persons—at least to more developed countries—historically has been tepid at best. An apt comparison might be to the grudging acceptance in the United States of the First Amendment rights of various extreme voices. Purveyors of offensive speech might have the right to do what they do, but—a good portion of society will assert—(1) they shouldn't do it, and (2) if they do, they should be subjected to the moral opprobrium of society. So too has it been with Catholic social teaching's acceptance of the right of educated and skilled persons to migrate from undeveloped to developed countries:

> Even though they have a right of emigrating, citizens are held to remember that they have the right and the duty . . . to contribute according to their ability to the true progress of their own community. Especially in underdeveloped areas where all resources must be put to urgent use, those men gravely endanger the public good, who, particularly possessing mental powers or wealth, are enticed by greed and temptation to emigrate. They deprive their community of the material and spiritual aid it needs.[16]

As this statement reveals, acceptance of the right is grudging because Church teachings also impose a duty on migrants to contribute their talents and abilities to their home countries. Educated and skilled migrants by their very nature are endowed with qualities that their home communities—developing countries—need. Viewing migrants as "crossing an unbridgeable gulf,"[17] those who choose to migrate are seen by the Church as abandoning their duties to their home countries.[18]

What does it mean when a body—in this case the Sacred Congregation for Bishops—possessing moral authority only, recognizes a technical right to perform an act, but makes a moral judgment tantamount to stating that exercise of the right reveals one as greedy and susceptible to temptation. Among other things, it likely means that the body will seek to undercut the right where possible, much as prosecutors and legislators periodically attempt to limit the First Amendment rights of disfavored speakers, especially through indirect means such as permit requirements, zoning restrictions, and burdensome regulations. The next section—concerning the obligation of states to accept immigrants—demonstrates that Catholic social teaching historically has endorsed exactly such an indirect limiting of the right of emigration.

WHERE CAN EMIGRANTS MIGRATE?

As noted, the right to immigrate into a particular country is analytically distinct from the right to emigrate out of a particular country. Catholic social teaching does not call for unregulated open borders; however, it holds that the discretion of receiving countries to regulate the right to immigrate generally should be limited.[19] Like the right to emigrate, as broadly defined by Catholic social teaching, the extent of the permissible limitation on the right to immigrate varies depending upon the class of individuals migrating.

With respect to refugees, the duty of sovereign states to accept refugees is essentially absolute. Catholic social teaching imposes an affirmative duty on the state to accept refugees, as well as a duty to help to integrate them into their new society.[20]

With regard to migrants, Catholic social teaching acknowledges that the right to immigrate to a particular country may be more limited for migrants than for refugees. In general, however, the teachings here also tend toward a relatively expansive conception of the right, encouraging countries to receive migrants openly. Indeed, while recognizing that a sovereign nation may have an interest in regulating migration across its borders because of the impact of migration on its citizens and residents, some statements suggest that the nation's discretion to block the movement of migrants is extremely limited.[21] When assessing the common good of the receiving countries and the right of individuals to migrate, Church teaching unmistakably favors the rights of migrants.

The exception to this general rule involves the Church's position on the migration of skilled and educated workers. In this one case, in contrast to its usually expansive stance, Catholic social teaching historically has taken a rather restrictive position with regard to the migration rights of skilled and educated migrants who seek to migrate from undeveloped to developed countries.[22] Indeed, not only has the Church suggested developed nations are within their rights to limit admission by STEP OUT migrants, it has affirmatively encouraged such nations to do so.[23]

HOW SHOULD IMMIGRANTS BE
TREATED IN THE RECEIVING COUNTRY?

In the final policy area concerning immigrants—their treatment upon arrival in their new country—Catholic social teaching again adopts a welcoming position. Moreover, this time there are no exceptions; according to Catholic social teaching, every migrant—including the educated and skilled—should be welcomed into their new community regardless of the motive for migrating.[24] In effect, upon arrival across the border, the Church merges all three types of migrants into a special fourth type—the newcomer—and insists that newcomers across the board are to be treated with dignity and respect.

In addition to the application of the abstract principles of Catholic social teaching (a topic which will begin to be addressed in chapter 5), a host of historical, institutional, and experiential factors support the Church's favorable disposition toward such newcomers.[25] Scripture, for example, seems to demand openness to arriving immigrants.[26] Indeed, from the Old Testament admonition to "treat the stranger who resides with you no differently than the natives born among you, have the same love for him as for yourself; for you too were once strangers in the land of Egypt,"[27] to Jesus's warning that those who do not "welcome" the "stranger" will face "eternal punishment,"[28] the biblical commands themselves constitute a type of unimpeachable social teaching that, given their unusual clarity, make an unwelcoming approach to newcomers most difficult to justify.

The Church's conception of itself as a universal Church, with a message for people of all nations, also orients it toward a position of openness to migrants.[29] Historically, long periods of deeply rooted Eurocentrism have undermined this message to some extent,[30] even recently some contend;[31] nevertheless, today the Church's professed universalism is expressly recognized as a basis for maintaining a pro-immigrant position.[32] Similarly orienting the

Church toward a position favorable to immigrants is the ancient conception, which still resonates, of Christians generally as *"paroikoi*—strangers, sojourners, or displaced people without a home."[33] This self-conception creates a type of philosophically or perhaps even theologically inspired *identification* with immigrants, who likewise are strangers in the land.[34]

Catholic social teaching also adopts a welcoming attitude toward immigrants because of the spiritual benefits such an attitude can bring to the members of the *receiving* country. As the U.S. Catholic bishops have stated, "Immigrants, new to our shores, call us out of our unawareness to a conversion of mind and heart through which we are able to offer a genuine and suitable welcome."[35] While the bishops' statement is potentially true on all occasions when one encounters an immigrant, it is especially likely when the immigrant is in an extreme position of vulnerability, as exposure to extreme events and circumstances can quite effectively open one's eyes to one's own excessive complacency, and create a personal incentive for positive change.[36]

While the reasons stated above apply to the entire Church, the individual members of the American Catholic Church and the American Church as an institution each have some additional reasons for advocating the welcoming of immigrants as part of Catholic social teaching. We make no contention that these additional reasons are uniquely American, only that they will tend to resonate especially well with those persons most familiar with the American experience.

First, the American Catholic Church itself, like many of its individual members, is highly aware of its immigrant roots.[37] Many individual members of the Church, as well as persons in the broader American society, share a background shaped by familial memories of the immigrant experience.[38] So, too, the institutional memory of the American Catholic Church is colored by its founding as an "immigrant Church."[39] This history cannot help but incline the Church and many of its members to be favorably disposed toward migrants in their midst.

Second, the Church and its members also share personal experiences with immigrants or as immigrants. For a long time, the Church in America has worked with immigrants every day and in many ways,[40] and, given the prevalence of immigrants in American life today, so, too, do its members. Indeed, many American Catholics are themselves immigrants.[41] This tends to create an enhanced sense of empathy for and solidarity with the newly arriving immigrant.

Third, the wealth of the American Catholic Church—which is largely a function of the wealth of its members—makes the American Church's message of generosity toward immigrants particularly likely to bear visible fruit, even when the persons the message is directed at are not members of immigrant communities themselves. It is always easier—if not more virtuous—to give out of one's abundance rather than out of one's need.

Finally, paralleling the Church's belief in the universality of its message, a widespread American belief undergirds the American Church's attitude of welcome toward immigrants. This is the belief—as fact or as ideal—in the United States as a nation united not on the basis of nationality, but on the basis of ideas of liberty and freedom universally open to people of all nations.[42] The ultimate physical representation of this belief, of course, is the Statue of Liberty, a symbol that resonates (and motivates) across the political spectrum.

In sum, the Church-wide rationales of scriptural command, universalist aspiration, philosophical identification, and personal conversion, combined with the history, experiences, wealth, and political ideals of the American people, establish an environment overwhelmingly likely to produce policies unusually propitious toward arriving immigrants. There is no mystery, then, in why the American Catholic Church has established an extensive social network designed to aid immigrants.[43] Nor is there any mystery in why Catholic social teaching, especially that by the United States bishops, is generally so pro-immigrant in its orientation.[44] This longtime, firmly established record of pro-immigrant action and sentiment, however—the latter of which was reaffirmed in 2004 in a major document[45]—raises the issue of why the emigration choice of one class of migrants, the skilled and educated, is decidedly not favored by Catholic social teaching. To explain this notable exception it is necessary to explore Catholic social teaching in more detail, including its foundational principles and the way in which those principles have been applied to specific immigration issues. The next two chapters do so.

NOTES

1. See Pope Pius XII, "The Apostolic Constitution, Exsul Familia" (Washington, D.C.: Catholic University of America, 1952), reprinted in *Exsul Familia: The Church's Magna Charta for Migrants*, ed. Rev. Giulivo Tessarolo (Staten Island: St. Charles Seminary, 1962): 23–60 (discussing the Church's history of assisting migrants and the work of Pope Leo XIII and his predecessors on behalf of migrants). For an overview of Catholic social teaching on immigration, see Terry Coonan, "There Are No Strangers Among Us: Catholic Social Teaching and U.S. Immigration Law," *The Catholic Lawyer* 40 (2000): 105.

2. See, e.g., Matthew 2:12–23 (the flight of Jesus, Mary, and Joseph into Egypt); Luke 10:29–37 (the parable of the good Samaritan); Exodus 23:9 ("You shall not oppress the alien; you well know how it feels to be an alien, since you were once aliens yourselves in the land of Egypt"); Leviticus 19:33–34 ("You shall treat the stranger who resides with you no differently that the natives born among you, have the same love for him as for yourself; for you too were once strangers in the land of Egypt"); Matthew 25:35 ("I was a stranger and you made me welcome"); Deuteronomy

10:17–19 ("For the Lord, your God . . . executes justice for the orphan and the widow, and befriends the alien, feeding and clothing him. So, you too must befriend the alien, for you were once aliens yourselves"); and Deuteronomy 27:19 ("Accursed be anyone who violates the rights of the foreigner, the orphan and the widow"). For more on scripture and migration, see Joseph A. Mindling, "Chosen People in Foreign Lands: Scriptural Reflections on Immigration and the Uprooted," *New Theology Review* 12 (1999): 4, *passim*; Jose Roberto Juarez, Jr., "The Challenge of Catholic Social Thought on Immigration for U.S. Catholics," *The Journal of Catholic Social Thought* 1 (2004): 461, 465–69; Michael Scaperlanda, "Who Is My Neighbor? An Essay on Immigrants, Welfare Reform, and the Constitution," *Connecticut Law Review* 29 (1997): 1,587, 1,620–21. See also Pontifical Council for the Pastoral Care of Migrants and Itinerant People, *Erga migrantes caritas Christi (The Love of Christ toward Migrants)*, pars. 14–15 (Vatican City: 2004) (discussing "Migration and the History of Salvation" and "Christ the 'foreigner' and Mary, a living symbol of the emigrant"), available at http://www.vatican.va.

   3. Charles E. Curran, *Catholic Social Teaching, 1891–Present: A Historical, Theological, and Ethical Analysis* (Washington, D.C.: Georgetown University Press, 2002), 44.

   4. Curran, *Catholic Social Teaching, 1891–Present* 44–45. See Thomas Massaro, *Living Justice: Catholic Social Teaching in Action* (Franklin: Sheed & Ward, 2000), 90–91 (asserting that "Scripture plays far less central a role [in Catholic social teaching] than it does in documents from parallel Protestant sources, such as the social teachings of the World Council of Churches or individual Protestant denominations"). Michael Novak has strongly defended Catholic social teaching's approach—which matches his own—by stating that "no one can deduce a system of political economy from the texts of the Bible alone. . . . One needs to add . . . a profound study of political philosophy, of social institutions, and of economic experiments throughout history." Michael Novak, *Catholic Social Thought & Liberal Institutions: Freedom with Justice*, 2nd edition (New Brunswick: Transaction, 1989), xv–xvi.

   5. Alan Dowty, *Closed Borders* (New Haven: Yale University Press, 1987), 8 (noting that "the right of emigration does not imply a corresponding right of immigration; the state does not have to let anyone in").

   6. Pontifical Council Cor Unum & Pontifical Council for the Pastoral Care of Migrants and Itinerant People, *Refugees: A Challenge to Solidarity*, sec. 14 (Libreria Editrice Vaticana, 1992) (stating that "[n]o person must be sent back to a country where he or she fears discriminatory action or serious life-threatening situations"). Pope John XXIII also charged states to accept refugees freely and to integrate them into society. Pope John XXIII, *Pacem in Terris* (1963), par. 106, available at http://www.vatican.va; see also U.S. Bishops' Committee on Migration, *One Family Under God* (Washington, D.C.: U.S. Catholic Conference, 1995), 10 (noting that people "fleeing persecution or other refugee-like situations require special consideration").

   7. United States Conference of Catholic Bishops and Conferencia del Episcopado Mexicano, *Strangers No Longer: Together on the Journey of Hope, A Pastoral Letter*

Concerning Migration from the Catholic Bishops of Mexico and the United States par. (Washington, D.C.: U.S. Conference of Catholic Bishops and Conferencia del Episcopado Mexicano 2003), par. 31.

8. Convention Relating to the Status of Refugees, July 28, 1951, art. 1(A)(2), 189 U.N.T.S. 150, 152–54 (hereinafter Refugee Convention). The Refugee Convention obligates its signatories not to return a refugee to her home country—an obligation known as *non-refoulment*—but it does not require the state to extend to refugees any particular rights in the country of protection.

9. Protocol Relating to the Status of Refugees, January 31, 1967, 19 U.S.T. 6223, 606 T.I.A.S. 6577 [hereinafter Refugee Protocol]. The Refugee Protocol provides that, by ratifying it, a nation also is bound by Articles 2–34 of the Refugee Convention.

10. Refugee Protocol, at art. 1(1). Similarly, the Immigration and Nationality Act defines a refugee as "any person who is outside any country of such person's nationality . . . and who is unable or unwilling to return to, and is unable or unwilling to avail himself or herself of the protection of that country because of persecution or a well-founded fear of persecution on account of race, religion, nationality, membership in a particular social group, or political opinion." INA sec. 101(a)(42), 8 U.S.C. sec. 1101(a)(42).

11. See, e.g., Pontifical Council Cor Unum and Pontifical Council for the Pastoral Care of Migrants and Itinerant People, *Refugees*, sec. 13 (calling for nation-states to consider as refugees individuals fleeing from systematic oppression and civil strife); Pope John Paul II, *Sollicitudo Rei Socialis* (1987), sec. 24 (speaking of refugees as those "whom war, natural calamities, persecution, and discrimination of every kind have deprived of home, employment, family, and homeland"). Drew Christiansen argues that the exclusion of victims of severe economic deprivation from the scope of the term "refugee" as defined in U.S. law is a critical legal failure; indeed, he posits that the "pejorative designation of 'economic refugee' in current U.S. practice is repugnant to the spirit of Catholic social teaching." Drew Christiansen, "Sacrament of Unity: Ethical Issues in the Pastoral Care of Migrants and Refugees," in *Today's Immigrants and Refugees: A Christian Understanding* (Washington, D.C.: National Conference of Catholic Bishops, 1988): 91.

With this in mind, in 1992, the Catholic Church called on the international community to expand the scope of internationally recognized refugees:

> The first international initiatives took place in a rather limited context. They demonstrated an interest for the suffering of specifically persecuted persons, which was limited to their individual reasons for leaving their countries. Now that forcibly uprooted people have become multitudes, international agreements must be revised, and the protection they guarantee must be extended to other categories as well.

Pontifical Council Cor Unum and Pontifical Council for the Pastoral Care of Migrants and Itinerant People, *Refugees*, sec. 8. See also Coonan, "There Are No Strangers Among Us," at 116 n. 31 & 133–34, n.102 (noting that "[n]either international refugee law nor U.S. asylum law recognizes severe economic deprivation as grounds for warranting refugee protection or the granting of asylum status" and detailing other ways in which the Church has "called for the recognition of refugee rights that far exceed the scope of protection under current international law").

12. Because of the sacredness of the family, church teachings extend the right to migrate to families of migrants. As the U.S. Bishops' Committee on Migration explains, "[I]t is important that, as a nation, we recognize the importance of affirming family within the immigration context as a means of not only affirming the family in the United States in general, but as a means of providing buffers for immigrants who seek to acclimate to this society." U.S. Bishops' Committee on Migration, *One Family Under God* (Washington, D.C.: United States Catholic Conference), 11. Accordingly, the U.S. Catholic bishops support U.S. immigration laws that provide preferences in migration to family members of newcomers to the United States and support efforts to reunite families. U.S. Bishops' Committee on Migration, *One Family Under God*, 16; see also National Conference of Catholic Bishops, W*elcoming the Stranger Among Us: Unity in Diversity* (Washington, D.C.: U.S. Catholic Conference, 2000), 12.

13. Pope John Paul II, *Laborem Exercens* (1981), sec. 23.

14. Coonan, "There Are No Strangers Among Us," 116. Catholic social thought shows particular concern for the plight of migrant workers and other unauthorized workers who are marginalized and voiceless in the mainstream polity. See, e.g., National Conference of Catholic Bishops, *Welcoming the Stranger Among Us*, 51 (discussing migrant workers); U.S. Bishops' Committee on Migration, *One Family Under God*, 10–11 (discussing undocumented migrants and migrant workers); NCCB Ad Hoc Committee on Migration and Tourism, "The Church and the Immigrant Today: The Pastoral Concern of the Church for People on the Move," in National Conference of Catholic Bishops, *The Pastoral Concern of the Church for the People on the Move* (Washington, D.C.: U.S. Catholic Conference, 1976) 5, 19–23 (discussing undocumented migrants) (herinafter "The Church and the Immigrant Today"), reprinted in National Conference of Catholic Bishops, *People on the Move: A Compendium of Church Documents on the Pastoral Concern for Migrants and Refugees* (Washington, D.C.: U.S. Catholic Conference, 1988), 61, 66–68. The U.S. bishops have called for the granting of legal immigration status to unauthorized individuals, particularly those who have "built equities and otherwise contributed to their communities." National Conference of Catholic Bishops, *Welcoming the Stranger Among Us*, 12.

15. The coupling of the right to migrate with the duty to sustain one's self and one's family is a theme repeated throughout modern Catholic social teaching. See chapter 6; see also Andrew Yuengert, "Catholic Social Teaching on the Economics of Immigration," *Journal of Markets & Morality* 3 (2000): 88, 89, available at http://www.acton.org/publicat/m_and_m/2000_spring/yuengert.html (adding that in addition to the right of the family to sustenance, the right to migrate is also grounded in the right to economic initiative and the priority of the family over the state).

16. Sacred Congregation for Bishops, "Instruction on the Pastoral Care of People Who Migrate" (Washington, D.C.: U.S. Catholic Conference, 1969), 8 par. 8 (citations and internal quotation marks omitted), reprinted in National Conference of Catholic Bishops, *People on the Move*, 83, 85.

17. See Yuengert, "Catholic Social Teaching on the Economics of Immigration," 90.

18. Dana W. Wilbanks, *Re-Creating America: The Ethics of U.S. Immigration and Refugee Policy in a Christian Perspective* (Nashville: Abingdon Press in cooperation with the Churches' Center for Theology and Public Policy, 1996), 151 ("From the standpoint of Catholic social teaching, [STEP OUT migrants] have a strong moral obligation to contribute to the common good of their homelands, not to take their skills elsewhere").

19. Some scholars assert that in Catholic social teaching "immigration is a right that the state cannot abridge." Yuengert, "Catholic Social Teaching on the Economics of Immigration," 88.

20. Pope John XXIII, *Pacem in Terris*, par. 106, available at http://www.vatican.va; Pontifical Council Cor Unum and Pontifical Council for the Pastoral Care of Migrants and Itinerant People, *Refugees*, at sec. 14 (stating that "[n]o person must be sent back to a country where he or she fears discriminatory action or serious life-threatening situations"); U.S. Bishops' Committee on Migration, *One Family Under God*, at 10 (noting that people "fleeing persecution or other refugee-like situations require special consideration").

21. See chapter 6. See also Juarez, Jr., "The Challenge of Catholic Social Thought on Immigration for U.S. Catholics," 464 (stating that, according to Catholic social teaching, the right to exclude economic migrants "is very limited"). Catholic social teaching conceives of the right of sovereign nations to regulate migration across their borders much more narrowly than the rights currently recognized under international and U.S. law, which give sovereign nations the unchallenged right to control their borders. See *Chae Chan Ping v. United States*, 130 U.S. 581, 603 (1889) (stating that "[j]urisdiction over its own territory to [exclude aliens] is an incident of every independent nation"); James A.R. Nafziger, "The General Admission of Aliens Under International Law," *American Journal of International Law* 77 (1983): 804, 804 (explaining that "sovereign decisions concerning the general admission of aliens are said to be immune from legal appraisal"). See also Dowty, *Closed Borders*, 14. Professor Dowty describes the general consensus as follows:

> Whatever the arguments over the authority of the state to block emigration, there is little dispute over its rights to limit *immigration*. The two issues are not symmetrical: departure ends an individual's claims against a society, while entry sets claims in motion. Control of entry is essential to the idea of sovereignty, for without it a society has no control over its basic character. Even in countries where the right of exit is taken for granted, few contest the right, or even duty, of the state to regulate the influx of newcomers.

Dowty, *Closed Borders*, 14 (emphasis in original)

22. See chapter 6.

23. U.S. Bishops' Committee on Migration, *One Family Under God*, 12–13; NCCB Ad Hoc Committee on Migration and Tourism, "The Church and the Immigrant Today," 14.

24. Pontifical Council for the Pastoral Care of Migrants and Itinerant People, *Erga migrantes caritas Christi (The Love of Christ toward Migrants)*, par. 28 ("Pastoral care of migrants means welcome, respect, protection, promotion and genuine love of every

person in his or her religious and cultural expressions"). See also Pope John Paul II, *Ecclesia in America* (Washington, D.C.: United States Catholic Conference, 1999), sec. 65 (reiterating that the human dignity of all migrants should be respected "even in cases of non-legal immigration"), available at http://www.vativan.va; Pope Paul VI, *Populorum Progressio* (1967), par. 67 ("We cannot insist too much on the duty of welcoming others—a duty springing from human solidarity and Christian charity—which is incumbent both on the families and the cultural organizations of the host countries"); United States Conference of Catholic Bishops and Conferencia del Episcopado Mexicano, *Strangers No Longer,* par. 38 (explaining that "[r]egardless of their legal status, migrants, like all persons, possess inherent human dignity that should be respected . . ."); National Conference of Catholic Bishops, *Welcoming the Stranger Among Us,* 11 (explaining that the "Church supports the human rights of all people and offers them pastoral care, education, and social services, no matter what the circumstances of entry into this country"). As Pope John Paul II explained, "So that every person's dignity is respected, the immigrant is welcomed as a brother or sister, and all humanity forms a united family which knows how to appreciate with discernment the different cultures which comprise it." Pope John Paul II, "Message for the World Migration Day, 2000" (Vatican, November 21, 1999), sec. 5, available at http://www.vatican.va. See generally Pontifical Council for the Pastoral Care of Migrants and Itinerant People, *Erga migrantes caritas Christi (The Love of Christ toward Migrants) passim* (detailing the many obligations every level of the Church has to ease migrants' burdens).

25. Some have characterized the abstract principles of Catholic social teaching and "the explicitly formulated theories of economic, political and social life that are expressed in papal, conciliar and other episcopal documents" as constituting the "high tradition" of Catholic social teaching, while the "low tradition" is formed by the lives and spiritual experiences of the broader faith community. See Kenneth R. Himes, *Responses to 101 Questions on Catholic Social Teaching* (New York: Paulist Press, 2001), 6–7.

26. See, e.g., U.S. Bishops' Committee on Migration, *One Family Under God,* 7 (noting that the Church "is required by the Gospel . . . to promote and defend the human rights and dignity of people on the move, to advocate social remedies to their problems and to foster opportunities for their spiritual and religious growth") (internal quotation marks omitted); National Conference of Catholic Bishops, *Together a New People: Pastoral Statement on Migrants and Refugees* (Washington, D.C.: U.S. Catholic Conference, 1987), 1–2 (approved November 8, 1986) (grounding the Church's efforts to extend care and protection to migrants on Gospel teachings), reprinted in National Conference of Catholic Bishops, *People on the Move: A Compendium of Church Documents,* 71, 72. See also Pontifical Council for the Pastoral Care of Migrants and Itinerant People, *Erga migrantes caritas Christi,* at par. 12–17 (citing numerous biblical passages relating to migrants). For an informative general discussion of the themes apparent in the Catholic Church's teachings on migration, see Donald Kerwin, "Catholic Social Teaching on Migration on the 40th Anniversary of Pacem in Terris," *Journal of Catholic Social Thought* 1 (2003): 129.

27. Exodus 23:9.

28. Matthew 25:31–46.

29. See Curran, *Catholic Social Teaching, 1891–Present*, 42 ("Catholic teaching by definition is universal. A Catholic ethic must include a concern for the whole world, all people in the world, and what is happening in it").

30. Pope John Paul II, "Address to the Conference of the *Centesimus Annus Pro Pontifice* Foundation" (Vatican: May 9, 1998) (noting that *Rerum Novarum* focused mainly on "the 'worker question' in a European context"). See Novak, *Catholic Social Thought and Liberal Institutions*, 222 (stating that prior to Vatican II, Catholic social thought "had been centrally addressed to the problems of industrialization, and especially to the workers of Europe," and that "[t]he Church and its terminology were Eurocentric"); David Hollenbach, *Justice, Peace, & Human Rights: American Catholic Social Ethics in a Pluralistic Context* (New York: Crossroad, 1988), 5 (explaining that the "early social encyclicals had Western Europe implicitly in mind as the 'world' to which the church's mission was to be directed"); Michael Evans, *An Analysis of U.N. Refugee Policy in Light of Roman Catholic Social Teaching and the Phenomena Creating Refugees* (Ann Arbor: University Microfilms International, 1991), 111 (noting that the early social encyclicals give "the idea that the workers whose rights are discussed are only those of the industrial, developed countries"); John A. Coleman, "The Future of Catholic Social Thought," *Modern Catholic Social Teaching: Commentaries and Interpretations*, ed. Kenneth B. Himes (Washington, D.C.: Georgetown University Press, 2005): 522, 523 (stating that up to Vatican II, "official Catholic social thought was an essentially Eurocentered project").

31. See Donal Dorr, *Option for the Poor: A Hundred Years of Catholic Social Teaching*, revised edition (Maryknoll: Orbis Books, 1992): 343 (noting criticism that the encyclical published after the end of the Soviet Union's domination of Eastern Europe, *Centesimus Annus*, was "unduly Eurocentric").

32. Pope John Paul II, Message for the 85th World Migration Day 1999, Feb. 2, 1999, available at www.vatican.va (stating that "the Church is in solidarity with the world of migrants who, with their variety of languages, races, cultures and customs, remind her of her own condition as a people on pilgrimage from every part of the earth to their final homeland. This vision helps Christians to reject all nationalistic thinking and to avoid narrow ideological categories.") National Conference of Catholic Bishops, *Together a New People*, at 1–3 (explaining that as a "church of many nations, the Catholic community was called to develop an attitude of welcome"); Pontifical Council for the Pastoral Care of Migrants and Itinerant People, *Erga migrantes caritas Christi (The Love of Christ toward Migrants)*, at par. 17 ("Foreigners are also a visible sign and an effective reminder of that universality which is a constituent element of the Catholic Church"). See also Pontifical Council for the Pastoral Care of Migrants and Itinerant People, *Erga migrantes caritas Christi*, at par. 103 (noting that migrants "offer the Church the opportunity to realize more concretely its identity as communion and its missionary vocation").

33. Dale T. Irvin and Scott W. Sunquist, *History of the World Christian Movement, Volume I: Earliest Christianity to 1453* (Maryknoll: Orbis Books, 2001), 69, 96. See Pontifical Council for the Pastoral Care of Migrants and Itinerant People, *Erga migrantes caritas Christi*, at par. 16 ("The believer is always a *paroikos*, a temporary resident, a guest wherever he may be"); Pontifical Council for the Pastoral Care of

Migrants and Itinerant People, *Erga migrantes caritas Christi*, at par. 101 (noting that "we are all pilgrims on our way towards our true homeland"). See also Michael Novak, *The Catholic Ethic and the Spirit of Capitalism* (New York: Free Press, 1993), 215–16 (stating that while "the Catholic tendency is to affirm every culture in which [the Church] finds itself," the Church also calls upon Catholics to "be in the world as a stranger"). Novak's statement echoes one found in the second-century Letter to Diognetus, which represented an attempt by a Christian to explain Christians to pagans. See Pope John Paul II, Message for the 85th World Migration Day 1999, Feb. 2, 1999, at par. 2, available at www.vatican.va (quoting the Letter to Diognetus to the effect that, for Christians, "[e]very foreign country is a homeland . . . and every homeland is a foreign country").

34. Curiously, then, both the Church's universalism *and* its apartness contribute to the Church's openness to immigrants. This apparent paradox springs from the differing objects of the universalist and separatist ambitions. For the Church, universalism describes the perspective of the Church vis-à-vis its relationship with all peoples of the world, while the separatist outlook is meant to preserve the unique independence of the Church and its members in their relations with other institutions. See Pontifical Council for the Pastoral Care of Migrants and Itinerant People, *Erga migrantes caritas Christi*, par. 22 (stating that the Church "is practically marked by the vocation to be in exile, in diaspora, dispersed among cultures and ethnic groups without ever identifying itself completely with any of these [because] [o]therwise it would cease to be the first-fruit and sign, the leaven and the prophecy of the universal Kingdom and community that welcomes every human being without preference for persons or peoples").

35. National Conference of Catholic Bishops, *Welcoming the Stranger Among Us*, 4, 7. See also United States Conference of Catholic Bishops and Conferencia del Episcopado Mexicano, *Strangers No Longer*, par. 40 (explaining that "[f]aith in the presence of Christ in the migrants leads to a conversion of mind and heart, which leads to a renewed spirit of communion and to the building of structures of solidarity to accompany the migrant"); Pontifical Council for the Pastoral Care of Migrants and Itinerant People, *Erga migrantes caritas Christi*, par. 101 ("The 'foreigner' is God's messenger who surprises us and interrupts the regularity and logic of daily life . . .").

36. Indeed, the importance to the conversion experience of confronting life as lived by persons in vulnerable states has achieved wide acceptance. Thus, the leading liberation theologian Gustavo Gutiérrez has favorably quoted "the most famous and moving statement of theology from the underside of history," Dietrich Bonhoeffer's statement that "[i]t is an experience of incomparable value to have learned to see the great events of history from beneath: from the viewpoint of the useless, the suspect, the abused, the powerless, the despised—in a word, from the viewpoint of those who suffer." John O'Brien, *Theology and the Option for the Poor* (Collegeville: The Liturgical Press, 1992), 30 n. 20. See also United States Conference of Catholic Bishops and Conferencia del Episcopado Mexicano, *Strangers No Longer*, par. 40 (explaining that "[p]art of the process of conversion of mind and heart deals with confronting attitudes of cultural superiority, indifference and racism; accepting migrants not as foreboding aliens, terrorists, or economic threats, but rather as persons with dignity and rights"); Curran, *Catholic Social Teaching 1891–Present*, 45–46 ("The tradition of

Catholic social teaching also recognizes, though in a comparatively minor key, the need for a change of heart").

37. As the U.S. Bishops' Committee on Migration explains, the "immigrant tradition of this nation has meant that the Catholic Church in the United States is a microcosm of the universal Church." U.S. Bishops' Committee on Migration, *One Family Under God*, at 7.

38. Americans whose families have lost such memories in any particularity still are usually aware that someone among their ancestors was an immigrant, and if they know the area from which that immigrant originated, they usually are sensitive to the plight of immigrants at least from that area.

39. Pope John Paul II, *Ecclesia in America*, sec. 65 (U.S. Conference of Catholic Bishops, 1999) (noting that "America has experienced many immigrations, as waves of men and women came to its various regions in the hope of a better future"); National Conference of Catholic Bishops, *Welcoming the Stranger Among Us*, at 7 (explaining that the Catholic community today is "rapidly re-encountering itself as an 'immigrant Church'"). The rapid growth of the American Catholic Church in the nineteenth and twentieth centuries is attributed in large part to continuous immigrant flows. See Charles R. Morris, *American Catholic: The Saints and Sinners Who Built America's Most Powerful Church* (New York: Time Books, 1997), 113, 268. The vast majority of American Catholics today are the direct descendants of several waves of immigrant flows, which peaked from Ireland in the 1850s, from Germany in the early 1880s, from Italy in the early 1900s, and from Poland and Slavic countries in the early 1920s. Morris, *American Catholic*, 268. More recently, large groups of immigrants are coming to the United States from the predominately Catholic countries of Latin America. National Conference of Catholic Bishops, *Welcoming the Stranger Among Us*, 15 (noting that "[p]robably more than 80 percent of Hispanic immigrants were raised in the Catholic faith" and that Hispanic Catholics "could make up the majority of U.S. Catholics" by the year 2020). In addition, Catholics represent large segments of immigrants coming from Vietnam, former Soviet republics, China, Korea, Sri Lanka, Indonesia, and African countries. National Conference of Catholic Bishops, *Welcoming the Stranger Among Us*, 15. As Pope John Paul II explained in *Ecclesia in America*,

> The [immigration] phenomenon [in America] continues even today, especially with many people and families from Latin American countries who have moved to the northern parts of the continent, to the point where in some cases they constitute a substantial part of the population . . . The Church is well aware of the problems created by this situation and is committed to spare no effort in developing her own pastoral strategy among these immigrant people, in order to help them settle in their new land and to foster a welcoming attitude among the local population, in the belief that a mutual openness will bring enrichment to all.

Pope John Paul II, *Ecclesia in America*, at sec. 65.

40. See generally Appendix B. See also National Conference of Catholic Bishops, *Together a New People*, 1 (noting that the "concern of the Church for immigrants and refugees is a thread that ties together more than three centuries of its history in the United States").

41. According to statistics from the Pew Charitable Trust, 50 percent of the 30 million immigrants in the United States are Catholic. "Telephone Interview with Mary Jane Smith," May 29, 2003 (interview summary on file with authors). The U.S. Catholic Bishops' Secretariat for Hispanic Affairs reports that there are 25 million Hispanic Catholics in the United States, comprising 40 percent of the U.S. Catholic population. See Agostino Bono, "Hispanic Growth Requires Bilingual Church Life, Says Bishop," *Catholic News Service*, November 18, 2002. While not all Hispanics are recent immigrants, the Catholic bishops attribute 71 percent of the post-1960 growth in the U.S. Catholic population to Hispanics.

42. Wilbanks, *Re-Creating America*, 14 ("Our national self-image is bound up with our immigrant heritage—a diverse people united by common allegiance to the United States, its Constitution, and its promise of freedom and opportunity"); Dowty, *Closed Borders*, 230 (noting that "Americans have traditionally perceived their country as a haven for people subject to persecution in other lands"). Indeed, one of the first documents collectively published by the U.S. bishops expressly invoked this view of the United States as a bastion of liberty open to all:

> Our country had its origins in a struggle for liberty. Once established as an independent republic, it became the refuge of those who preferred freedom in America to the conditions prevailing in their native lands. Differing widely in culture, belief, and capacity for self-government, they had as their common characteristic the desire for liberty and the pursuit of happiness.

"Pastoral Letter of September 26, 1919," in *Pastoral Letters of the United States Catholic Bishops* 1, ed. Hugh J. Nolan (Washington, D.C.: National Conference of Catholic Bishops, 1984): 272, 319–20.

43. See Appendix B for a discussion of the origins, history, and extent of the American Catholic Church's social network for immigrants.

44. See this chapter; see also Pope Paul VI, "Responsibility of Local Churches Regarding the Problems of Migration," *L'Osservatore Romano* (Vatican, November 1, 1973), at 5 (advocating that states "guarantee the rights of migrants to respect of their personality, security of work, vocational training, family life, schooling for their children adapted to their needs, social insurance and freedom of speech and association").

45. Pontifical Council for the Pastoral Care of Migrants and Itinerant People, *Erga migrantes caritas Christi* (2004). The Pontifical Council for the Pastoral Care of Migrants and Itinerant People was established in 1988, as the successor to the Pontifical Commission for the Pastoral Care of Migration and Tourism. Pontifical Council for the Pastoral Care of Migrants and Itinerant People, *Erga migrantes caritas Christi*, at par. 31. The Council is charged with guiding "the pastoral solicitude of the Church to the particular needs of those who have been forced to abandon their homeland as well as those who have none." Pontifical Council for the Pastoral Care of Migrants and Itinerant People, *Erga migrantes caritas Christi*, at Juridicial Pastoral Regulations, Art. 22, sec. 1 (internal quotation marks and citation omitted).

Chapter Five

Foundational Principles

In this chapter, the focus will be on what is sometimes called Catholic social *doctrine*. Although the term has been the subject of some controversy, for our purposes Catholic social doctrine is best thought of as Catholic social teaching but with stress on the theoretical aspects of the teaching, rather than on its historical and practical aspects.[1] These differing aspects—theoretical, historical, and practical—have been distinguished as follows:

> Under the heading of [the] theoretical dimension, the Vatican lists organic and systematic reflection, universal criteria which can be accepted by all, and permanent ethical principles. The historical dimension is that in which the use of these ethical principles is framed in a real view of society and its problems at a particular point in time. Finally, the practical dimension proposes the effective application of these ethical principles, based on the interpretation of historical conditions, to concrete circumstances.[2]

As this work progresses, it will become apparent that its challenge is not to the social doctrine as such, but to the practical position the Church has taken on STEP OUT migration. Nonetheless, it is necessary to discuss the social doctrine in its narrow sense, that is, the theoretical dimension of Catholic social teaching, in order to render meaningful the subsequent discussion concerning how the Church's specific position on STEP OUT migration was deemed consonant with the general principles.

Turning then to the theoretical aspects of Catholic social teaching, it might first be noted that, while the Church rarely attempts to systematically explain the methodology of the social doctrine portion of its social teaching,[3] the two foundational concerns of Catholic social teaching are plain. The first of these concerns is the principle of human dignity. Indeed, the Church's most systematic treatment of Catholic social teaching, *Gaudium et Spes*, regards "human

dignity" as the grounding of the whole teaching.[4] The other foundational principle, also noted in *Gaudium et Spes*, is "the common good."[5] An understanding of these two principles, which are discussed below, provides the key for
grasping how Catholic social teaching could develop a generally pro-immigration policy, yet adhere to a restrictive position on the migration of skilled
and educated persons from developing countries.

HUMAN DIGNITY

The sacredness of the human person, which grants everyone a fundamental human dignity, is at the foundation of Catholic social teaching.[6] Unlike capital-
istic or some other contemporary notions of dignity or worth, Catholic social
teaching views human dignity as a gift of creation. Every human being pos-
sesses it, and it is not dependent on achievement, worth, or value of any kind.[7]
The most fundamental effect of this principle on the social teaching is a focus
on the subjectiveness of the human experience. Thus, for example, in Pope
John Paul II's encyclical on work, *Laborem Exercens*, the Pope emphasized
again and again that the most important consideration in regard to work is
never the object or output of the work, but the fact that a *person* is doing it.[8]

From the human being's essential dignity, certain fundamental human
rights flow.[9] These human rights are "universal and inviolable, [and] cannot
in any way be surrendered";[10] *a fortiori*, they belong to migrants as they belong to all others.[11] Individuals are endowed with these fundamental rights in
order to fulfill their duties to themselves and the community.[12] Grounded in
the dignity of the human person, rights are not considered to be creations of
society or the state. Nor are they primarily immunities that protect one's freedom.[13] Rather, "they are empowerments that give freedom for a particular end
or purpose."[14]

The state's purpose therefore is not to endow individuals with rights.
Rather, with respect to individual rights, the state's purpose is to protect the
inherent rights of persons and foster an environment in which people can live
with dignity.[15] As explained by the U.S. Catholic bishops, "These rights are
bestowed on human beings by God and grounded in the nature and dignity of
human persons. They are not created by society. Indeed, society has a moral
duty to secure and protect them."[16] American lawyers today, trained to assert
that the first amendment grants a right to free speech, and that the Constitution mandates due process, might at first consider these assertions regarding
the origin of rights as alien to U.S. "rights talk," but really they are not. Indeed, modern Catholic social teaching on this subject echoes the statement articulated at the inception of the United States, in the Declaration of Indepen-

dence: "We hold these Truths to be self-evident, that all Men are created equal, that they are endowed by their Creator with certain inalienable Rights, that among these are Life, Liberty, and the Pursuit of Happiness."[17] More recent articulations of the same idea are plentiful as well, including a prominent mention by America's only Catholic President, John F. Kennedy, in his inaugural Address.[18]

In the body of Catholic social teaching, the most extensive delineation of human rights appears in Pope John XXIII's *Pacem in Terris*.[19] Rights listed in this encyclical include, among many others, the rights to subsistence,[20] a basic education,[21] family life,[22] worship,[23] work,[24] food,[25] shelter,[26] security in cases of sickness and old age,[27] private property,[28] assembly and association,[29] emigration and immigration,[30] and bodily integrity[31]—indeed, "all the rights enumerated in the United Nations Universal Declaration and its two accompanying covenants."[32] The listed rights are said to derive from one's inherent human dignity.[33]

Notably, the set of rights that the human person enjoys, as interpreted through Catholic social teaching, is broad and expands beyond traditional notions of human and civil rights commonly found in U.S. domestic law. Domestic law bestows predominately negative, or "liberty," rights, such as freedoms from intervention by the government in one's speech, religion, and associations. Catholic social teaching extends beyond the class of negative rights to the understanding that the natural law bestows on the human person positive, or "entitlement," rights that are necessary for the human person to live in dignity. Examples of such rights are the rights to food and to shelter.[34]

THE COMMON GOOD

While the dignity of the human being is fundamental, Catholic social teaching also recognizes that individuals live in community with others. The social nature of the person and her relationships with family and community form an essential part of human existence that is necessary in order for the individual to flourish and develop.[35] The second foundational principle of Catholic social teaching, the principle of the "common good," flows from this communitarian nature of humans, which reflects the trinitarian nature of the faith.

As described by Pope John XXIII, the common good is "the sum total of those conditions of social living, whereby [persons] are enabled more fully and more readily to achieve their own perfection."[36] The recognition of human beings as living and "only truly flourish[ing] in the context of a community"[37]—interestingly, recent research on brain development provides a biological foundation for this view[38]—is evident throughout Catholic social teaching. As explained in the Vatican II document, *Gaudium et Spes*:

> Man's social nature makes it evident that the progress of the human person and the advance of society itself hinge on each other. . . . This social life is not something added on to man. . . . Among those social ties which man needs for his development, some, like the family and political community, relate with greater immediacy to his innermost nature.[39]

According to Catholic social teaching, the state is entrusted with promoting and protecting the common good. Rather than being regarded as a necessary evil, the "state or the political community . . . has a positive function to promote public well-being."[40] Thus, the Catholic Church views the state not merely as a coercive or authoritative power, but also as one that is necessary to achieve the common good. Indeed, as Pope John XXIII explained in *Mater et Magistra*, the whole raison d'être of the state "is the realization of the common good in the temporal order."[41]

THE RELATIONSHIP BETWEEN AND THE SOCIAL POLICY IMPLICATIONS OF THE PRINCIPLES OF HUMAN DIGNITY AND THE COMMON GOOD

Although it may seem to some that these two principles of human dignity and the common good might naturally be in opposition to each other, in Catholic social teaching they work hand in hand. That is because the social teaching conceives human dignity as being attainable only in community with others, while it simultaneously views the "commitment to serve the common good [as] a means whereby the dignity of each person [can be] given its due."[42] On this basis, the Church can speak of "the *integral* promotion of the human person and the common good."[43]

In general, the highlighting of both of these twin concerns puts the Church in good stead, helping it to help the world avoid both the horrors of collectivism—in which the dignity of the individual person is denied in pursuit of a collectivist good—and the excesses of rampant individualism, in which the good of the greater society is discounted in pursuit of idiosyncratic personal ends.[44] In isolation, both of these alternative orientations are misguided, in the view of the Church, because they are incomplete: the inherent dignity of the human person and humanity's social nature both must be respected and considered.[45] To do otherwise results in distortions that, because they are founded on an incomplete and, hence, untruthful assessment of human nature, cannot help but bring about misfortune and even, periodically, catastrophe.[46]

Appropriate social policy, then, is a matter of appropriately considering both human dignity and the common good.[47] Oftentimes, this task appears to be a clear one, as when both key concerns point in the same direction, or when one concern is implicated strongly and the other weakly or not at all. On many issues, however, consideration of human dignity and the common good yields no definitive policy; rather, "a plurality of morally acceptable policies and solutions [may] arise . . . because of the contingent nature of certain choices regarding the ordering of society, the variety of strategies available for accomplishing or guaranteeing the same fundamental value, the possibility of different interpretations of the basic principles of political theory, and the technical complexity of many political problems."[48]

The Church's sound inclination in such cases is to remain silent. This is why, among other reasons,[49] there are no encyclicals on issues such as how far off the coastline international waters should begin,[50] and why the U.S. bishops have yet to articulate exactly how much arsenic should be permitted in drinking water, or how big a percentage of U.S. energy use should come from nuclear power. In these types of cases, the Church recognizes the complexity of the issues, and understands that it has no special contribution to offer.[51]

The root of this humility, or perhaps prudence,[52] is not that the issues noted above cannot ever be assessed through the prism of Catholic social teaching; rather, it is that crucial facts about each issue are, at present, insufficiently understood, so that the moral dimensions of the issues have yet clearly to emerge[53] within a particular "historical, geographic, economic, technological and cultural context."[54] But they conceivably could; for example, "international laws that unduly punish landlocked countries . . . could provoke a justified appeal to the lessons of Catholic social teaching."[55] In the meantime, however, a cautious approach seems wise, and yet, absent an unbroken policy of unyielding silence—an eternal "no comment"—there is always the chance that in some cases the Church unwittingly could assert positions prematurely or without a full understanding of the facts. The next chapter explores the possibility of factual error with relation to Catholic social teaching's positions on the rights of refugees, migrants, and STEP OUT migrants, as part of a larger discussion concerning how the principles of human dignity and the common good apply to immigration.

NOTES

1. Fred Kammer, *Doing Faith Justice: An Introduction to Catholic Social Thought* (New York: Paulist Press, 1991), 72. Interestingly, Pope John Paul II used both terms, as well as a third, i.e., "social magisterium," without seeming to distinguish between them. See Pope John Paul II, *Centesimus Annus* (1991), sec. 2. Others have distinguished

between "teaching" and "doctrine," however, to the general disadvantage of the latter term, which has fallen out of favor since the 1960s. The principal objection to "social doctrine" is that "it smack[s] of a timeless dogmatism which would be particularly inappropriate in matters of social morality where the emphasis of Church teaching has changed so much over the years." Donal Dorr, *Option for the Poor: A Hundred Years of Catholic Social Teaching*, revised edition (Maryknoll: Orbis Books, 1992), 10. "Teaching," on the other hand, has won favor as "less rigid, and less oppressively authoritative." Philip S. Land, *Catholic Social Teaching As I Have Lived, Loathed, and Loved It* (Chicago: Loyola University Press, 1994), 109. "Social doctrine" retains some utility, however, at least as we use it here, not as a complete alternative to the term "social teaching," but in the more limited sense of invoking the teaching's more theoretical aspects.

2. Kammer, *Doing Faith Justice*, 72.

3. Charles E. Curran, *Catholic Social Teaching, 1891–Present: A Historical, Theological, and Ethical Analysis* (Washington, D.C.: Georgetown University Press, 2002), 48 (noting that the "documents of Catholic social teaching generally do not propose a well-integrated theological methodology," due to "the fact that Catholic social teaching by definition deals with teaching, not with a systematic ethical approach").

4. Second Vatican Council, *Gaudium et Spes* (1965), sec. 12 (discussing, in part one, chapter 1, "The Dignity of the Human Person"). See also Curran, *Catholic Social Teaching, 1891–Present*, 75; David Hollenbach, *Claims in Conflict: Retrieving and Renewing the Catholic Human Rights Tradition* (New York: Paulist Press, 1979), 42.

5. Vatican Council, *Gaudium et Spes*, at sec. 23 (discussing, in part one, chapter 2, "The Human Community"). See "Address of His Holiness Benedict XVI to the Delegates of the Academy of Moral and Political Sciences of Paris," Feb. 10, 2007 (stating that "the reflections and actions of the Authorities and of the citizens must be centered on two elements: respect for the human being and the quest for the common good"), available at www.vatican.va.

6. Vatican Council, *Gaudium et Spes*, sec. 12. As the U.S. Catholic Bishops explain: "The human person is the clearest reflection of God's presence in the world; all of the Church's work in pursuit of both justice and peace is designed to protect and promote the dignity of every person. For each person not only reflects God, but is the expression of God's creative work and the meaning of Christ's redemptive ministry." U.S. Catholic Bishops, *The Challenge of Peace: God's Promise and Our Response* (1983), par. 15. Pope John XXIII explained human dignity in this way: "Any human society, if it is to be well-ordered and productive, must lay down as a foundation this principle, namely that every human being is a person; that is, his nature is endowed with intelligence and free will. Indeed, precisely because he is a person he has rights and obligations flowing directly and simultaneously from his very nature." Pope John XXIII, *Pacem in Terris* (1963), par. 9.

7. Pope John Paul II, *Centesimus Annus* (1991), sec. 11 (stating that "there exist rights which do not correspond to any work [a person] performs, but which flow from his essential dignity as a person").

8. Pope John Paul II, *Laborem Exercens* (1981), secs. 3, 6, 7, 8, 9, 10, 12, 13. See also Pope John Paul II, "Speech to the Pontifical Academy of Social Sciences" (Vat-

ican, April 27, 2001) (stating the human person "must always be an end and not a means, a subject, not an object, not a commodity of trade"); Pope John Paul II, *Homily at Mass for the Jubilee of Workers* (Vatican, May 1, 2000) (asserting that workers must not "become tools but the protagonists of their future").

9. Pope John XXIII, *Pacem in Terris*, par. 9; Pope John Paul II, *Centesimus Annus*, sec. 11. See Archbishop Celestino Migliore, *Statement Before the Third Committee of the U.N. General Assembly* (November 14, 2003) (stating that "[t]he universality of human rights springs from the unquestionable truth that all human beings are equal in nature and in dignity").

10. Pope John XXIII, *Pacem in Terris*, par. 9.

11. Pontifical Council for the Pastoral Care of Migrants and Itinerant People, *Erga migrantes caritas Christi (The Love of Christ toward Migrants)* (Vatican City: 2004), sec. 5 ("Every migrant enjoys inalienable fundamental rights which must be respected in all cases."), available at http://www.vatican.va.

12. David Hollenbach, *Claims in Conflict*, 48 (noting that "to each of [the enumerated] rights corresponds a duty").

13. Curran, *Catholic Social Teaching, 1891–Present*, 217.

14. Curran, *Catholic Social Teaching, 1891–Present*, 217.

15. The best-known articulation of this is Pope Leo XIII's famous formulation: "Man is older than the State." Pope Leo XIII, *Rerum Novarum* (1891), sec. 6. As Pope John XXIII asserted: "The cardinal point of this teaching is that individual men are necessarily the foundation, cause, and end of all social institutions." Pope John XXIII, *Mater et Magistra* (1961), par. 219. Similarly, Professor Lisa Sowle Cahill has explained that human rights are "owed the protection of law and the support of some degree of institutionalization by the state." Lisa Sowle Cahill, "The Catholic Tradition: Religion, Morality, and the Common Good," *Journal of Law & Religion* 5 (1987): 75, 77.

16. National Conference of Catholic Bishops, *Economic Justice for All: Pastoral Letter on Catholic Social Teaching and the U.S. Economy* (Washington, D.C.: U.S. Catholic Conference, 1986) par. 79 [hereinafter *Economic Justice for All*]; see Archbishop Celestino Migliore (stating that human "rights and freedoms are not contingent upon the State or upon its recognition of any particular right. Rather, they are intrinsic to human nature itself and to what is essential to this nature."). See also Curran, *Catholic Social Teaching, 1891–Present*, 219 (discussing the grounding of rights in Catholic social teaching).

17. The Declaration of Independence (U.S. 1776), par. 2. See also Edward Dumbauld, *The Declaration of Independence and What It Means Today* (Oklahoma: University of Oklahoma Press, 1950), 157.

18. John F. Kennedy, "Inaugural Address" (January 20, 1961) (stating that "the rights of man come not from the generosity of the state but from the hand of God"), reprinted in David Newton Lott, *The Presidents Speak: The Inaugural Addresses of the American Presidents, from Washington to Clinton* (New York: Henry Holt & Co, 1994): 311, 312.

19. Hollenbach, *Claims in Conflict*, 66.

20. Pope John XXIII, *Pacem in Terris*, par. 11.

21. Pope John XXIII, *Pacem in Terris*, par. 13.

22. Pope John XXIII, *Pacem in Terris*, pars. 15–17.

23. Pope John XXIII, *Pacem in Terris*, par. 14.

24. Pope John XXIII, *Pacem in Terris*, par. 18. Individuals also have the right to working conditions that are fair and in which their physical health is not endangered, and the right to a proper wage. Pope John XXIII, *Pacem in Terris*, pars. 18–20.

25. Pope John XXIII, *Pacem in Terris*, par. 11.

26. Pope John XXIII, *Pacem in Terris*, par. 11.

27. Pope John XXIII, *Pacem in Terris*, par. 11.

28. Pope John XXIII, *Pacem in Terris*, par. 21.

29. Pope John XXIII, *Pacem in Terris*, par. 23.

30. Pope John XXIII, *Pacem in Terris*, par. 25.

31. Pope John XXIII, *Pacem in Terris*, par. 11.

32. David Hollenbach, *Justice, Peace, & Human Rights: American Catholic Social Ethics in a Pluaralistic Context* (New York: Crossroad, 1988), 94.

33. Pope John XXIII, *Pacem in Terris*, pars. 11–27. See Hollenbach, *Claims in Conflict*, 68 (noting that "[t]he thread which ties all [the rights listed in *Pacem in Terris*] together is a fundamental norm of human dignity").

34. Marvin L. Krier Mich, *Catholic Social Teaching and Movements* (Mystic: Twenty-Third Publications, 1998), 105 (noting that "civil and political rights are . . . generally given priority in the U.S. setting and have been enshrined in the Bill of Rights" whereas economic and social rights are "emphasized in socialist countries"). Indeed, some U.S. commentators, including Michael Novak, argue that "rights that require the provision of goods and or services to carry them out, do not qualify as real rights." *Catholic Social Teaching and Movements*, 105. Others, including David Hollenbach, "have no trouble accepting the concept of economic rights." *Catholic Social Teaching and Movements*, 105. Hollenbach interprets the rights enumerated in *Pacem in Terris* as "unambiguously affirm[ing] the recognition of specifically economic rights to be religiously and politically mandatory." *Catholic Social Teaching and Movements*, 105. Interestingly, Hollenbach would categorize the rights recognized by Catholic social teaching substantively not into two but into eight categories: (1) rights related to life and one's standard of living; (2) rights concerning moral and cultural values; (3) rights in the area of religious activities; (4) rights in the area of family life; (5) economic rights; (6) rights of assembly and association; (7) rights of freedom of movement; and (8) political rights. See Hollenbach, *Claims in Conflict*, 66–67.

35. As the Second Vatican Council explained, "God did not create man for life in isolation, but for the formation of social unity." Second Vatican Council, *Gaudium et Spes*, sec. 32.

36. Pope John XXIII, *Mater at Magistra*, par. 65.

37. Kenneth R. Himes, *Responses to 101 Questions on Catholic Social Teaching* (New York: Paulist Press, 2001), 36.

38. Dartmouth Medical School, Institute for American Values and YMCA of the USA, *Hardwired to Connect: The New Scientific Case for Authoritative Communities* (New York: Institute for American Values, 2003), 8 (stating that "a complex neurological system . . . biologically predisposes human beings to form long-term relationships, to bear and nurture children, and to seek deeper meaning in life," and that the

nurture received from relationships with others has the ability to "change the way particular genes operate so that what would otherwise be genetic vulnerabilities are neutralized or even transformed into strengths"). See also Daniel Goleman, *Social Intelligence: The New Science of Human Relationships* (New York: Bantam Dell, 2006), 4 (explaining that recent discoveries in neuroscience show that "we are wired to connect" as "our brain's very design makes it *sociable*").

39. Second Vatican Council, *Gaudium et Spes*, sec. 25.

40. Curran, *Catholic Social Teaching, 1891–Present*, 138. David Hollenbach explains that "the state may and should legitimately intervene to protect the common good, which consists in the mutual respect of rights and the fulfillment of duties by all citizens." Hollenbach, *Claims in Conflict*, 48–49.

41. Pope John XXIII, *Mater et Magistra*, par. 20. See also *Pacem in Terris*, at par. 63 (explaining that "[i]t is also demanded by the common good that civil authorities should make earnest efforts to bring about a situation in which individual citizens can easily exercise their rights and fulfill their duties as well").

42. Himes, *Responses to 101 Questions on Catholic Social Teaching*, 36. Even given this understanding, difficulties arise in "reconciling what appears to be a contradiction: respect for free persons and attainment of the common good." Michael Novak, *Free Persons and the Common Good* (Lanham: Madison Books, 1989), 9. Michael Novak has noted that the difficulties, while "late in being confronted," have now "moved center stage." Novak, *Free Persons and the Common Good*,150; see also Novak, *Free Persons and the Common Good*, at *passim* (providing a powerful analysis of the common good and the difficulties in applying the concept, while ultimately concluding that the common good "is compatible both with the right of individuals to define the good for themselves and also with an unplanned and uncoerced social order").

43. Congregation for the Doctrine of the Faith, *The Participation of Catholics in Political Life* (Vatican, 2002), Part III, sec. 6 (emphasis added), available at http://www.vatican.va.

44. "[I]t is safe to say that Catholic social teaching never gives its unconditional support or approval to any existing economic system," Thomas Massaro, *Living Justice: Catholic Social Teaching in Action* (Franklin: Sheed & Ward, 2000), 176; indeed, as Pope John Paul II wrote, "The Church's social doctrine adopts a critical attitude toward both liberal capitalism and Marxist collectivism," Pope John Paul II, *Sollicitudo Rei Socialis* (1987), sec. 21, and in fact has done so since the beginning of modern Catholic social thought, see David J. O'Brien & Thomas A. Shannon, *Introduction, in Catholic Social Thought: The Documentary Heritage* (Maryknoll: Orbis Books, 1992): 12, 13 (noting, in an introductory essay to *Rerum Novarum* that, in that 1891 encyclical, "[i]n a remarkably even-handed manner the pope laid anathemas on both liberal capitalism, which released the individual from social and moral constraints, and socialism, which subordinated individual liberty to social well-being without respect for human rights or religious welfare"). See also, e.g., *Centesimus Annus*, sec. 13 (criticizing socialism for completely subordinating the good of individuals to the "socioeconomic mechanism" and eliminating "the concept of the person as the autonomous subject of moral decision"); *Gaudium et Spes*, sec. 30 (stating that it is "urgent that no one . . . content himself with a merely

individualistic morality"); Pope Pius XI, *Quadragesimo Anno* (1931), sec. 120 (noting that while socialism "contains a certain element of truth," it is fundamentally "opposed to true Christianity").

45. Indeed, the Church has insisted that these two concerns—by definition—are linked. Thus, in *Pacem in Terris*, Pope John XXIII stated that "[t]he dignity of the human being involves the right to . . . contribute one's part to the common good of the citizens." Pope John XXIII, *Pacem in Terris*, par. 26. See also *Economic Justice for All*, par. 79 ("In Catholic social thought, therefore, respect for human rights and a strong sense of personal and community responsibility are linked, not opposed."). See also Michael A. Evans, *An Analysis of U.N. Refugee Policy in Light of Roman Catholic Social Teaching and the Phenomena Creating Refugees* (Ann Arbor: University Microfilms International, 1991), 87 (defining the common good as "that principle which seeks to counter the perceived philosophical excesses of individualism with the emphasis on the dignity and rights of human persons *in* community") (emphasis in original). For an informed discussion of the consequences of liberal egalitarianism's decoupling of human dignity from its religious roots, see Michael A. Scaperlanda, "Immigration Justice: A Catholic Christian Perspective," *Journal of Catholic Social Thought* 1 (2004): 535.

46. See Massaro, *Living Justice*, 208 (stating that Catholic social teaching "attempts to balance the extremes of a radical individualism (the blind spot to which capitalist systems are prone) and collectivism (one of the errors of communism) [on the ground that] [i]f we go too far in either of these directions, our approach to life is incomplete and potentially harmful to ourselves and others"). It should be noted that the radical individualist-collectivist dichotomy, as perceived by the Church, does not necessarily break along what modern U.S. politics would consider right-left lines. Certainly, the Church recognizes what the twentieth century made horrifyingly apparent, that modern variants of "the old organistic conception of the state, in which the individual is seen as only a cog in the whole . . . may spring from either the left or the right; neither end of the political spectrum has a monopoly on collectivist zeal." Alan Dowty, *Closed Borders* (New Haven: Yale University Press, 1987), 58–59. Similarly, excesses stemming from excessive individualism also are perceived on both the right and left—the Church's view of economic rights, on the one hand, and sexual rights, on the other, provide examples here.

47. Hollenbach, *Claims in Conflict*, 65 (noting that "[t]he rights which protect human dignity . . . are the rights of persons *in* community [and] are neither exclusively the rights of individuals against the community nor are they the rights of the community against the individual") (emphasis in parenthetical in original).

48. Congregation for the Doctrine of the Faith, *The Participation of Catholics in Political Life* (Vatican, November 24, 2002, Part II(3)).

49. See this chapter at note 53 (providing other potential reasons why the Church might not articulate a policy on a particular issue).

50. See Massaro, *Living Justice*, 175 (giving the international waters issue and the question of "the proper rate for sales taxes" as examples of issues on which the Church has remained silent).

51. See Congregation for the Doctrine of the Faith, *The Participation of Catholics in Political Life*, at Part II(3) ("It is not the Church's task to set forth specific political

solutions—and even less to propose a single solution as the acceptable one—to temporal questions that God has left to the free and responsible judgment of each person"). This position is longstanding; as Professor Curran has noted, "Throughout the corpus of Catholic social teaching, popes have insisted that the church does not have teaching competence in political, economic, and social issues as such." Curran, *Catholic Social Teaching, 1891–Present*, 109; see, e.g., Pope John Paul II, *Sollicitudo Rei Socialis* (1987), sec. 41 (stating that "[t]he Church does not have *technical solutions* to offer for the problem of underdevelopment as such [nor does it] propose economic and political systems") (emphasis in original).

52. Catholic social teaching is intended as an authoritative teaching of the Church, and, at least to some degree, binding of Catholics. Curran, *Catholic Social Teaching, 1891–Present*, 109, 112. See Evans, *An Analysis of U.N. Refugee Policy*, 77 (noting that "Roman Catholics are obliged to consider [the social teachings] seriously in the formation of their individual consciences"); Land, *Catholic Social Teaching As I Have Lived, Loathed, and Loved It*, 263–64 n. 15 (stating that "[e]ncyclical writing, [while] the most authoritative of [the social teaching documents], is of ordinary magisterium unless a pope intended to define or solemnly declare"). See also Terry Coonan, "There Are No Strangers Among Us: Catholic Social Teaching and U.S. Immigration Law," *The Catholic Lawyer* 40 (2000): 105, 160 (noting the "theological consensus that the greater the degree of particularity in a church social teaching, the less morally obligatory the teaching"). See generally W. J. Smith, "Interpreting Papal Documents," in *The Church and Social Progress*, ed. Benjamin L. Masse (Milwaukee: The Bruce Publishing Company, 1966): 28–33 (distinguishing various types of papal pronouncements and the degree of deference claimed by them). One consequence of the Church's insistence upon the authoritative status of its social teaching is that it places a very high premium on the maintenance of the Church's credibility, and hence a very high priority on avoiding any obvious missteps. The fear is that focusing on specific policy choices could "mortgage the moral authority of the church." J. Bryan Hehir, "The Right and Competence of the Church in the American Case," in *One Hundred Years of Catholic Social Thought: Celebration and Challenge*, ed. John Coleman (Maryknoll: Orbis Books, 1991): 55, 68. Prudence, then, accordingly may counsel that, in order to avoid obvious missteps, Catholic social teaching "by its very nature must be somewhat general and cannot be specific." Curran, *Catholic Social Teaching, 1891–Present*, 112.

53. See Pope John Paul II, *Address to the Members of the Centesimus Annus Pro Pontifice Foundation* (September 12, 1999) (noting the difficulty of forming Catholic social teaching, "due to the complexity of the phenomena at issue and the speed with which they arise and develop"). Generally, "there can be no single Catholic approach or answer" when complex and specific issues require the independent collection and analysis of factual and scientific data. Curran, *Catholic Social Teaching, 1891–Present*, 112. Of course, many other reasons might also explain an absence of Church writings on a particular topic, including a lack of interest by the Church, a lack of resources in the Church, an agreement with the status quo (especially if unchallenged in the broader society), and a conclusion that the topic has been or is being adequately explored by others. See generally Michele R. Pistone, "The Devil in the Details: How Specific Should Catholic Social Teaching Be?,"

Journal of Catholic Social Thought 1 (2004): 507, 508–11 (discussing reasons for and extent of Church silence on specific issues). In addition, Charles Curran has noted that the Church generally is reluctant to detail "the exact relationship between rights and duties," and usually avoids the "thorny problem" of rights in conflict. Curran, *Catholic Social Teaching, 1891–Present*, 222.

    54. See "Congregation for the Doctrine of the Faith," *The Participation of Catholics in Political Life*, at Part II(3).

    55. Massaro, *Living Justice*, 175.

Chapter Six

Applying Human Dignity and the Common Good to Immigration

The general methodology of Catholic social teaching, with its insistence on assessing issues through the prism of the two fundamental principles of human dignity and the common good, provides a fruitful framework for assessing immigration issues. This chapter will undertake such an assessment. Because the specific issues of human dignity and the implications for the common good change as the specific immigration issue changes, the chapter is divided into three sections, corresponding to the three types of immigration decisions discussed by Catholic social teaching: those of (1) refugees, (2) economic migrants, and (3) skilled and educated migrants.

REFUGEES

Refugees, by definition, are persons fleeing conditions, such as persecution, war, or famine, in which their human dignity and basic human rights have been deeply violated.[1] The Church's position on their right to migrate is correspondingly categorical: "[Refugees] are persons and . . . all their rights as persons must be recognized, since they do not lose those rights on losing the citizenship of the states of which they are former members."[2]

Catholic social teaching's assessment of the common good in this context is equally definitive, albeit less plainly stated:

[The refugee's rights] include his right to enter a country in which he hopes to be able to provide more fittingly for himself and his dependents. It is therefore the duty of State officials to accept such immigrants and—so far as the good of their own community, rightly understood, permits—to further the aims of those who may wish to become members of a new society.[3]

There is much said in the paragraph quoted above (from *Pacem in Terris*), a good part of it by implication. Note, for example, the extreme succinctness of the discussion of the common good. In its express terms, it is limited to noting that a receiving country might consider the common good of its own citizens in determining whether to accept the refugees *as citizens*, as opposed to providing them with some type of non-citizen status within the country. The only fair interpretation of this limited express mention of the common good is not that consideration of the common good is otherwise irrelevant here, but that its import is obvious. People are persecuted, starving, or threatened by war—given the wealth in the world today, by what conception of the common good could one possibly argue that the proper response is to deny them refuge from their horrors?

SOME NOTES ON SOURCES AND TRANSLATIONS

Does the following sentence, which we quote and discuss in the main text of this chapter:

> It is therefore the duty of State officials to accept such immigrants [,i.e., refugees,] and—so far as the good of their own community, rightly understood, permits—to further the aims of those who may wish to become members of a new society.

have the same meaning as the sentence below?

> Wherefore, as far as the common good rightly understood permits, it is the duty of that State to accept such immigrants and to help to integrate them into itself as new members.

The two sentences are different translations of the final sentence of paragraph 106 of *Pacem in Terris*. The version on top, which suggests that acceptance of refugees is mandatory and that only the particulars of their treatment is a matter for the exercise of discretion in light of a correctly formed conception of the common good, is taken from the Vatican's website; the version below, which indicates that even the decision to admit a refugee is a matter for discretionary judgment, is taken from the collection edited by David O'Brien and Thomas Shannon. As we have used the O'Brien and Shannon versions of encyclicals elsewhere in this book, one might have expected us to use the same source when discussing paragraph 106. We have not, however, and the reader is due an explanation. Here it is.

Although each is generally reliable, neither the Vatican's English version of *Pacem in Terris* nor the version provided in the book by O'Brien and Shannon is a definitive source. Rather, the definitive authority is the version published by the Vatican in the *Acta Apostolicae Sedis*, formerly known as the *Acta Santae Sedis*. The definitive authority is usually, although not always, in Latin.

In the case of *Pacem in Terris*, the definitive version, that is, the one published in the *Acta*, is in fact in Latin. It reads as follows:

> *Quare rei publicae moderatorumm officium est alienos venientes excipere, et, quantum suea communitatis sinit non fucatum bonum, eorum proposito favere, qui forte novae societati sese velint aggregare.*

We each claim no more than a lawyer's understanding of Latin, *inter alia*, but knowledgeable persons we have consulted agree that the Vatican's English version of paragraph 106 is truer to the definitive Latin than is our usual source of O'Brien and Shannon. Given this, we think it is better to use a second source in this limited instance than to engage in the foolish consistency of using only one source in all instances. Of course, if one finds oneself using this logic very often with regard to a particular translation, one might best be advised to reject the problematic translation altogether. Homer nodded, it is true, and so can everyone else, but a translator who engages in more than an occasional nod is about as helpful as a more than occasionally insolvent insurer. If possible, neither should be relied upon at all.

Based on the foregoing, one might wonder whether the Vatican's translations should always be preferred—after all, in this case, the Vatican's English version does seem to have gotten it right, while O'Brien and Shannon appear to have erred. Unfortunately, no simple response is possible. While Vatican translations are certainly generally reliable, they are not always the most reliable. Indeed, even other Vatican translations of paragraph 106 demonstrate why. The Italian translation provided by the Vatican, for example—*[D]i conseguenza quella comunità politica, nei limiti consentiti dal bene commune rettamente inteso, ha il dovere di permettere quell'inserimento, come pure di favorire l'integrazione in se stessa delle nuove membra*—more closely resembles O'Brien and Shannon's version than it resembles the official Latin. (Incidentally, in the particular matter of concern to us, the Vatican's Spanish translation conveys the meaning of the Latin and the English translations, rather than the meaning of the Vatican's Italian version.). In sum, no one has ever suggested that the widely used collection by O'Brien and Shannon is sloppily or carelessly translated and, while it may not be perfect, neither can any of the English-language alternatives be expected to be perfect. It is therefore appropriate to use the O'Brien–Shannon book and to assume its accuracy as one would use, and assume the reliability of, other respected translations, but that assumption need not and should not prevail in a particular case in the face of specific and persuasive evidence to the contrary.

Sources: *Catholic Social Thought: The Documentary Heritage*, eds. David J. O'Brien and Thomas A. Shannon, 1992); Pope John XXIII, *Pacem in Terris*, *Acta Apostolicae Sedis* (April 20, 1963) 286; http:www.vatican.va.

Indeed, this is a striking example of how, "[i]n Catholic social thought, . . . respect for human rights and a strong sense of both personal and community responsibility are linked, not opposed."[4] One example of that linkage, we would assert, can be found in the way that the seriousness of the offense to human rights effectively enlarges the community whose "good" must be considered.[5] A genuine respect for human rights and human dignity demands that, in the face of the most critical suffering, the more fortunate communities claim the suffering one as their own. In the face of extreme need, such a change in perspective becomes a duty. Earlier in *Pacem in Terris*, in fact, Pope John XXIII alluded to this idea, noting that

> every human being . . ., when there are just reasons for it, [has] the right to emigrate to other countries and take up residence there. The fact that he is a citizen of a particular state does not detract in any way from his membership in the human family as a whole, nor from his citizenship in the world community.[6]

This understood background is why Pope John XXIII, in his specific discussion of the rights of refugees, was content simply to note that "[i]t is therefore the duty of State officials to accept such immigrants." Once the immediate life-threatening danger has been averted, however, resort to the usual nation-state perspective, "rightly understood," may again become appropriate in ascertaining the common good. But surely not before, which is why the U.S. and Mexican Catholic bishops could recently reiterate, forty years after *Pacem in Terris*, that "[t]he right to asylum must never be denied when people's lives are truly threatened in their homeland."[7]

Finally, there is no basis for asserting that Catholic social teaching's assessment of refugee policy is tainted by any faulty factual understandings. Refugees by definition are displaced persons in great need, threatened with death or other catastrophe. In abundance they exist; recent estimates range from ten to twenty million at-risk refugees, many of whom may have been refugees for several years.[8] In any case, however, Catholic social teaching is not dependent on any particular number, except perhaps a number so large that it would be impossible for more fortunate countries to respond to the crisis. The world's population is thirty to sixty *thousand* percent larger than the current refugee population, and much of the larger population is extremely wealthy, especially by refugee standards. Given these facts, Catholic social teaching's adamant insistence upon the necessity of welcoming refugees is entirely appropriate and reasonable.

ECONOMIC MIGRANTS

Catholic social teaching's liberality regarding the rights of non-refugees to emigrate similarly stems from the right's conception as a natural law right based upon one's dignity as a human person.[9] In this case, the Church links the right to migrate to the denial in the sending country of certain rights and duties that the Church sees as fundamental for humans to live with dignity, the most important of these being the right to sustain oneself and the duty to support one's family.[10]

Dating back to the first mention of the right to migrate in modern Catholic social teaching and continuing to today, the Church has linked migration to the right to subsistence and the duty to sustain one's family.[11] Thus, in 1961, Pope John XXIII explained that it is in the duty to provide for the physical, spiritual, and religious needs of one's family that "the right of the family to migrate" is rooted, and traced this view to the writings of his predecessors, Popes Leo XIII and Pius XII.[12] More recently, Pope John Paul II reiterated again the connection between the right to migrate and the search for an improvement in one's standard of living: "Man has the right to leave his native land for various motives—and also the right to return—in order to seek better conditions of life in another country."[13]

The notion that the world was provided for all to use and enjoy guides this position. Noting that the "goods of creation are destined for the whole human race,"[14] Catholic social thought teaches that

> God intended the earth and all that it contains for the use of every human being and people. Thus, as all men follow justice and unite in charity, created good should abound for them on a reasonable basis. Whatever the forms of ownership may be . . . attention must always be paid to the universal purpose for which created goods are meant. In using them, therefore, a man should regard his lawful possessions not merely as his own but also as common property in the sense that they should accrue to the benefit of not only himself but of others.
> . . . [T]he right to have a share of earthly goods sufficient for oneself and one's family belongs to everyone.[15]

Ensuring the concrete realization of this right "demands a cooperative effort on the part of people to bring about a quicker exchange of goods, or of capital, *or the migration of people themselves.*"[16]

The nature of this "cooperative effort" to realize the human dignity of economic migrants implicates, of course, questions of the common good.[17] In contrast to the Church's discussion of refugees, here the Church admits the issues may be more murky, and that line drawing may be necessary. Thus, for example, a number of Church documents have conceded, as the U.S. and Mexican bishops did in their 2003 letter, that "a sovereign state [has the right] to control its borders in furtherance of the common good."[18]

However, while the issue of economic migration may be recognized as complicated, a liberal orientation toward allowing that immigration may clearly be discerned. For example, *Together, a New People*, the U.S. bishops' 1986 statement on migration, recognizes that "[w]hile the government has a right to safeguard the common good by controlling immigration, an effort should be pursued to regularize as many undocumented immigrants as possible."[19] This is because, in the words of *The Church and the Immigrant Today*, "human solidarity, the norms of Christian charity and justice favor a broad application of the states' regulative affirmative laws."[20] The Sacred Congregation for Bishops, consisting of Catholic bishops from around the world, similarly has placed a type of high burden of proof on those who would limit migration, stating that "[p]ublic authorities unjustly deny the rights of human persons if they block or impede emigration or immigration except where *grave* requirements of the common good, *considered objectively*, demand it."[21] Importantly, as a joint statement by U.S. and Mexican bishops has noted, this high burden is not met when the immigration controls are instituted "merely for the purpose of acquiring additional wealth."[22]

The statements of these various bishops' organizations are fully consistent with statements by Pope John Paul II, in which the late Pope repeated the fundamental Catholic social teaching principle that every human being has a right to migrate, while recognizing that such rights cannot be exercised without some sort of limited regulation by the receiving country.[23] However, as with the bishops, an appreciation for the burdens immigration places on receiving countries did not alter the position of Pope John Paul II that in weighing the parties' rights, greater value should be placed on the needs of the migrants than on the desire to protect the receiving country's prosperity.[24]

Interestingly, this strong support for the right of economic migration predates the Church's acceptance of modern human rights at Vatican II. Indeed, as the following excerpt from the U.S. Catholic bishops' 1976 resolution, *People on the Move*, indicates, Pope Pius XII had fully articulated the Church's current position as early as 1952, when in that year's Christmas Address he

> returned to the interplay between the individual right to migrate and the common good of a country and implied the possibility that the Church might have to take a position for the defense of this right which would be opposed to enacted legislation. He deplored the fact that "the natural right of the individual to be unhampered in immigration or emigration is not recognized or, in practice, is nullified under the *pretext of a common good which is falsely understood or falsely applied*, but sanctioned and made mandatory by legislative or administrative measures."[25]

Finally, as is the case with the Church's position on refugees, the factual underpinnings of the Church's position on economic migrants appear sound. This is partly due to the fact that the generality of the Church's position eludes factual dispute by avoiding factual assertion, while taking care to subject the assertion of the right to generally noted practical limits. That is not to say, of course, that the position is unassailable. It might, for example, be challenged on its idea that it is illegitimate to restrict immigration for the purpose of acquiring additional wealth. Or the Church's position might be challenged on cultural grounds. But these arguments have to do with values, not facts per se. On a factual basis, the Church's position is as secure as that of someone who takes a position against war because war "kills people." In a particular case, the ultimate position may be wrongheaded, but its asserted factual basis is indisputable.

STEP OUT MIGRANTS

In contrast to Catholic social teaching's enthusiastic backing for the emigration rights of refugees and migrants generally, recognition of the emigration rights of STEP OUT migrants—who are referred to in Catholic social teaching by various names[26]—historically has been grudging at best. For example, the Sacred Congregation for Bishops has discouraged STEP OUT migration by asserting that such migrants can "gravely endanger the public good" by "depriv[ing] their community of the material and spiritual aid it needs."[27] Expressly invoking "the problem of 'brain drain,'" the U.S. bishops likewise have discouraged STEP OUT migration by suggesting that exercise of the right to migrate can imperil the fulfillment of "the duty to serve the common good, especially in developing countries."[28]

The U.S. bishops also have implied that U.S. policies allowing "brain drain" were designed intentionally and for selfish reasons to exploit the developing world's talent. In *One Family Under God*, for example, the U.S. Bishops' Committee on Migration stated that "[w]hile Catholic social teaching is not averse to labor migration in general, it is clearly in opposition to policies that *explicitly and intentionally tap* the third world's reservoir of trained, educated individuals *in pursuit of selfish interests*."[29]

In 1976, the U.S. bishops expressed these same sentiments in *The Church and the Immigrant Today*. That document notes that

> the United States should not encourage the movement of skilled and professional people from developing countries. Thus, the special preference afforded by the U.S. to highly skilled persons should be restricted. Our immigration policy should not encourage a flow of educated persons needed for development in

other countries . . .. It does not make good sense to direct foreign aid to developing countries and at the same time receive reverse foreign aid in the form of professional persons whose talents are badly needed in the same countries.[30]

Indeed, the U.S. bishops' position has been remarkably consistent over the years. Thus, perfectly bookending the bishops' 1976 declaration are the following two statements. In 1959, the U.S. bishops asserted that the laws allowing STEP OUT migration "in effect bleed a nation troubled with population problems of its best citizens, leaving behind those who can contribute least to national prosperity. Such ungenerous laws seem to bespeak a spirit of selfishness rather than a genuine desire by a privileged people to help those in need."[31] Forty-one years later, in 2000, the U.S. bishops made the same point regarding the consequences of STEP OUT migration, by "remind[ing] our government that the emigration of talented and trained individuals from the poorer countries represents a profound loss to those countries."[32]

In combination, these statements reveal that Catholic opposition to STEP OUT immigration is based on two factual assertions: first, underdeveloped sending countries, on the whole, are injured by the emigration of skilled and educated citizens; and second, developed countries that allow such individuals to immigrate are greedily enriching themselves at the expense of poorer nations. These factual assertions are more problematic than the matters discussed earlier in this chapter, that is, the factual underpinnings of Catholic social teaching on refugees and economic migrants. Were the factual underpinnings of the current position on STEP OUT migration free from substantial doubt, however, the principle of the common good likely *would* be advanced by a more restrictive policy on STEP OUT migration. The position of Catholic social teaching on STEP OUT migration, in other words, is not logically wrong *assuming the correctness of its factual predicates*.

The conclusion that the common good is disserved by STEP OUT migration might have been deemed sufficient to justify Church opposition to brain drain in spite of possible offense to human dignity, and certainly would have been sufficient if opposition to STEP OUT migration were deemed to aid human dignity. Catholic social teaching, however, has declined to make any affirmative case that opposition to STEP OUT migration enhances human dignity. But Catholic social teaching has not relied only on common good grounds; in opposing brain drain, it at times also has affirmatively *discounted* the affront to human dignity that may occur when a skilled and educated person from a poor country is forbidden from emigrating to a richer one. Indeed, it has at times done so in an unusually aggressive manner, insinuating that elites who seek to migrate from developing countries often act in selfishness and greed, rather than from any positive motivation. The root of this conclusion is another factual assumption, namely, that a STEP OUT migrant, while living abroad, cannot make a meaningful contribution to her home country and therefore cannot fulfill her duty to do so. Indeed, as one commentator has explained, the Church's position implies "that the migrant crosses an un-bridgeable gulf, cutting himself off completely from his homeland, unable and unwilling to contribute to its economic life."[33]

This inability to contribute constitutes a serious deficiency under Catholic social teaching "[e]specially in underdeveloped areas where all resources must be put to urgent use."[34] Yet, this deficiency does not inhibit migration by refugees and non-elite economic migrants, for their duty to their homelands may appropriately be outweighed by their right to subsistence and their duty to support their families. STEP OUT migrants, however, as presumably elite members of the home country, are assumed to be able to support their families above a subsistence level without leaving home. Accordingly, their duty "to contribute according to their ability to the true progress of their own community"[35] remains a central obligation. And, Catholic social teaching indicates, this is an obligation that generally can be met only by those who choose to stay, rather than leave and "deprive their community of the material and spiritual aid it needs."[36]

Catholic social teaching, then, while holding that consideration of the common good and human dignity should favorably dispose one toward immigration and immigrants in every other case, holds that consideration of each of the same two factors should cause one to oppose STEP OUT migration. Our view is that this position, while historically understandable (*see* chapters 7 and 8) is no longer tenable, and that the fundamental principles of Catholic social teaching, that is, the common good and human dignity, do not mandate continued opposition to STEP OUT migration (*see* chapters 9 to 16).

NOTES

1. See chapter 4 (discussing legal definition of the term "refugee").

2. Pope John XXIII, *Pacem in Terris* (1963), par. 105. This view, of course, is consistent with Catholic social teaching's position that states do not grant rights; rather, rights are bestowed by God, so they cannot be diminished by acts of government or natural disasters. See Charles E. Curran, *Catholic Social Teaching, 1891–Present: A Historical, Theological, and Ethical Analysis* (Washington, D.C.: Georgetown University Press, 2002), 219, citing National Conference of Catholic Bishops, *Economic Justice for All: Pastoral Letter on Catholic Social Teaching and the U.S. Economy* (Washington, D.C.: U.S. Catholic Conference, 1986), par. 79.

3. Pope John XXIII, *Pacem in Terris*, par. 106, available at http://www.vatican.va.

4. National Conference of Catholic Bishops, *Economic Justice for All*, par. 79.

5. Cf. William R. O'Neill and William C. Spohn, "Rights of Passage: The Ethics of Immigration and Refugee Policy," *Theological Studies* 59 (1998): 84, 100 ("The graduated urgency of human rights and duties provides that those whose basic rights are most imperiled have the strongest claim").

6. Pope John XXIII, *Pacem in Terris*, par. 25.

7. United States Conference of Catholic Bishops and Conferencia del Episcopado Mexicano, *Strangers No Longer: Together on the Journey of Hope, A Pastoral Letter Concerning Migration from the Catholic Bishops of Mexico and the United States* (Washington, D.C., United States Conference of Catholic Bishops and Conferencia del Episcopado Mexicano, 2003), par. 31. The absolutism of Catholic social teaching's rhetoric on the need to allow immigration of refugees could be misinterpreted as allying it—on a rhetorical level—with the extreme individualist camp, which generally resists any limitation on personal rights. The argument would be that the Church's rhetoric, filled with imperatives, on behalf of the rights of refugees, echoes the individualists' rhetoric on behalf of every individual. We disagree. There is a difference between an argument that rights can never be infringed and thus must always—when there is a perceived conflict—trump the common good, with the position of Catholic social teaching that certain fundamental rights—such as the right to life—must be vindicated in the face of a narrow conception of the common good.

8. See, e.g., U.S. Committee for Refugees, *2004 World Refugee Survey* (estimating that there were 11,999,000 refugees and asylum seekers worldwide in 2004), available at http://www.refugees.org/article.aspx?id=1156; U.S. Committee for Refugees, *2003 World Refugee Survey* (estimating that there were 14,900,000 refugees and asylum seekers worldwide in 2001), available at http://www.refugees.org/data/wrs/03/stats/ SSRefugeesWorldwide.pdf. According to the United Nations High Commissioner for Refugees (UNHCR), in the year 2002, 19,783,100 people fell within its mandate to assist refugees, asylum seekers, and internally displaced persons (those who are displaced internally within the confines of their country's national borders) to find refuge and, when appropriate, to return to their countries of origin. United Nations High Commissioner for Refugees, *Refugees by Numbers, 2002 Edition*, August 8, 2002. Estimates of refugee populations in a particular time period often vary because different formulas for measuring total refugee populations are used. For example, individuals who are internally displaced in their home countries, refugees who do not need assistance, and "those who do not meet the strict U.N. definition of refugees" are all sometimes excluded and sometimes included in refugee calculations. Alan Dowty, *Closed Borders* (New Haven: Yale University Press, 1987), 181. "The strict U.N. definition" means, of course, the requirement that the refugee be fleeing persecution on account of race, religion, nationality, membership in a particular social group, or political opinion. Interestingly, the UNHCR does not follow the strict definition when calculating refugees worldwide. "In fact, the scope of the UNHCR's protection has been extended in practice to include all persons uprooted by external aggression, occupation, foreign domination or events seriously disturbing public order." Dowty, *Closed Borders*, 108 (internal quotations omitted). An additional cause of differing estimates, even when using the same standards, is the rapidity with which events can cause the figures to fluctuate; hence, UNHCR's 2004 estimate of the refugee population at the

beginning of 2004 was "only" 17.1 million, United Nations High Commissioner for Refugees, *Refugees by Numbers, 2004 Edition*, a number almost three million less than its 2002 estimate.

9. Pope John XXIII, *Pacem in Terris*, par. 25; NCCB Ad Hoc Committee on Migration and Tourism, "The Church and the Immigrant Today: The Pastoral Concern of the Church for People on the Move," in National Conference of Catholic Bishops, *The Pastoral Concern of the Church for People on the Move* (Washington, D.C.: U.S. Catholic Conference, 1976): 5, 10 (stating that "emigration is a natural right"), reprinted in National Conference of Catholic Bishops, *People on the Move: A Compendium of Church Documents on the Pastoral Concern for Migrants and Refugees* (Washington, D.C.: U.S. Catholic Conference, 1988): 61, 62.

10. NCCB Ad Hoc Committee on Migration and Tourism, "The Church and the Immigrant Today," 10 (stating that "if a deficiency [of earthly goods] exists in his or her own country, a person has a right to emigrate to another"); Michael A. Evans, *An Analysis of U.N. Refugee Policy in Light of Roman Catholic Social Teaching and the Phenomena Creating Refugees* (Ann Arbor: University Microfilms International 1991), 99 (noting that, in Catholic social teaching, "the right to emigration stems from the right to subsistence, and the rights of families to have their basic needs met by the family's breadwinner(s)").

11. Pope Leo XIII, *Rerum Novarum* (1891), sec. 35; Pope Pius XII, Radio Address, June 1, 1941, cited in Evans, *An Analysis of U.N. Refugee* Policy, 102–3. See U.S. Bishops' Committee on Migration, *One Family Under God* (Washington, D.C.: U.S. Catholic Conference, 1995), 4 (noting that "*Rerum Novarum* ('On the Condition of Labor') was partially a response to the great European migration to the United States," and that, in "articulat[ing] the principles of private property and the dignity of human labor," *Rerum Novarum* also provided a corollary "right to migrate to sustain one's family").

12. Pope John XXIII, *Mater et Magistra* (1961), pars. 41–45. Summarizing the views of Pope Pius XII, one scholar has written that

> Pius XII took the social teaching of his predecessors concerning the rights of workers and families to subsistence, to bodily integrity, and especially to private property and usufruct and sees within these rights the accompanying right to migration. When a person is denied the right to a living wage for the worker and his/her family, . . . then their human dignity is seriously affronted and migration is the only recourse. This is what one normally would refer to as economic refugees or migrants.

Evans, *An Analysis of U.N. Refugee Policy*, 107.

13. Pope John Paul II, *Laborem Exercens* (1981), sec. 23.

14. *Catechism of the Catholic Church* (New York: Doubleday, 1995), sec. 2402.

15. Second Vatican Council, *Gaudium et Spes* (1965), sec. 69.

16. Pope John XXIII, *Pacem in Terris*, par. 101 (emphasis added).

17. It will be noted that the discussion that follows this note in the main text focuses exclusively upon the Church's assessment of the common good of the receiving country, not the sending country. The omission of any discussion regarding the sending country's common good accurately reflects the Church's writings in the

context of subsistence-level economic and refugee migration. Apparently, the Church does not contest the generally accepted view that since "welfare is an increasing function of income *per caput*, emigrating workers taking along no capital raise the welfare of the people remaining behind as well as their own." Herbert G. Grubel, "Reflections on the Present State of the Brain Drain and a Suggested Remedy," *Minerva* 14 (1976): 209, 217.

18. United States Conference of Catholic Bishops and Conferencia del Episcopado Mexicano, *Strangers No Longer*, at par. 39. See also National Conference of Catholic Bishops, *Welcoming the Stranger Among Us: Unity in Diversity* (Washington, D.C.: U.S. Catholic Conference, 2000), 11 (recognizing that "nations have the right to control their borders."); U.S. Bishops' Committee on Migration, *One Family Under God*, at 5; NCCB Ad Hoc Committee on Migration and Tourism, "The Church and the Immigrant Today," at 10 (considering the common good of the country of destination in migration decisions); Pontifical Council for the Pastoral Care of Migrants and Itinerant Workers, *Erga migrantes caritas Christi (The Love of Christ for Migrants)* (2004), par. 21 (summarizing the position of the Second Vatican Council as "reaffirm[ing] the right to emigrate" but "recognis[ing] the right of public authorities, in a particular context, to regulate the flow of migration"), available at www.vatican.va.

19. National Conference of Catholic Bishops, *Together a New People: Pastoral Statement on Migrants and Refugees* (Washington, D.C.: U.S. Catholic Conference 1987): 10 (approved Nov. 8, 1986), reprinted in National Conference of Catholic Bishops, *People on the Move: A Compendium of Church Documents on the Pastoral Concern for Migrants and Refugees* (Washington, D.C.: U.S. Catholic Conference 1988): 71, 75.

20. NCCB Ad Hoc Committee on Migration and Tourism, "The Church and the Immigrant Today," 10.

21. Sacred Congregation for Bishops, *Instruction on the Pastoral Care of People Who Migrate* (Washington, D.C.: U.S. Catholic Conference, 1969), at 8, sec. 7 (emphasis added), reprinted in National Conference of Catholic Bishops, *People on the Move: A Compendium of Church Documents*, 83, 85. Pope Paul VI approved this Instruction by the Apostolic Letter, *Pastoralis Migratorum Cura*. See Pope Paul VI, *Apostolic Letter in the Form of Motu Proprio Establishing New Norms for the Care of Migrants* (Vatican, 1969) (*motu proprio* means "of his own accord," and signifies that the provisions of the document were decided on by the pope personally, not simply approved on the advice of cardinals or others), reprinted in National Conference of Catholic Bishops, *People on the Move: A Compendium of Church Documents*, 79. "Grave requirements of the common good" might include, for example, situations in which migration flows are regulated due to compelling national security concerns.

22. United States Conference of Catholic Bishops and Conferencia del Episcopado Mexicano, *Strangers No Longer*, par. 36.

23. Pope John Paul II, *Message of the Holy Father for the 87th World Day of Migration, 2001* (Vatican, 2001), 3, available at http://www.vatican.va/holy_father/john_paul_ii/messages/migration/documents/hf_jp-ii_mes_20010213_world-migration-day-2001_en.html.

24. Pope John Paul II, *Message of the Holy Father for the 87th World Day of Migration*, 3 (stating that immigration limits by developed countries "cannot be based solely on protecting their own prosperity").

25. NCCB Ad Hoc Committee on Migration and Tourism, "The Church and the Immigrant Today," 10 (emphasis added).

26. The terms that have been used in official Catholic social teaching documents, in the context of discussing migration, to describe STEP OUT migrants include (1) "highly skilled persons," see NCCB Ad Hoc Committee on Migration and Tourism, "The Church and the Immigrant Today," 14; (2) "skilled and professional people," see NCCB Ad Hoc Committee on Migration and Tourism, "The Church and the Immigrant Today," 14; (3) "educated persons," see NCCB Ad Hoc Committee on Migration and Tourism, "The Church and the Immigrant Today," 14; (4) "professional persons," see NCCB Ad Hoc Committee on Migration and Tourism, "The Church and the Immigrant Today," 14; (5) "best citizens," see National Catholic Welfare Conference, *Statement on World Refugee Year and Migration* (Washington, D.C., 1959), par. 31, reprinted in National Conference of Catholic Bishops, *People on the Move: A Compendium of Church Documents*, 17, 19, at par. 31; (6) "talented and trained individuals," see National Conference of Catholic Bishops, *Welcoming the Stranger Among Us*, 8; (7) "skilled workers [such as] nurses, computer professionals, and scientists," see National Conference of Catholic Bishops, *Welcoming the Stranger Among Us*, 8; (8) individuals "possessing mental powers or wealth," see Sacred Congregation for Bishops, *Instruction on the Pastoral Care of People Who Migrate*, at 8, par. 8; (9) "trained, educated individuals," see U.S. Bishops' Committee on Migration, *One Family Under God*, at 12; and (10) "highly skilled and educated persons," see *One Family Under God*, at 12.

27. Sacred Congregation for Bishops, *Instruction on the Pastoral Care of People Who Migrate*, at 8, par. 8. As a fuller quotation reveals, the position of the Sacred Congregation for Bishops essentially amounts to a statement that while STEP OUT migrants may have the technical right to migrate, they generally have a duty not to:

> Even though they have a right of emigrating, citizens are held to remember that they have the right and the duty . . . to contribute according to their ability to the true progress of their own community. Especially in underdeveloped areas where all resources must be put to urgent use, those men gravely endanger the public good, who, particularly possessing mental powers and wealth, are enticed by greed and temptation to emigrate. They deprive their community of the material and spiritual aid it needs.

Instruction on the Pastoral Care of People Who Migrate at 8, par. 8 (citations and internal quotation marks omitted). See also National Conference of Catholic Bishops, *Policy Statement on Employer Sanctions* (Washington, D.C.: U.S. Catholic Conference 1988), 4 (noting that the only type of migration opposed by the Church is that perceived to be "based on excessively selfish interests").

28. National Conference of Catholic Bishops, *Resolution on the Pastoral Concern of the Church for the People on the Move* (Washington, D.C.: U.S. Catholic Conference, 1976), 1, reprinted in National Conference of Catholic Bishops, *People on the Move: A Compendium of Church Documents*, 59, 60.

29. U.S. Bishops' Committee on Migration, *One Family Under God*, 12–13 (emphasis added).

30. NCCB Ad Hoc Committee on Migration and Tourism, "The Church and the Immigrant Today," 14. The National Conference of Catholic Bishops' Ad Hoc Committee on Migration and Tourism authored *The Church and the Immigrant Today*, which document was expressly endorsed by the National Conference of Catholic Bishops, and published along with the endorsement. See National Conference of Catholic Bishops, *Resolution on the Pastoral Concern of the Church for the People on the Move* (Washington, D.C.: U.S. Catholic Conference 1976), 1, 3, reprinted in National Conference of Catholic Bishops, *People on the Move: A Compendium of Church Documents*, 59, 60.

31. National Catholic Welfare Conference, *Statement on World Refugee Year and Migration*, at par. 31.

32. National Conference of Catholic Bishops, *Welcoming the Stranger Among Us*, at 8.

33. Andrew M. Yuengert, "Catholic Social Teaching on the Economics of Immigration," *Journal of Markets & Morality* 3 (2000): 88, 90, available at http://www.acton.org/publicat/m_and_m/2000_spring/yuengert.html.

34. Sacred Congregation for Bishops, *Instruction on the Pastoral Care of People Who Migrate* (Vatican City: August 22, 1969), at 8, par. 8 (internal quotation marks omitted).

35. Sacred Congregation for Bishops, *Instruction on the Pastoral Care of People Who Migrate*, at 8, par. 8 (internal quotation marks omitted).

36. Sacred Congregation for Bishops, *Instruction on the Pastoral Care of People Who Migrate*, at 8, par. 8 (internal quotation marks omitted)

Part Three

EVENTS AND UNDERSTANDINGS INFLUENCING THE FORMATION OF THE CHURCH'S STEP OUT MIGRATION POLICY

Chapter Seven

Political Developments

The formation of Catholic social teaching's position against STEP OUT migration unquestionably was influenced by contemporaneous political, economic, and social events. Looming large in the formation of the position were two developments in particular. The first was a worldwide change in attitude toward the importance and feasibility of economic development by poor countries. The second was a change in the immigration laws of leading developed countries, which increased STEP OUT migration to those nations.

The combination of these developments powerfully affected the Church's analysis of STEP OUT migration. Indeed, as always, "[t]his social context shaped both the content and the tone of the teachings. The documents cannot be adequately understood without attending to this context."[1] This chapter discusses the relevant political developments in greater detail. Chapter 8, the next chapter, discusses simultaneous developments in the Roman Catholic Church that made it particularly receptive to interpreting these political developments as reasons for opposing STEP OUT migration.

The usefulness of our inquiry in these two chapters is two-fold. Most immediately, it helps to paint a fuller picture of why the Church adopted its policy. In showing how strong the pull of contemporaneous political events and political interpretations can be, it also demonstrates the limits of the influence of the more deeply rooted historical, institutional, and experiential factors noted previously in chapter 4. The inquiry plainly shows that these more deeply rooted factors, which ordinarily can be expected to push the Church toward policies favoring immigrants, are certainly not controlling when, in a particular case, other considerations conspire to convince the

Church that a "pro-immigration" policy would not serve human dignity and the common good.

As for those other considerations, the Church's position on STEP OUT migration was initially articulated during the same time period that world economic development was first recognized as an important issue.[2] The roots of this new period in economic thought were in the 1950s, when an "enormous change in the thinking of government leaders and their advisers [occurred, which] affected the views of industrialists, trade unionists, agriculturists, and 'ordinary people.' Essentially this change was the widespread acceptance of the belief that each individual country, and the world as a whole, can 'grow' out of poverty."[3] As this idea reached critical mass, the 1960s was optimistically labeled the "Development Decade" at the United Nations.[4] Development experts, who had ignored impoverished nations for centuries, now called attention to their "urgent problems"[5] and confidently devised solutions.[6] Assistance was available in unprecedented amounts, in large part because the United States and the U.S.S.R., the two opposing superpowers, were using development aid as a means to gain allies in the developing world.[7] During this time, economists "began to measure 'human capital' and its role in economic growth."[8]

Based upon the perceived value of human capital, migration researchers placed new emphasis on the international migration of highly skilled and educated individuals.[9] At that time—and for many years afterward—most commentators and interested organizations were critical of "brain drain."[10] The criticism originated in Europe and the developed world.[11] Encouraged by Soviet Bloc countries seeking to make "common cause against Western 'exploitation,'"[12] developing nations quickly adapted the theme to their own situations, "complaining that they were losing substantial numbers of their own skilled personnel" to developed countries.[13] And, in point of fact, during the 1960s migration of highly trained and skilled workers from developed to developing countries did increase significantly.[14]

The dramatic increases in STEP OUT migration that began in the 1960s were attributable in large part to amendments to immigration laws and policies in several of the largest receiving countries. The U.S. immigration laws, for example, were almost completely overhauled in 1965. At that time, U.S. immigration laws changed from a quota system, which largely established admission preferences based upon the intending migrant's country of nationality, to a system that increasingly evaluated qualities that the migrant possessed, rather than her nationality. In particular, the Immigration and Nationality Act of 1965 (1965 Act) increasingly awarded visas according to preference categories based upon employment skills.[15]

A SHORT HISTORY OF THE
IMMIGRATION LAWS OF THE UNITED STATES

Until the passage of the notorious Chinese Exclusion Acts in the 1880s, there was essentially no federal immigration law in the United States. But when the late 1800s and early 1900s saw a substantial increase in the rate of immigration, Congress responded by enacting a series of laws of general applicability to regulate immigration. Among other things, the new laws defined excludable groups of intending immigrants, including anarchists and subversive classes; instituted penalties; and took steps to prevent unregulated entry. However, these laws did not establish specific immigration quotas. That changed in 1921 and 1924, when specific immigration quotas were first established.

In particular, pursuant to the Immigration Act of 1924, approximately 150,000 immigrant visas were available for allocation annually to nationals of specific countries based on the number of American citizens who traced their ancestry to those nations in the 1920s census. Each country received a minimum of one hundred visas per year. Groups that represented a large percentage of the U.S. population in the 1920s census, predominately from countries of Northern and Western Europe, such as England, Ireland, and Germany, were granted quota numbers so large that they sometimes went unused. On the other hand, individuals from those nations whose predecessors had not migrated in large numbers before 1920, including migrants from Asia, Africa, some parts of Eastern and Southern Europe, and other countries, often found the that the quotas had the effect of curtailing their freedom of movement. Notably, for a law that quite obviously was intended to maintain the racial status quo, African Americans were not counted for purposes of awarding quotas; rather, the 1924 act expressly stated that "the term 'inhabitants in the continental United States in the 1920's does not include . . . the descendants of slave immigrants."

The Immigration and Nationality Act of 1952 adjusted the formula so that nations were awarded quotas of one-sixth of 1 percent of the number of inhabitants of the United States who traced their ancestry to that country. Although more recent figures were of course available, census numbers from 1920 continued to guide the calculations. Gladly, the 1952 law did not keep the discriminatory exception for descendants of African Americans.

In 1965, Congress enacted a new series of immigration laws that ended the national origins quota system. In place of the quota system, the new laws for the first time gave preference to professionals. Under the 1965 laws, 10 percent of the available visas were set aside for members of professions, scientists, and artists. Preferences were also given to those who could prove family

(*continued*)

relationships to United States citizens or permanent residents. As opposed to
the previous systems, all of which favored, in fact or in law, European and
specifically Northern and Western European immigration, the 1965 laws for
the first time made it possible for immigration from outside Europe to exceed
immigration from Europe.

Sources: Immigration Act of 1924, Pub. L. No. 139, 43 Stat. 153; Immigration and Nationality Act of 1952,
Pub. L. No. 414, 66 Stat. 163 (1952); Immigration and Nationality Act of 1965, Pub. L. No. 89-236, 79
Stat. 911; Gabriel Chen, "The Civil Rights Revolution Comes to Immigration Law: A New Look at the
Immigration and Nationality Act of 1965," 75 *N.C.L. Review* (1996) 273; E.P.Hutchingson, *Legislative
History of American Immigration Policy, 1798–1965* (1981).

Other developed countries enacted similar laws. In 1967, Canada eliminated its racial quotas and imposed a point system, which gave preference to
professional and skilled workers.[16] The United Kingdom, in 1962 and again
in 1965,[17] and Australia, in 1958 and 1966,[18] also amended their immigration
laws to provide preferences to skilled and educated migrants. These new immigration laws had an almost immediate effect; as early as the mid-1960s,
"both the numbers of highly trained and skilled workers from developing to
developed countries, as well as the proportions of such persons from developing countries, increased significantly."[19] For example, between 1965 and
1970, the movement of STEP OUT migrants to the United States increased
from 37 to 70 percent of total skilled immigration,[20] with large gains in migration from developing countries in Asia (most significantly from Korea, India, Taiwan, and the Philippines) accounting for much of the change.[21] These
new waves of migration, particularly of STEP OUT migrants at a time when
international development was receiving worldwide interest, caught the attention of the international community.[22]

The early consensus view of international organizations was negative toward the trend of increased STEP OUT migration. The critical "nationalistic" view of the brain drain phenomenon saw the migration of skilled and
educated individuals from developing countries as a "reinjection" in the
developed world of the benefits of aid originally granted to the developing
countries.[23] In the United States, then-Senator Walter Mondale captured
the prevailing "nationalistic" sentiment in 1966 when he said, "I feel that
the brain drain from developing countries is particularly urgent. It com-
promises our commitment to development assistance, by depriving new
nations of high-level manpower indispensable to their progress. It runs
counter to the education and training programs which are so vital in our
foreign aid."[24] Similarly, another commentator explained "that a society, a
country or a region which is exporting skilled, trained adults with high

learning potential is losing human capital and it is usually the case that societies which are receiving these people are gaining human capital and gaining potential for growth."[25]

The losses to the sending countries were perceived to stem from several sources. First, there were direct losses in future tax revenues and past educational costs. As Professor Harry Johnson noted in 1965,

> There is one directly obvious way in which the residents of a region may lose by the emigration of trained people. If education is financed wholly or partly by general taxation of the resident population, every emigrant takes with him a gift—in the form of the education he has received—from the place he leaves to the place he goes to. To put the point another way, the region of immigration gets the right to tax the high income made possible by an educational investment it has not paid for, while the region of emigration loses the opportunity to recoup by taxation the cost of the educational investment it has made."[26]

Second, it was noted that the loss of skilled personnel, by virtue of a negative multiplier effect, could increase unemployment across the skill spectrum:

> The employment of less skilled workers is often complementary to that of highly trained personnel. The emigration of a highly trained technician, for instance, may result in the unemployment of a large number of other workers who might otherwise be employed under him. . . . There may be cases, [moreover], where, but for the emigration of highly trained personnel, a new enterprise could be launched absorbing a large number of hitherto unemployed workers.[27]

Third, economists noted that productivity could suffer because the migration of skilled labor from developing countries could leave large gaps in the supply of highly skilled workers. Indeed, some economists argued that at "the core of the argument about the brain drain lies the fear that it will retard the economic development of the home country by creating or aggravating shortages of vitally needed high-level personnel."[28]

Finally, economists argued that long-term productivity also would suffer from the loss of skilled and educated workers. They asserted that skilled and educated individuals often exhibit leadership and entrepreneurial skills that are necessary for a country to develop and prosper. When people with those skills migrate from a country, the citizenry suffers long-term adverse impacts. As one commentator explained, "In the [long] run, the loss of human abilities like leadership, initiative and entrepreneurship will have very serious effects" on the sending countries.[29] Similarly, a United Nations study of the phenomenon noted in 1970 that the most important losses, however, centre around the contributions trained persons make not only professionally but creatively in terms of leadership and talent. Without such qualities development cannot take place and the demands of leadership, politics, planning and imaginative management cannot be met. In addition, trained men have now become masters of these techniques of management, control and planning which are the keys to modern national wealth and power. Though unappraisable because the potential contribution is a result which did not take place and because means for assessing the exact relationship of trained men to development have not been found losses of talent certainly have profound developmental repercussions.[30]

Based upon this understanding of the costs of STEP OUT migration, the negative outlook of the nationalistic position was adopted by the United Nations and formed the basis for numerous international policy proposals.[31] The international community proposed systems both to compensate sending countries for what was perceived as a loss to them at the hands of developed countries and to discourage emigration from developing sending countries.

Most of the proposals involved mechanisms for rendering financial compensation to the sending states perceived to be victims of STEP OUT migration.[32] For example, one well-known proposal was a scheme of taxation that called for each receiving country to recover a surtax from the incomes of professionals who had migrated there from developing countries. One version of the proposal would have "routed [the funds] to the United Nations for disbursement in . . . developmental programmes" of sending countries.[33] Another proposed remedy suggested the formation of tax-exempt private foundations, funded by contributions from STEP OUT migrants, who would receive a tax deduction in their receiving country.[34]

More direct methods of solving the problem also were suggested. Indeed, the most direct method already had been implemented by the Soviet Union and the Eastern European countries, with their imposition of drastic emigration restrictions.[35] The Berlin Wall, of course, was both an important means of enforcing this type of restriction and the paramount symbolic representation of it,[36] although onerous bureaucratic rules, interminable administrative delays, and misuse of the criminal code also played large roles.[37] Concern about STEP OUT migration was such that some scholars suggested that developing countries impose harsh restrictions of their own.[38] Receiving countries also were encouraged to adopt laws restricting immigration of skilled and educated individuals into their countries.[39]

In sum, the 1960s saw concerns about STEP OUT migration peak, with the general consensus—as the many proposed remedies indicate—"underlin[ing] the negative impact of migration on emigration countries."[40] At the same time, there was a pre-existing "presumption in economic thought . . . that the poor [would] catch up to the rich."[41] Indeed, "[b]oth the wealthy and the deprived had assumed that what had been achieved by some could soon be achieved by others, and eventually by all";[42] the Roman Catholic Church shared "[t]his optimism towards Third World economic development."[43] When reality failed to match this expectation, STEP OUT migration appeared as an obvious and ready-made villain.[44] The apparent and unprecedented successes of STEP OUT migrants seemed to confirm this assignment of blame—after all, if the STEP OUT migrants could succeed in the developed countries, wasn't it apparent that they would have succeeded at home as well, to the great benefit of the source country? This impression was further reinforced by advocates of the new immigration laws' opening up of immigration to skilled and educated persons from the entire world. In their arguments, such advocates emphasized the economic necessity of winning in the "international market of brains," thereby implying that the losers would suffer economic loss.[45] Strikingly, the more positive arguments advanced today on behalf of STEP OUT migration—such as the positive economic effects that can accrue to sending countries,[46] and the positive social effects that can accrue to receiving countries when "more just patterns of multiracial diversity [are created] than would be the case if immigrants were almost entirely low wage workers"[47]—were almost entirely absent from the debate.[48] Given this environment, it is hardly surprising that the Church's social teachings reflected a stance against the migration of skilled workers from the developing to the developed world and a view that decisions to migrate or accept such migrants were selfish and greedy.

NOTES

1. David Hollenbach, *Claims in Conflict: Retrieving and Renewing the Catholic Human Rights Tradition* (New York: Paulist Press, 1979), 42 (discussing generally the connection between political and social events and the development of Catholic social teaching). See Patricia A. Lamoureux, "Immigration Reconsidered in the Context of an Ethic of Solidarity," in *Made in God's Image: The Catholic Vision of Human Dignity*, eds. Regis Duffy and Angelus Gambatese (New York: Paulist Press, 1999): 105, 115 (noting "the growing awareness of historicity and the contextual, dynamic, conflictual nature of social problems" in Catholic social teaching documents following Pope John XXIII and Vatican II).

2. Catholic social teaching first warned about the dangers of STEP OUT migration in 1959. See National Catholic Welfare Conference Administrative Board, *Statement on World Refugee Year and Migration* (Washington, D.C., 1959), par. 31, reprinted in

People on the Move: A Compendium of Church Documents on the Pastoral Concern for Migrants and Refugees (Washington, D.C.: U.S. Catholic Conference, 1988), 17, 19, at par. 31. See also Sacred Congregation for Bishops, *Instruction on the Pastoral Care of People Who Migrate* (1969), reprinted in *People on the Move*, 83, 85, at pars. 7-8. This effort coincided with the identification by economists of poor country development as a leading economic issue. See William Easterly, *The Elusive Quest for Growth: Economists' Adventures and Misadventures in the Tropics* (Cambridge: MIT Press, 2001), xi (stating that "[f]ifty years ago . . . we economists began our own audacious quest: to discover the means by which poor countries . . . could become rich"); see also John Kay, "These Are Desolate Times for the Dismal Science," *Financial Times*, June 5, 2003, 21 (stating that when he taught economics at Oxford in the 1960s, "The most popular option was euphemistically described as the economics of developing countries").

3. Donal Dorr, *Option for the Poor: A Hundred Years of Catholic Social Teaching*, rev. ed (Maryknoll: Orbis Books, 1992), 179 (internal quotation marks in original). See Gurcharan Das, *India Unbound* (New York: Alfred A. Knopf, 2001), 296 (noting that "development economists [and] sociologists were an optimistic lot in the 1950s and early 1960s"). As hopes of quick development were repeatedly dashed, however, disillusionment arose and the prior optimism faded. See Paul Krugman, "Good News on Poverty," *International Herald Tribune*, November 29, 2003, 8 (asserting that, because of the lack of successful examples, "in the mid-1970's, development economics was just too depressing to pursue").

4. G.A. Res. 1710, U.N. GAOR 2nd Comm., 16th Sess., Supp. No. 17, at 248, U.N. Doc. A/5100 (1961), available at http://daccessdds.un.org/doc/RESOLUTION/GEN/NR0/167/63/IMG/NR016763.pdf; see Herbert G. Grubel, "A Sober View of the Brain Drain," *Minerva* 11 (1973): 147, 148 (book review) (noting that 1960–69 was the Development Decade at the United Nations). See Michael Novak, *Catholic Social Thought & Liberal Institutions: Freedom with Justice*, 2nd edition (New Brunswick: Transaction Publishers, 1989), 126 (noting that in the 1960s, "a sense of hope swept the entire world . . . [as] [t]he ideals of democracy and development were young and bright").

5. Easterly, *The Elusive Quest for Growth*, 30. Before World War II, economists essentially ignored the concerns of developing countries: "The League of Nations 1938 World Economic Survey, prepared by future Nobel Prize winner James Meade, included one paragraph on South America. Poor areas in Asia and Africa received no coverage at all."

6. Easterly, *The Elusive Quest for Growth*, xi, 23, 30 (noting economists have "had many theories as to how the newly independent poor countries could grow and catch up to the rich," including foreign aid, investment in machines, education, population control, conditional loans, and conditional debt relief, but "[n]one has delivered as promised"). See Das, *India Unbound*, 72–73 (noting that in the early 1960s "even the usually gloomy economists were hopeful" that "poor nations could rise out of poverty—and quickly at that").

7. John G. Stoessinger, *The Might of Nations: World Politics in Our Time* (Columbus: McGraw-Hill, 1965), 192–93. The U.S. bishops criticized the policy—

which persisted until the demise of the Soviet Union—"mak[ing] national security the central policy principle" behind development assistance to poor countries. National Conference of Catholic Bishops, "Economic Justice for All" (1986), par. 262.

8. Grubel, "A Sober View of the Brain Drain," 148 (reviewing *Education and Emigration*, by R.G. Myers).

9. Grubel, "A Sober View of the Brain Drain," 147-48 (concluding that attention given to "brain drain" in the late 1960s was based on a "simplified" view of "the importance of human capital in development"); see D. Chongo Mundende, "The Brain Drain and Developing Countries," in *The Impact of International Migration on Developing Countries*, ed. Reginald Appleyard (Paris: Development Centre of the Organisation for Economic Co-operation and Development, 1989): 183 (explaining that the movement of highly skilled workers began to receive a great deal of attention from international migration scholars in the 1960s and 1970s); Peter Vas-Zoltan, *The Brain Drain: An Anomaly of International Relations* (Leyden: A.W. Sijthoff, 1976), 8 (noting the study of "brain drain" exploded in the 1960s); Don Patinkin, "A 'Nationalist' Model," in *The Brain Drain*, ed. Walter Adams (New York: Macmillan, 1968): 92 (paper presented in 1967 notes "increased" and "intensive concern with the 'brain drain' in recent years").

10. Kenneth Hermele, "The Discourse on Migration and Development," in *International Migration, Immobility and Development*, eds. Tomas Hommar et al. (Oxford: Berg Publishers, 1997): 133, 134 (stating that "[u]ntil quite recently the customary position [among migration researchers] was to underline the negative impact of migration on emigration countries," and noting that the conclusion that "the emigration of skilled people hurts development in emigration countries" has been especially common); J. d'Oliveira e Sousa, "The Brain Drain Issue in International Negotiations," in *The Impact of International Migration on Developing Countries*, ed. Reginald Appleyard: 197, 201 (citing U.N. and international conference documents opposed to STEP OUT migration; for example, the author quotes a 1974 World Population Conference resolution holding that "[s]ince the outflow of qualified personnel from developing to developed countries seriously hampers the development of the former, there is an urgent need to formulate national and international policies to avoid the 'brain drain' and to obviate its adverse effects"); Mundende, "The Brain Drain and Developing Countries," 186 ("On the whole, brain drain immigration has been found to be detrimental to developing countries"); N.K. Onuoha Chukunta, "Human Rights and the Brain Drain," *International Migration* 11 (1977): 281, 281 (noting the "loud voice" of opposition to STEP OUT migration among international organizations); Subbiah Kannappan, "The Brain Drain and Developing Countries," *International Labour Review* 98 (July 1968): 10 (arguing that "every item in the brain drain represents a deplorable loss"); 112 Cong. Rec. 21477-80 (daily ed., August 31, 1966) (statement of Sen. Walter Mondale) at 21478, ("[T]he fact remains that the brain drain is an international problem of the first magnitude, and a problem which we have hardly begun to deal with").

11. See, e.g., Alan Dowty, *Closed Borders* (New Haven: Yale University Press, 1987), 148 (noting that "[t]he loss of skilled manpower first became a concern around 1960—not in the Third World but in Europe"). In fact, the first use of the term "brain

drain" in relation to migration was by the British Royal Society in the early 1960s in reference to "scientists and intellectuals who migrated to the United States." Anne Marie Gaillard and Jacques Gaillard, *International Migration of the Highly Qualified: A Bibliographic and Conceptual Itinerary* (Washington, D.C.: Center for Migration Studies, 1998), 22.

12. Dowty, *Closed Borders*, 152.

13. Dowty, *Closed Borders*, 148. Indeed, in the major international body largely controlled by developing nations—the General Assembly of the United Nations—as early as 1968 a resolution was passed seeking an official study by the secretary-general to "'formulate suggestions for ways of tackling the problems arising from the outflow of trained personnel at all levels from developing to developed countries within the framework of the proposed strategy for development of the Second United Nations Development Decade'"; e Sousa, "The Brain Drain Issue in International Negotiations," 201 (quoting General Assembly resolution 2417). One skeptic of the motives of poor countries has contended, however, that those countries' claims of harm should not be unquestionably accepted:

> [I]t is also important to realise that official representations by governments in international organizations, such as the United Nations or UNCTAD, cannot be taken at face value as indication of the seriousness of the problem of the brain drain from developing countries. It is well known that such agencies to some extent serve as a forum for political pronouncements and efforts by poor countries to bring about transfers of income from industrial countries. . . . The spokesmen for poor countries have every incentive to exaggerate and none to understate the seriousness of the problem of the brain drain.

Herbert G. Grubel, "Reflections on the Present State of the Brain Drain and a Suggested Remedy," *Minerva* 14 (1976): 209, 220. See also Patinkin, "A 'Nationalist' Model," 93 (noting that the increase in attention given to complaints of poor countries in the 1960s was due to "political developments since World War II").

14. See this chapter, notes 19-21 and accompanying text.

15. *Immigration and Nationality Act of 1965*, Pub. L. No. 89-236, 79 Stat. 911 (1965). Articulating a rationale for the new law, former Secretary of State Dean Rusk explained that "we are in the international market of brains." Congressional Research Service for the House Subcommittee on National Security Policy and Scientific Developments, 93d Congress, *Brain Drain: A Study of the Persistent Issue of International Scientific Mobility* (Washington, D.C.: U.S. Government Printing Office, 1974), 36.

16. Before 1967, Asians could migrate to Canada only if sponsored by a Canadian citizen relative, while a relative of European immigrants did not need to be a citizen but merely a resident. See Don DeVoretz and Dennis Maki, "The Brain Drain and Income Taxation: Canada," in *Taxing the Brain Drain I: A Proposal*, eds. Jagdish Bhagwati and Martin Partington (Amsterdam: North-Holland Publishing, 1976): 53, 55. Under the new system, intending immigrants had to demonstrate that they warranted at least 50 points out of the 100 total in order to gain admission, unless sponsored by a Canadian relative. 101 C. Gaz. 1359 (September 13, 1967). "Points were assigned for education and training, occupational skills, occupational demand in Canada, arranged employment in Canada, age and other factors." 101 C. Gaz. 1359 (Septem-

ber 13, 1967). As Canada's Jean Marchand, Minister of Manpower and Immigration, explained: "The high cost of training professional and skilled people—engineers, doctors, skilled technicians, etc.—is a measure of the benefit derived upon [their] arrival in Canada. Other countries are in competition with us for immigrants." Congressional Research Service for the House Subcommittee on National Security Policy and Scientific Developments, 93d Congress, *Brain Drain: A Study of the Persistent Issue of International Scientific Mobility* (Washington, D.C.: U.S. Government Printing Office, 1974), 36. See also Hon. Jean Marchand, Canadian Minister of Manpower and Immigration, *White Paper on Immigration* (October 1966), 8, 11, cited in Gregory Henderson, No. 74-39002, *The Emigration of Highly Skilled Manpower from the Developing Countries* 7, n.1 (UNITAR, 1970).

17. Congressional Research Service for the House Subcommittee on National Security Policy and Scientific Developments, 93rd Congress, *Brain Drain: A Study of the Persistent Issue of International Scientific Mobility* (Washington, D.C.: U.S. Government Printing Office, 1974), 34-35. In 1962, for the first time the United Kingdom limited migration from Commonwealth countries and gave preference to, among others, "those with prescribed professional, academic, or other qualifications, coming to the U.K. to seek employment." Peter Balacs and Anne Gordon, "The Brain Drain & Income Taxation: The U.K.," in *Taxing the Brain Drain I: A Proposal*, eds. Jagdish Bhagwati & Martin Partington, 71, 73-74.

18. Australian immigration laws were highly discretionary. Essentially, the Immigration Minister was authorized to admit individuals according to his or her own preferences. Gregory Henderson, No. 74-39002, *The Emigration of Highly-Skilled Manpower from the Developing Countries*, 6 n.2 (UNITAR 1970). "[U]ntil 1938, encouragement was usually given only to British migration. [Starting in 1947] the range of immigration from Europe [increased somewhat]." Henderson, *The Emigration of Highly Skilled Manpower from the Developing Countries*, 6 n. 2. Indeed, in 1956 regulations were enacted that provided for the admission of "distinguished and highly qualified non-Europeans . . . for indefinite stay." Henderson, *The Emigration of Highly Skilled Manpower from the Developing Countries*, 6-7, n.2. The following year, those admitted for temporary residence became eligible for naturalization. Henderson, *The Emigration of Highly Skilled Manpower from the Developing Countries*, 6–7 n. 2. Then, in 1958, the "'dictation test' in a European language was abolished" and, in 1966, the Australian government "announced the provision for the admission of non-Europeans capable of integration and of contribution to the [country's] progress." Henderson, *The Emigration of Highly Skilled Manpower from the Developing Countries*, 6–7 n. 2. "[Q]ualifications which [were] in fact positively useful to Australia," including such qualities as technical skills and "high attainment in the arts, sciences or other fields," were favorably considered. Hon. Hubert Opperman, Minister for Immigration, "Paper Delivered to Student Seminar," Canberra, May, 28, 1966, cited in Gregory Henderson, No. 74- 39002, *The Emigration of Highly Skilled Manpower from the Developing Countries*, 6-7, n.2 (UNITAR, 1970).

19. Mundende, "The Brain Drain and Developing Countries," 183. In the early to mid-1900's, a large majority of migrants to the United States were agricultural and industrial workers. Brinley Thomas, "'Modern' Migration," in *The Brain Drain*, ed.

Walter Adams (1968): 33. For example, from 1907 through 1923 only 2.6 million of the close to 7 million migrants to the United States were professionals. By 1965, the percentage of migrants to the United States and Canada classified as being among the professional or technical classes increased to 22 percent. Brinkley Thomas, "'Modern' Migration," 33.

20. Jagdish N. Bhagwati, "The International Brain Drain and Taxation," in *The Brain Drain and Taxation II: Theory and Empirical Analysis*, ed. Jagdish N. Bhagwati (Amsterdam: North-Holland Publishing, 1976): 3, 6-7. Records from the Immigration and Naturalization Service indicate that the number of professional and technical migrants to the United States increased significantly within just a few years of the 1965 Act. Bhagwati, "The International Brain Drain and Taxation," 6–7.

21. Jagdish Bhagwati, "The Brain Drain," *International Social Science Journal* 28 (1976): 691, 695-97, and Tables 1 & 2 (showing large increases in migration to the United States from African and Asian developing countries, most significantly from Korea, India, Taiwan, and the Philippines). Professor Bhagwati attributes the increase in migration of STEP OUT migrants from less developed countries to the 1965 act legislative changes. Bhagwati, "The Brain Drain," 695. For statistical information on more recent migration flows, see Immigration and Naturalization Service, U.S. Department of Justice, *2000 Statistical Yearbook of the Immigration and Naturalization Service*, Table 1 (2000), available at http://uscis.gov/graphics/shared/statistics/yearbook/2000/Yearbook2000.pdf. See also Susan Martin, B. Lindsay Lowell, and Philip Martin, "U.S. Immigration Policy: Admission of High-Skilled Workers," *Georgetown Immigration Law Journal* 16 (2002): 619, 621-22 (outlining U.S. immigration laws on skilled migration with tables of statistics showing migration patterns to the United States).

22. See chapter 2, at note 31, and this chapter, at notes 13 and 31-40, and text accompanying these notes.

23. Gaillard and Gaillard, *International Migration of the Highly Qualified*, 24.

24. 112 Congressional Record 21477-80 (daily ed., August 31, 1966) (statement of Sen. Mondale), at 21477. Senator Mondale went on to explain: "Were our objective simply to siphon off the world's most talented people—to draw them to the United States—we would consider the brain drain an unmixed blessing. But in today's world it is barely a mixed blessing. It may be a brain gain for us in the short run, but it threatens one of the paramount long-run objectives of American foreign policy, progress in underdeveloped lands. . . . World security—and American security—depends on development in these countries, development at sufficient speed to satisfy at least a portion of their rising aspirations. Since the brain drain threatens development, it is ultimately a threat to the security of our own land." 112 Congressional Record 21477-80 (daily ed., August 31, 1966) (statement of Sen. Mondale), at 21478 (internal quotation marks omitted). These sentiments were also repeated in the popular press. The *Christian Science Monitor*, for example, criticized immigration policies, saying that "[w]ith one hand the United States is giving these countries millions to develop themselves. And with the other it is casually taking away the seed corn of future leaders in natural science, health, and technical knowledge. These are even more precious to the country than food or machinery." Walter Adams, "Introduction," in *The Brain Drain*, ed. Walter Adams (1968): 1, 3 (quoting article in the *Christian Science Monitor*).

25. Kenneth E. Boulding, "The 'National' Importance of Human Capital," in *The Brain Drain*, ed. Walter Adams (1968): 109, 113.

26. Harry G. Johnson, "The Economics of the 'Brain Drain': The Canadian Case," *Minerva* 3 (1965): 299, 302. See also S. Wantanabe, "The Brain Drain from Developing to Developed Countries," *International Labour Review* 99 (1969): 401, 407-08 (noting the losses to the sending countries in terms of education costs).

27. Wantanabe, "The Brain Drain from Developing to Developed Countries," 410.

28. Wantanabe, "The Brain Drain from Developing to Developed Countries," 401.

29. Wantanabe, "The Brain Drain from Developing to Developed Countries," 417. But see Herbert G. Grubel, "The Reduction of the Brain Drain: Problems and Policies," *Minerva* 6 (1968): 541, 546 (arguing that "the quality of 'leadership' is difficult to define, and requires special conditions to develop and become effective").

30. Henderson, *The Emigration of Highly Skilled Manpower from the Developing Countries*, 119.

31. Gaillard and Gaillard, *International Migration of the Highly Qualified*, 24; B. Lindsay Lowell, International Migration Papers 46: "Some Developmental Effects of the International Migration of Highly Skilled Persons," 2, International Migration Branch, International Labour Office (Geneva, 2002) (noting that "[e]arly international interest in the causes and consequences of the brain drain resulted in debates and resolutions in the United Nations starting from about 1967").

32. As a general guide, the likelihood of implementation for proposals of this sort depended, first of all, on whether a particular proposal required agreement among nations or could be implemented unilaterally. Broad compensatory schemes requiring international cooperation, such as Jagdish Bhagwati's plan for receiving countries to levy a special tax on the income of migrants and pass the proceeds on to sending countries (see Bhagwati, "The Brain Drain Tax Proposal and the Issues," in *Taxing the Brain Drain I: A Proposal*, 3-5; see also Jagdish Bhagwati, *In Defense of Globalization* (New York: Oxford University Press, 2004), 215 (noting Bhagwati's continued support for the "so-called Bhagwati tax" first proposed by him in the 1960s)), and various other proposals calling for rich countries to establish an international fund to benefit sending countries (see Sudha Shenoy, "The Movement of Human Capital," in *Economic Issues in Immigration* (London: Institute for Economic Affairs, 1970): 45, 58)—while garnering support among the latter group of nations—tended to languish unenacted in the face of international resistance. As one writer noted, commenting upon the plethora of international proposals and the paucity of international action,

> It would need many times the volume of this book to present all the proposals aimed at decreasing brain drain that have come to light since this process was first recognized. There have been numerous individual proposals to curb it in nearly every publication of the international organizations . . . .
>
> None of these proposals have been realized.

Vas-Zoltan, *The Brain Drain: An Anomaly of International Relations*, 107.

However, proposals not demanding international cooperation, such as a requirement that emigrants pay for their education upon departure, occasionally have been enacted. See, e.g., Reginald Appleyard, "International Migration and Developing Countries," in

The Impact of International Migration on Developing Countries, ed. Reginald Appleyard (Paris: Development Centre of the Organisation For Economic Co-operation and
Development, 1989): 19, 23 (noting Romanian requirement that emigrants from Romania repay the state for secondary and college education). See also Dowty, Closed
Borders, 214, 234 (noting Romania's retreat from imposition of its "education tax" in
light of U.S. threats to withdraw most-favored nation trade status).

    33. Jagdish N. Bhagwati, "Preface," in The Brain Drain and Taxation II—Theory
and Empirical Analysis, vii. See also Jagdish Bhagwati and Koichi Hamada, "The Brain
Drain, International Integration of Markets for Professionals and Unemployment: A
Theoretical Analysis," Journal of Development Economics 1 (1974): 19; Jagdish N.
Bhagwati and William Dellalfar, "The Brain Drain and Income Taxation: The U.S.," in
Taxing the Brain Drain I: A Proposal, 33. The International Monetary Fund "examine[d] the effect of alternative tax and subsidy policies of economic growth in the presence of brain drain." The study showed that, based on a two-country endogenous
growth model, in the absence of brain drain, "a tax-financed increase in education subsidy that preserves the fiscal balance will induce a positive growth effect, while in the
presence of human capital flight such a policy can have a negative impact on growth."
Nadeem Haque and Se-jik Kim, "Human Capital Flight: Impact of Migration on Income
and Growth," 9/1/95, IMF Staff Papers 577, at 3 (WP/94/155) (1994).

    Another proposal called for "either the individual whose education is publicly fi-
nanced on the assumption that he will remain in the country of his origin, or his employer or the government in his country of immigration . . . to repay the cost of his
education to the country that educated him, or perhaps to repay that cost plus an estimate of the amount of his income projected in the future in his own country of origin,
which he would have been obliged to redistribute via excess taxation to his fellow citizens." Harry G. Johnson, 'An 'Internationalist Model,'" in The Brain Drain, ed. Walter Adams (1968), 69, 87. These and other similar proposals were largely abandoned
at the United Nations in 1987 after much study. See Gaillard and Gaillard, International Migration of the Highly Qualified, 25.

    34. Grubel, "Reflections of the Present State of the Brain Drain and a Suggested
Remedy," 209, 223-24.

    35. Gaillard and Gaillard, International Migration of the Highly Qualified, 25,
n.25. Prior to the collapse of the Soviet Bloc in the late 1980s and early 1990s, more
than twenty countries essentially denied everyone the right to emigrate. Dowty,
Closed Borders, 3. All were "ideologically doctrinaire one-party states," and almost
all "define[d] themselves as Marxist-Leninist." Dowty, Closed Borders, 185.

    36. Approximately 270 people died trying to cross the Berlin Wall into West
Berlin. "Berlin Wall Remembrance," San Francisco Chronicle, August 14, 2001, A7.
Incredibly, the Berlin Wall may have represented the milder side of East German bor-
der patrol policy, as this description, written in 1987, indicates:

In most places, the border between the German Democratic Republic and the Federal Republic of Germany is marked by parallel metal trellis fences with contact mines between
them. . . . Immediately to the east of the fence is an antivehicle ditch, then a tracking strip

to detect footprints or other tracks, then a relief road to provide guards easy access, and finally another fence outfitted with electric and acoustic warning devices. . . . [W]here observation is difficult, attack dogs help out. Border guards have standing orders to shoot to kill anyone within fifty yards of the metal trellis fence.

Dowty, *Closed Borders*, 205. And, indeed, the number of East Germans killed trying to escape to the West over the Berlin Wall is dwarfed by the number killed trying to cross the border elsewhere. Kate Connolly, "More than 1000 died" trying to flee East Germany, *Daily Telegraph*, August 16, 2003, at http://www.telegraph.co.uk/news/main.jhtml?xml=/news/2003/08/13/weast13.xml.

37. Dowty, *Closed Borders*, 117, 207 (citing examples).

38. See, e.g., V.M. Dandekar, "India," in *The Brain Drain*, ed. Walter Adams (1968), 203, 229 (arguing that because "[i]t is not fair to permit the young men to be lured away and then to expect them to resist the easy temptations," India should "help [them] by closing the doors" to emigration). Indeed, some developing countries tried to adopt a restrictive approach, to disappointing and often counter-productive results. Dowty, *Closed Borders*, 154-55 (discussing restrictions by Mozambique, Haiti, Ethiopia, India, Pakistan, and Sri Lanka).

39. See Grubel, "The Reduction of the Brain Drain," 541, 548-556 (noting recommendations to impose "on all foreign students the requirement that upon completion of their education they leave the country of study presumably to return home for a period of two years before they can apply for an immigrant's visa" and to eliminate "provisions in the immigration laws which discriminate in favour of highly skilled persons"). U.S. immigration laws incorporate some of these concerns, for example, by requiring certain participants in student exchange programs to return to their country of nationality to live for at least two years before they can apply for permanent residency status and certain business visas. See 8 U.S.C. sec. 1182(e), INA sec. 212(e). See also Inna Tachkalova, Comment, "The Hardship Waiver of the Two-Year Foreign Residency Requirement Under Section 212(e) of the INA: The Need for a Change", *American University Law Review* 49 (1999): 549, 550.

Finally, some scholars encouraged the governments of sending countries to improve the political, social, and economic conditions in their countries, thus making the home country more attractive to its nationals. For example, one supporter of the nationalist position argued that sending countries could non-coercively discourage STEP OUT migration in three ways. "First, these countries must encourage a high degree of identification of their skilled and scientific manpower with the development of their country; second, they must demonstrate to this manpower that it can fulfill a vital role in promoting this development; and third, they must provide them with the conditions necessary to fulfill their scientific aspirations to at least a minimum extent." Patinkin, "A 'Nationalist Model,'" 95. Others suggested increasing salaries and improving working conditions, increasing professional opportunity, and reaching out to nationals abroad, including provision of information about employment opportunities in the sending countries. Mundende, "The Brain Drain and Developing Countries," 188-89; see also Walter Adams and Joel B. Dirlam, "An Agenda for Action," in *The Brain Drain*, ed. Walter Adams (1968): 247, 248-61 (listing a number of desired economic and social changes).

40. Hermele, "The Discourse on Migration and Development," 134. See, e.g., Congressional Research Service for the House Subcommittee on National Security Policy and Scientific Developments, 93rd Cong., *Brain Drain: A Study of the Persistent Issue of International Scientific Mobility* (Washington, D.C.: U.S. Government Printing Office, 1974), 9 (noting that a 1968 House report titled "Scientific Brain Drain from the Developing Countries" predicted "serious adverse consequences in the long run").

41. Easterly, *The Elusive Quest for Growth*, 64. See Pope John Paul II, *Sollicitudo Rei Socialis* (1987), par. 12 (noting that, in the 1960s, "there was a certain widespread optimism about the possibility of overcoming, without excessive efforts, the economic backwardness of the poorer peoples, of providing them with infrastructures and assisting them in the process of industrialization").

42. Dorr, *Option for the Poor*, 232.

43. Michael A. Evans, *An Analysis of U.N. Refugee Policy in Light of Roman Catholic Social Teaching and the Phenomena Creating Refugees* (Ann Arbor: University Microfilms International, 1991), 112; Philip S. Land, *Catholic Social Teaching As I Have Lived, Loathed, and Loved It* (Chicago: Loyola University Press, 1994), 37 (noting that "an undeniable, perhaps somewhat excessive, optimism [about development emerged] from Vatican II").

44. William A. Glaser, *The Brain Drain: Emigration and Return* (Oxford: Pergamon Press, 1978), 1-2 (noting that when the optimism of the 1950s toward the development of Asia, Latin America, and Africa turned to disillusionment in the late 1960s, "brain drain" was identified as the culprit in academia, the press, and the United Nations). The failure of economic reality to match economic expectations had other consequences as well. For example, as "poverty in Latin America . . . worsened in the 1960s," Latin Americans responded by developing and popularizing the tenets of liberation theology. Marvin L. Krier Mich, *Catholic Social Teaching and Movements* (Mystic: Twenty-Third Publications, 2000), 241.

45. See Congressional Research Service for the House Subcommittee on National Security Policy and Scientific Developments, 93rd Congress, *Brain Drain: A Study of the Persistent Issue of International Scientific Mobility* (Washington, D.C.: U.S. Government Printing Office, 1974), 36 (quoting former Secretary of State Dean Rusk).

46. See chapters 11–14.

47. Dana W. Wilbanks, *Re-Creating America: The Ethics of U.S. Immigration and Refugee Policy in a Christian Perspective* (Nashville: Abingdon Press, 1996), 150. Professor Wilbanks further explains that "[t]o relegate immigrants entirely to the lower rungs of employment and social position is to perpetuate unequal divisions between residents and immigrants."

48. See, e.g., E. P. Hutchinson, *Legislative History of American Immigration Policy, 1798-1965* (Philadelphia: University of Pennsylvania Press, 1981), 366-379 (in a discussion of arguments in Congress regarding the 1965 Immigration Act, no mention is made of positive economic benefits accruing to sending countries, nor is any mention made of social benefits created by the admission of professionals from developing countries).

Chapter Eight

Developments in the Church

It is especially unsurprising that Catholic social teaching took a position against STEP OUT migration given the fact that, at the time that studies denouncing "brain drain" migration were gaining prominence, the Church's social teachings were also undergoing a transition of sorts which made the Church highly receptive to the complaints of sending countries. This transition had two major elements: first, a change in content, namely a greater concern with the development of the entire world, especially with that of poorer nations; and second, an attempted change in perspective, to see the world through the eyes of the developing world, especially beginning with the Second Vatican Council's *Gaudium et Spes* in 1965.[1]

Both of these elements represented major differences with the Church's prior approach. Historically, Catholic social teaching had set a tone for the Church that one scholar has characterized as "generally introspective, defensive and self-righteous toward the 'world.'"[2] But this introspective perspective changed during the papacy of John XXIII, who served as Pope from 1958 to 1963. During these years, Pope John XXIII moved the Church away from its historically internal emphasis and "brought the official church into a new relationship with other churches and the contemporary society."[3]

The Church's new concerns and new perspective is clearly reflected in Pope John XXIII's two encyclicals.[4] For example, in the first "social encyclical to deal extensively with global poverty," *Mater et Magistra*,[5] "[s]ome of the most original thoughts . . . concern the demands of justice and the common good in the relations between nations at different stages of economic development."[6] The same focus is evident in Pope John XXIII's second social encyclical, *Pacem in Terris*.[7] *Pacem in Terris* clearly articulated an understanding of mutual cooperation and dependence among nation-states. In it, Pope John XXIII called upon the public authorities in nation-states to realize that their actions do not operate in isolation, but rather impact the rest of the human community, and that one state's development and progress is dependent upon development and progress in other states. He explained it in this way:

> [T]he social progress, order, security, and peace of each country are necessarily connected with the social progress, order, security, and peace of all other countries. . . . Given these conditions, it is obvious that individual countries cannot rightly seek their own interests and develop themselves in isolation from the rest, for the prosperity and development of one country follows partly in the train of the prosperity and progress of all the rest and partly produces that prosperity and progress.[8]

The call in *Pacem in Terris* for nation-states, especially the more economically developed states,[9] to concern themselves with the common good of all countries is elaborated upon in subsequent encyclicals. For example, the Church's concerns about world poverty and development took center stage with *Populorum Progressio* and *Octogesima Adveniens*, which were authored by Pope Paul VI in 1967 and 1971, respectively.[10] As David Hollenbach explains, the "problems of economic development, international economic relationships, and, above all, the poverty of developing nations are the central concerns of these documents."[11] In them, Pope Paul VI stated baldly that "the principal fact that we must all recognize is that the social question has become worldwide," and that human solidarity should be demonstrated through "the aid that the rich nations must give to developing countries."[12] Clearly, the perspective and subject matter in these documents was no longer primarily Eurocentric.[13]

In "brain drain" migration, the Church found an issue that dovetailed nicely with its new concerns. If it opposed STEP OUT migration, the Church would find itself in agreement with developing nations' views that STEP OUT migration impoverished developing nations, that rich nations benefited from STEP OUT migration, and that STEP OUT migration effectively took back the aid that was necessary for poor countries to develop. Moreover, not only would opposition to STEP OUT migration perfectly demonstrate the Church's new dedication to the development of poor countries, but since that opposition came equipped with mainstream economists' seal of approval, there also was little apparent risk in the position. Not surprisingly, as the many Church writings opposing STEP OUT migration attest, this apparent confluence of warmhearted moral sentiment[14] with dispassionate (and widespread) economic analysis proved too tempting for the Church to resist. Unfortunately, as with many a temptation, what seemed like a good idea at the time eventually proved problematic.

The source of the problem was not in the Church's application of the foundational principles of human dignity and the common good. Indeed, the conclusion of Catholic social teaching that the common good is not served by STEP OUT migration because such migration necessarily leads to a failure of duty by the migrant which results in the rich getting richer and the poor getting poorer is, assuming the validity of the factual predicates, theoretically sound and, in its intended effect of aiding the poor, actually consistent with other immigration teachings. The problem, especially today, is that there is little compelling evidence that STEP OUT migration in fact causes either a failure of duty by STEP OUT migrants to their home communities or an overall loss in poor nations. Indeed, there is considerable evidence to the contrary, and this evidence undermines the Church's conclusion that considerations of human dignity and the common good clearly counsel against STEP OUT migration.

NOTES

1. See Donal Dorr, *Option for the Poor: A Hundred Years of Catholic Social Teaching*, revised edition (Maryknoll: Orbis Books, 1992), 152 (noting that "Gaudium et Spes represents a considerable advance on earlier Church documents—even those of John XXIII—in so far as it begins to recognize more clearly that Third World countries have their own history, traditions, and social structures, as well as their own problems; and that none of these are to be treated as though they were no more than adjuncts to those of the West"). See also Patricia A. Lamoureux, "Immigration Reconsidered in the Context of an Ethic of Solidarity," in *Made in God's Image: The Catholic Vision of Human Dignity*, eds. Regis Duffy and Angelus Gambatese (Mahwah: Paulist Press, 1999): 105, 115–16 (stating that "the conciliar-era documents of John XXIII and Vatican II . . . led to a more global vision of solidarity"). It has been suggested that *Gaudium et Spes*, a document that emerged from the Second Vatican Council and that "represented the opinion of the overwhelming majority of the world's bishops" (David J. O'Brien and Thomas A. Shannon, "Introduction," in *Catholic Social Thought: The Documentary Heritage*, eds. David J. O'Brien and Thomas A. Shannon (Maryknoll: Orbis Books, 1992): 164, 165, introductory essay to *Gaudium et Spes*), reflected a broader perspective due to the fact that "the bishops at Vatican II . . . shared close quarters for many months, [and] had ample opportunity to consult with one another [and] talk frequently about . . . the desperate poverty that discouraged, disrupted, and even claimed millions of lives in their various homelands." Thomas Massaro, *Living Justice: Catholic Social Teaching in Action* (Franklin: Sheed & Ward, 2000), 145.

2. Marvin L. Krier Mich, *Catholic Social Teaching and Movements* (Mystic: Twenty-Third Publications, 2000), 90. Noting that the pre-Vatican II methodology for Catholic social teaching "was largely the fashioning of abstract universals," Philip Land stated that "[t]he post-Vatican II method of theologizing about society shifted dramatically to emphasize the historical, the concrete, the individual, together with stress on

creativity in making social order." Philip S. Land, *Catholic Social Teaching As I Have Lived, Loathed, and Loved It* (Chicago: Loyola University Press, 1994), 110.

   3. Krier Mich, *Catholic Social Teaching and Movements* (2000), 91.

   4. Pope John Paul II often noted the change in orientation marked by the encyclicals of Pope John XXIII. See, e.g., Pope John Paul II, *Laborem Exercens* (1981), sec. 2 (noting that with *Mater et Magistra*, "the church's teaching widen[ed] its horizon to take in the whole world"); Pope John Paul II, *Sollicitudo Rei Socialis* (1987), sec. 9 (noting that *Mater et Magistra* "entered into [a] wider outlook").

   5. Massaro, *Living Justice*, 143.

   6. Joseph Joblin, "The Papal Encyclical Mater et Magistra," *International Labour Review* 84 (International Labour Organization, 1961): 124, 140.

   7. Pope John XXIII, *Pacem in Terris* (1963). *Pacem in Terris* was praised by individuals representing groups far and wide, including "Protestant, Greek Orthodox, and Jewish leaders." "Chorus of Praise in U.S.," *The New York Times* (April 12, 1963), 6; see also Michael Novak, *Catholic Social Thought & Liberal Institutions: Freedom with Justice*, 2nd edition (New Brunswick: Transaction Publishers, 1989), 144 (noting the "worldwide headlines and renewed secular influence won by . . . *Pacem in Terris*").

   8. Pope John XXIII, *Pacem in Terris*, pars. 130–31. Moreover, the phenomenon of emigration was linked to "social development in explicit terms." NCCB Ad Hoc Committee on Migration and Tourism, "The Church and the Immigrant Today: The Pastoral Concern of the Church for People on the Move," in National Conference of Catholic Bishops, *The Pastoral Concern of the Church for the People on the Move* (U.S. Catholic Conference, 1976), 5, 10, reprinted in National Conference of Catholic Bishops, *People on the Move: A Compendium of Church Documents on the Pastoral Concern for Migrants and Refugees* (U.S. Catholic Conference, 1988), 61, 62.

   9. Pope John XXIII, *Pacem in Terris*, par. 88.

   10. Pope Paul VI, *Populorum Progressio* (1967); Pope Paul VI, *Octogesima Adveniens* (1971). Pope John Paul II stated that *Populorum Progressio* affirmed with unprecedented "clarity that the social question ha[d] acquired a worldwide dimension." Pope John Paul II, *Sollicitudo Rei Socialis*, sec. 9.

   11. David Hollenbach, *Claims in Conflict: Retrieving and Renewing the Catholic Human Rights Tradition* (New York: Paulist, 1979), 78. See also Michael Novak, *Catholic Social Thought and Liberal Institutions*, 134 ("The horizon of *Populorum Progressio* is no longer that of Europe, but of the developing world").

   12. Pope Paul VI, *Populorum Progressio*, pars. 3, 44. The 1971 document by the international Synod of Bishops, *Justice in the World*, also addressed development concerns from a broad perspective. Synod of Bishops, *Justice in the World* (Vatican City: Pontifical Commission of Justice and Peace, 1971).

   13. See chapter 4 at note 30 (compiling sources noting the traditional Eurocentrism of earlier Catholic social teaching). This change in perspective has been maintained into the current era, and was strongly reaffirmed by Pope John Paul II in *Sollicitudo Rei Socialis*: "Today more than in the past, the Church's social doctrine must be open to an *international outlook*, in line with the Second Vatican Council, the most recent encyclicals, and particularly in line with [*Populorum Progressio*]." *Sollicitudo Rei So-*

cialis, at sec. 42 (emphasis in original; footnotes omitted). See also Michael Novak, *Catholic Social Thought and Liberal Institutions,* 4 (noting that while the early encyclicals focus "on the political economies of Western Europe . . . later ones assume worldwide perspectives"); Lamoureux, "Immigration Reconsidered in the Context of an Ethic of Solidarity," 126 (noting that Pope John Paul II valued highly "the ability to listen to the other in mutual respect . . . especially to the voices of poor people and nations").

14. Herbert G. Grubel, "Reflections of the Present State of the Brain Drain and a Suggested Remedy," *Minerva* 14 (1976): 209, 220 ("The issue of the brain drain appeals to ethical ideas and sentiments"). Cf. Jagdish Bhagwati, "Sanctuary," in *A Stream of Windows: Unsettling Reflections on Trade, Immigration, and Democracy* (Cambridge: MIT Press, 1998): 343, 344 (noting that immigration in general "is par exellence an issue that is at the crossroads of economics and ethics").

Part Four

THE CASE FOR STEP OUT MIGRATION

Chapter Nine

An Overview

The economic evidence undermining Catholic social teaching's opposition to STEP OUT migration falls into two general categories. The first category consists of evidence showing that prior understandings effectively exaggerated losses to sending countries. Prominent among the errors here was an exaggerated belief in the permanence of migration.

The second and even more important category consists of evidence that makes an affirmative case for the benefits of STEP OUT migration. It demonstrates that, while overestimating the negative effects of STEP OUT migration, critics also underestimated the phenomenon's positive effects. This underestimation by early critics should not be judged too harshly since, at the time of their criticism in the 1960s, by and large the positive effects of STEP OUT migration had not yet obviously emerged. Nonetheless, Catholic social teaching's methodological shift away "from an ahistorical, deductive arguing from natural law principles to one marked by inductive reasoning from historical developments"[1] makes it imperative that these beneficial effects be taken into account by Catholic social teaching now that they obviously have emerged as part of the historical experience of the last few decades.[2] All others in the immigration debate who claim to argue inductively must, of course, do the same.

As part of the building of our own inductive argument, both categories of evidence are discussed in the chapters that follow. In chapter 10, the focus is on how and why the negative effects of STEP OUT migration were exaggerated, while chapter 11 focuses on the overlooked positive effects of STEP OUT migration to sending countries. The benefits discussed in chapter 11 are explained in greater detail in subsequent chapters in the next part of this book. In particular, chapter 12 shows how STEP OUT migrants contribute to their home countries through the transfer of knowledge and information, and the development of contacts; chapter 13 examines the ability of STEP OUT migrants to contribute to their home countries through various types of monetary transfers; and chapter 14 demonstrates how STEP OUT migration can stimulate the development of new technologies that can aid underdeveloped nations.[3] Individually, each of these contributions bolsters the case for STEP OUT migration—collectively, they make a strong case that, because of the ability of STEP OUT migrants to contribute to their home countries when abroad, the effects of STEP OUT migration can be broadly beneficial for those countries and the people who live in them.

NOTES

1. Michael A. Evans, *An Analysis of U.N. Refugee Policy in Light of Roman Catholic Social Teaching and the Phenomena Creating Refugees* (Ann Arbor: University Microfilms International, 1991), 77. Pope John Paul II noted the necessity of taking new information into account when formulating Catholic social teaching:

> [T]eaching in the social sphere . . . [o]n the one hand . . . is *constant*, for it remains identical in its fundamental inspiration, in its "principles of reflection," in its "criteria of judgment," in its basic "directives for action," and above all in its vital link with the Gospel of the Lord. On the other hand, it is ever *new*, because it is subject to the necessary and opportune adaptations suggested by the changes in historical conditions and by the unceasing flow of the events, which are the setting of the life of people and society.

See Pope John Paul II, *Sollicitudo Rei Socialis* (1987), sec. 3 (emphasis in original; footnote omitted).

2. The Jesuit Philip Land, who played an important role in the formation of several important social teaching documents of the 1960s and 1970s, remarked upon this obligation to take into account new circumstances:

> Even with the Spirit's guidance the Church arrives at most of its statements in the social field slowly, painfully, and with an intermix of error or of very contingent changeable judgments. The role of the believing community as well as the hierarchy is a further reception of revelation through reading signs of the times.

Philip S. Land, *Catholic Social Teaching As I Have Lived, Loathed, and Loved It* (Chicago: Loyola University Press, 1994), 217.

3. Some of the examples given in the chapters that follow, particularly those dependent upon migrant creativity, may seem *sui generis*, the chance consequences of events that, in their particulars, cannot be duplicated. "Yet the sources of economic dynamism, invention, and progress are typically serendipitous, depending upon the creativity of talented members of a free citizenry." Michael Novak, *Catholic Social Thought & Institutions: Freedom with Justice*, 2nd ed. (New Brunswick: Transaction, 1989), 53. The question is, is the system in which one is working one that, for whatever reason, discourages the serendipitous insight, or one that encourages it? STEP OUT migration typically is to the latter type of society, in which, paradoxically, serendipitous creative insights occur at a predictably high level of frequency.

Chapter Ten

A History of Accentuating the Negative

Direct negative losses due to STEP OUT migration were exaggerated in the 1960s for two reasons, namely the use of both a flawed theoretical paradigm and bad data. Each of these reasons is discussed in this chapter.

THE OBSOLETE PARADIGM

First, either explicitly or implicitly, many researchers worked from false assumptions—for example, that migration by skilled workers was overwhelmingly permanent, or that the opportunity to migrate does not itself "stimulate students in sending countries to pursue higher education."[1] The former assumption is worth pursuing in some detail, because it was both very important and very prevalent. Indeed, "[t]he popular legend . . . that migrants move to a receiving country, settle there permanently and are assimilated into a new culture"[2] so permeated the culture that popular humor could be based on it; it spawned, for example, "the oft-repeated phrase that 'there is nothing so permanent as a temporary migrant.'"[3]

Now, it may be true that all good humor contains a kernel of truth, but sound policy and sound social science should be based on something more. Unfortunately, in this case, it was not. Rather, as Professor Charles B. Keely has noted, along with many other scholars,[4] the governing assumption of many analysts was or soon became seriously outdated:

> Some highly skilled persons migrate with the intention of settling in a new country, mirroring the traditional international migrations of the 19th century from Europe to North and South America. But today's migrants for business, culture, and educational reasons are more likely to be making a temporary move, intending to live and work in a foreign country, perhaps in a series of

countries, but eventually returning home. Many maintain ties and identities with their native country and continue to think of themselves as belonging to and identifying with their birth place.[5]

Indeed, return migration is now such a common phenomenon among STEP OUT migrants that a host of phrases have arisen to describe it, among them "brain circulation,"[6] "circular migration",[7] "brain return," and "return of skills."[8] Whatever the name, it is now well established among researchers that immigrants who migrate to developed countries to attend institutions of higher education, to work, or both, often return to their countries of origin.[9] In fact, STEP OUT migrants have among the highest rates of return of all migrants.[10] Instead of being unidirectional, in a "growing proportion migration is circular."[11]

Return migration is so strong in some countries that they experience or are approaching a net "reverse brain drain." Ireland,[12] South Korea[13] and Taiwan[14] are three examples of this phenomenon. India is now beginning to trend in the same direction, with one writer even stating that "Indian professionals [are] returning home in droves . . . after stints that last anywhere between three and 20 years in the US."[15] Moreover, it is clear that many more Indians hope to return. Job fairs in California, for example, featuring Indian firms hoping to recruit Indian STEP OUT migrants, have attracted up to 1,000 attendees,[16] and even mid-size companies in Bangalore, the information technology center in India, "receive between 10 and 20 resumes a month from Indians in the U.S. seeking to return."[17] Taking the "skill-set and work culture" from their experience in the United States, the returnees are seen as improving the business climate in India.[18]

And yet, despite these developments, "the prevailing mindset" in the popular mind and to some extent elsewhere remains the discredited "19th century" idea that, generally, "highly skilled persons migrate with the intention of settling in a new country" and forever leaving the old one behind.[19] What accounts for the persistence of the "obsolete, binary models of migration"? Why is so much immigration "theory . . . anchored in a permanent settlement migration paradigm"[20] that effectively causes STEP OUT migration—and hence its negative direct effects—both to be overestimated? Why is all this so more than six years into the twenty-first century and three decades or more after the problem with the nineteenth-century notion of permanent immigration was first identified?[21] It seems a mystery.

We think there are two main explanations for the persistence of the assumption that migration by skilled workers is overwhelmingly permanent. The first is related to why the nineteenth-century notion was able to gain so much resonance in the 1960s in the first place: like Korean barbecue and Thai rice noodles, it was still another byproduct of the 1965 Immigration Act,[22] one made easily digestible by the fact that as the 1965 Act opened up immigration to the world, it also made immigrants much more visible than they previously were—especially in professional positions—and hence helped to create the overall cumulative impression to the citizenry that the new post–1965 Act immigration involved moves of at least relative permanence. (This impression would necessarily be conveyed as long as all the new immigrants did not leave or die each year and as long as no precipitous multi-year drops in immigration levels occurred. Not surprisingly, the first event never occurred, and the second occurred only in narrow subsets of the overall immigration population.)

Admittedly, this explanation seems more powerfully to explain the persistence of the "permanent settlement migration paradigm" among the general public than among researchers, who presumably would rely on data and not on a general impression created through an accident of immigration history. Ah, but there is the rub: what about the data? The next section will address this question for two purposes: (1) as earlier promised, to provide the second reason why direct losses due to STEP OUT migration have been exaggerated; and (2) to explain the persistence of "obsolete, binary models of migration" even among those who say things like "binary models of migration."

THE FLAWED DATA

The second reason that negative impacts were exaggerated is that researchers assumed erroneous statistics used to measure STEP OUT migration were reliable. In many important respects, they were not, and the errors were of a kind that tended to exaggerate the negative impact; again, the issue of return migration provides an informative example, as departures from poor countries were recorded more frequently than returns.[23] The use of such unreliable data caused "the consequences of the brain drain [to be] grossly overestimated."[24] To be sure, potential statistical problems were identified in the 1960s,[25] but when more rigorous studies were made in the late 1970s, the results still were surprising, even—in one "uniquely broad study" of student migration—to the point of "call[ing] into question the very notion of brain drain as postulated in economic analyses."[26]

Professor Herbert Grubel captured the environment and the problem well in an article published in 1976:

> During the 1960s when public concern with the brain drain was at its peak, the most readily available, seemingly reliable and comprehensive statistics on the flow of highly skilled persons to the United States were those published by the United States Immigration and Naturalization Service; these were used in the reports published by the United States National Science Foundation. They continue to be used uncritically by many analysts. . . . Yet, these statistics are very misleading; they overstate to a significant degree the gains of the United States and the losses of the rest of the world in migrants—human capital—because

they [among other things] do not include information about re-migration. . . . The reasons for this omission are simple. The United States immigration authorities do not keep a record of highly skilled persons leaving the United States. . . . Similarly, foreign governments do not record the return of native-born persons who in most countries can re-enter simply by showing their passports.[27]

In retrospect, then, even limiting the analysis to direct negative effects, it is clear that the general assessment, on which the Church relied, of the damage that STEP OUT migration causes poor nations was exaggerated. The cause of the exaggeration was a widespread reliance on both a bad model and on bad data, which combined to create the illusion that a firm factual foundation existed for Catholic social teaching's position on STEP OUT migration. In truth, however, the foundation was a shaky one, and one not built to withstand the stresses that would come in the form of updated facts and new events. Hence, Catholic social teaching's analysis of human dignity and the common good, in this particular context, is more compelling as an abstract case study in the methods of applied moral philosophy than it is as a description of human reality. This conclusion is even more inescapable when one considers the potential positive effects of STEP OUT migration on developing nations, which were either entirely ignored or severely discounted by most analysts at the time that the Church formed its position.

These ignored positive effects will be discussed shortly.[28] First, however, it is necessary to make a brief return to the matter left hanging at the end of the previous subsection: the mystery of why trained researchers would persist in utilizing "obsolete, binary models of migration." Being of Italian descent,[29] and in particular being from that part of Italy where the children wake up in the morning asking, "Hey mom, what's for dinner?"[30] we believe food, and sometimes food metaphors, hold the key to unlocking all the great mysteries of life. This one is no different, although, alas, as thoroughly assimilated Italian-*Americans*, the food we will be using to approach this mystery is very bad junk food. There are three reasons to eat bad food: (1) you don't care that it's bad; (2) you don't know any better; and (3) you do care and you do know better, but it's 3 a.m., and there's nothing else left in the refrigerator.

Permit us to indulge the fanciful conceit that the three reasons you might eat bad food correspond almost exactly to the reasons analysts or anyone else might use bad, that is, unreliable, statistics. The first reason—applicable to researchers who do not care that their data is bad—need not be discussed at length, since it surely applies to very few people.[31] Although some interested parties to the STEP OUT migration debate might have had every incentive to be indifferent to the accuracy of certain statistics,[32] there is no reason to assume any kind of widespread indifference to fact. Certainly, the latter two reasons we discuss provide ample explanation for the vast majority of usages of flabby statistics.

Of these two remaining reasons, the first—applicable to researchers who do not know that their statistics are bad—may apply in many more cases, but may similarly be disposed of quickly. In any research endeavor, honest mistakes are inevitable; researchers can be and are many times surprised to find that their data is flawed. In the wake of the Supreme Court's expert witness cases, *Daubert v. Merrell Dow Pharmaceutical, Inc.*[33] and *Kumho Tire Co. v. Carmichael*,[34] lawyers are learning this more and more, sometimes happily and sometimes to their chagrin.[35] And, of course, in the debate on STEP OUT migration, especially early in the debate, such mistakes *were* made. In a matter as complex and as diffuse as STEP OUT migration, that is to be expected.

As the debate matured, however, another dynamic emerged, one that corresponds to our final category, the 3 a.m. trip to the refrigerator. This occurred when researchers began to realize that the available data on STEP OUT migration was problematic. What to do? Back at the refrigerator, some might choose to eat the unhealthy food, even though they know it is bad for them. Some researchers, too, might do the same, though they might take a stab at virtue by qualifying their use of the data, without really challenging it. The food equivalent of this approach would be to tell yourself that that pint of chocolate chip ice cream really isn't very fattening because you covered it with a sliced-up banana, which is, after all, a fruit. But this only hides the problem.

Another approach would be to close the refrigerator door, and go back to bed, but only after waking your spouse to ask him or her to *please* buy something healthy for the house. This is essentially the approach taken by Professor Grubel in his 1976 article, quoted above, noting the problems with the available data.[36]

Finally, some would simply close the door and silently turn to something else. This happened, too, and it seems to have happened a lot. It is no coincidence that by all accounts interest in "brain drain" flagged in the 1970s,[37] when the data problems became more generally known. For most people, life is too short and their list of interests too long to continue too far down a research dead end.

It is here, at last, that we have found the key to directly answering why "obsolete, binary models of migration" survived: it was too much trouble to develop the data collection necessary to change the paradigm. It was too much trouble, first, because it will prove a huge undertaking. As Professor Graeme Hugo has written recently,

> From a research perspective, we have to confront the situation that the bulk of our international migration data collection, much of our empirical knowledge and theory is anchored in a permanent settlement migration paradigm. We need to rethink our data collection systems regarding migration flows that often have failed to capture non-permanent migrations, or limit the amount of detail sought regarding them. . . . Most conventional collections of information regarding stocks of migrants such as population censuses either exclude temporary residents altogether, or if they collect information from them, it is not processed or tabulated.[38]

Kevin O'Neil echoes the point, noting in 2003 that "[c]urrent migration data . . . relies too heavily on census and administrative sources [such as] visa information, census data and the stated intentions of migrants [which] do not accurately reflect actual migration behavior over time. Data from multiple sources and time points and new types of analysis are needed."[39] It is no criticism of these (and other)[40] researchers to note how closely their observations echo those of Professor Grubel twenty-seven years before;[41] it illustrates the relative stagnation in the field over that long time period regarding the measurement of STEP OUT migration's direct negative effects.

Yet, it was not only the difficulty of the task that discouraged tackling it. Probably at least as great a problem was the minimal reward expected. As long as the focus was almost entirely on the negative side of the "brain drain" calculation, not much could be accomplished by making that discrete calculation more accurate; necessarily, the bottom line would still show a loss for sending countries. If you only look at one side of the ledger, your bottom line is never going to change from red to black or vice versa; the best you can hope for is a slightly different shade of the same hue. In such an environment, most researchers will conclude greener pastures are everywhere.

THE EBBS AND FLOWS OF SCHOLARLY RESEARCH

Research into STEP OUT migration declined in the 1970s when shortcomings in the available data frustrated advances in the field. The seeming paradox of a field of inquiry becoming less attractive to scholars as the need for new scholarly explanation becomes more evident is a phenomenon with numerous precedents. The economist Paul Krugman, for instance, has noted that as improvements in mapmaking techniques raised standards in cartography, maps of Africa became less informative in certain respects because cartographers stopped trying to map lightly explored areas. As a result, "the crowded, if confused, continental interior of the old maps became . . . an empty space."

A similar phenomenon occurred in the field of development economics between the 1940s and 1970s. With respect to that discipline, as Krugman again has noted, "A rise in the standards of rigor and logic led to a much improved level of understanding of some things, but also led for a time to an unwillingness to confront those areas the new technical rigor could not yet reach. Areas of inquiry that had earlier been filled in, however imperfectly, became blanks. Only gradually, over an extended period, were those dark regions reexplored."

Accordingly, neither the relative pause in STEP OUT scholarship that began in the 1970s, nor the reason for the pause, was unusual. But it is evident that

that period of stagnation has ended, and that the time for re-exploration of all aspects of the STEP OUT phenomenon—from the most highly theoretical matters to the most basic data measurements—is now at hand.

Source: Paul Krugman, "The Fall and Rise of Development Economics," *Rethinking the Development Experience: Essays Provoked by the Work of Albert O. Hirschman,* eds. Lloyd Rodwin and Donald A. Schon (Washington, D.C.: The Brookings Institution, 1994): 39, 44. See also, e.g., Frédéric Docquier and Abdeslam Marfouk, "International Migration by Education Attainment, 1990–2000," in *International Migration, Remittances, & The Brain Drain,* eds. Çağlar Özden and Maurice Schiff (Washington, D.C.: World Bank, 2005): 151, 153 (noting that, until recently, "there has been no systematic empirical assessment of the brain-drain magnitude," and taking the first steps to remedy that deficiency).

As the years passed by, however, something very interesting happened with the STEP OUT debate. In the 1980s, as time allowed evidence of the positive effects of STEP OUT migration to emerge, the predominant focus began to swing away from the negative side of the ledger. The concept of "brain return" began to be developed.[42] And then, as technology advanced, the "diaspora option" emerged.[43] This model, which "integrates present and past citizens into a web of rights and obligations in the extended community defined with the home country as the center"[44] would not have been possible without "the systematic and multiple contacts that can be established through the development of modern communications technology."[45] Today, that technology, in "its many and more extensive configurations, [allows] a far greater number of members of the diaspora [to] inter-relate and exchange information."[46]

The identification of these positive aspects of STEP OUT migration re-energized the field. Ironically, the focus on these positive aspects has created a heightened interest in accurately measuring the negative aspects, and especially in retiring the "obsolete, binary models of migration" that heretofore have been the dominant paradigm.[47] This is because the stakes are high again. With both sides of the ledger open for inspection, the accuracy or inaccuracy of data collection methods could be the difference between the determination that STEP OUT migration is a net plus or a net minus for a developing country.

The next chapter introduces the numerous factors that make up the positive side of the ledger. Subsequent chapters—12, 13 and 14—address the same factors in greater detail and with specific examples.

NOTES

1. B. Lindsay Lowell, "Skilled Migration Abroad or Human Capital Flight?" *Migration Information Source* (Washington, D.C.: Migration Policy Institute, June 1, 2003) (boxed text), at http://www.migrationinformation.org/Feature/display.cfm?ID=135. The problem with the latter assumption, of course—beyond its invalidity (noting "support for

the notion [called 'optimal brain drain' theory] that the possibility of emigration for higher wages induces more students in the sending country to pursue higher education")—is that the researcher ends up overestimating losses attributable to the phenomenon of STEP OUT migration because some of the migrants used in the loss calculation would never have become educated but for "brain drain." Indeed, failing to account for this phenomenon produces something of a statistical double whammy. Not only does one end up overestimating negative effects of STEP OUT migration, but one also ends up underestimating the positive effects because not everyone who is induced to pursue a higher education by the prospect of migration will in fact leave; indeed, "[m]any end up staying and improving the country's educational profile." Lowell, "Skilled Migration Abroad or Human Capitol Flight?"; see Philip Martin, *Copenhagen Consensus: Challenge Paper on Population and Migration* (2004), 8 (noting that the "emigration of professionals" can "inspir[e] more young people to get educated, not all of whom will emigrate"); Michel Beine, Frederic Docquier, and Hillel Rapoport, "Brain Drain and Economic Growth: Theory and Evidence," *Journal of Development Economics* 64 (2001): 275, 288; Andrew Mountford, "Can a Brain Drain Be Good for Growth in the Source Economy?" *Journal of Development Economics* 52 (1997): 287; see also Fareed Zakaria, "Amid Disaster, New Confidence," *Newsweek*, January 17, 2005, 35 (noting that the hope of emigration provides a substantial impetus for education efforts by individuals throughout India, even though the hope may not be realized).

2. Kevin O'Neil, "Using Remittances and Circular Migration to Drive Development," *Migration Information Source* (Washington, D.C.: Migration Policy Institute, June 1, 2003), at http://www.migrationinformation.org/Feature/display.cfm?ID=133.

3. Graeme Hugo, "Circular Migration: Keeping Development Rolling?" *Migration Information Source* (Washington, D.C.: Migration Policy Institute, June 1, 2003), at http://www.migrationinformation.org/Feature/display.cfm?ID=129.

4. O'Neil, "Using Remittances and Circular Migration to Drive Development," at http://www.migrationinformation.org/Feature/display.cfm?ID=133; Hugo, "Circular Migration: Keeping Development Rolling?" at http://www.migrationinformation.org/Feature/display.cfm?ID=129; William J. Carrington and Enrica Detragiache, "How Extensive is the Brain Drain?" *Finance & Development* 36 (June 1999): 46, 46; Herbert G. Grubel, "Reflections on the Present State of the Brain Drain and a Suggested Remedy," *Minerva* 14 (1976): 209, 209–10.

5. Charles B. Keely, "Migration for Professional, Cultural, and Academic Reasons," *Migration at the Threshold of the Third Millennium, IV World Congress on the Pastoral Care of Migrants and Refugees*, (Vatican City: Pontifical Council for the Pastoral Care of Migrants and Itinerant People 1998): 101, 103.

6. See, e.g., AnnaLee Saxenian, *Local and Global Networks of Immigrant Professionals in Silicon Valley* (San Francisco: Public Policy Institute of California, 2002), vii.

7. See, e.g., O'Neil, "Using Remittances and Circular Migration to Drive Development," at http://www.migrationinformation.org/Feature/display.cfm?ID=133.

8. See, e.g., Anne Marie Gaillard and Jacques Gaillard, *International Migration of the Highly Qualified: A Bibliographic and Conceptual Itinerary* (Staten Island: Center for Migration Studies, 1998), 27 (noting the development in the 1980s of the concept of "'brain return' or 'return of skills'") (internal quotation marks in original).

9. Because most countries, including the United States, do not maintain data on emigration, researchers on the subject of return migration must make do without precise statistics. Several researchers nonetheless have found that the rate of return is significant. For example, the U.S. Social Security Administration currently assumes that annual emigration from the United States amounts to 30 percent of yearly legal immigration. Harriet Orcutt Duleep, "Social Security and the Emigration of Immigrants," *Social Security Bulletin* 57 (1994): 37; see also Amelie Constant and Douglas S. Massey, "Return Migration by German Guestworkers: Neoclassical versus New Economic Theories," *International Migration* 4 (2002): 5, 8. Another recent study of STEP OUT migrants found that 40 percent of highly skilled immigrants who responded to the survey would consider returning to their home country to live and work. Saxenian, *Local and Global Networks of Immigrant Professionals in Silicon Valley*, 32. Forty-five percent of individuals from India and 43 percent from China responded that it was likely they would return. And 73 percent of highly skilled Indian immigrants and 68 percent of highly-skilled Chinese immigrants know between one and ten returnees. Saxenian, *Local and Global Networks of Immigrant Professionals in Silicon Valley*, 23, 32. Cf. Harrry G. Johnson, "The Economics of the 'Brain Drain': The Canadian Case," *Minerva* 3 (1965): 299, 304 (noting the tendency of economists "to argue as if the problem is one of all or nothing and to ignore the fact that some proportion of its educated professional talent does stay in the region of origin").

10. See, e.g., Constant and Massey, "Return Migration by German Guestworkers: Neoclassical versus New Economic Theories," 22 (studying German migrants); Yaohui Zhao, *Causes and Consequences of Return Migration: Recent Evidence from China*, (China Center for Economic Research No. E2001010, 2001), 8 (studying Chinese migrants); Adrienne Roberts, "Can SA Recycle Lost Resources?" *Financial Mail*, November 19, 1999, 16 (reporting that "newly industrialized countries such as India, Singapore, South Korea, and Taiwan have managed to reverse some of their brain drain"); Guillermina Jasso and Mark R. Rosenzweig, "How Well Do U.S. Immigrants Do? Vintage Effects, Emigration Selectivity and Occupational Mobility of Immigrants," in *Research in Population Economics*, ed. T. Paul Schultz (1988): 229–253 (finding that skilled immigrants have a higher probability of return migration).

11. O'Neil, "Using Remittances and Circular Migration to Drive Development," http://www.migrationinformation.org/Feature/display.cfm?ID=133.

12. See "International Migration," *Financial Times ExPat*, April 1, 2002 (reporting that although Ireland had been a sending country for years, the tide changed between 1995 and 2000 when "around half of the 250,000 immigrants . . . were returning Irish nationals—a large proportion of which were skilled workers"); see also Alan Barrett and Fergal Trace, "Who Is Coming Back? The Educational Profile of Returning Migrants in the 1990s," *Irish Banking Review*, Summer 1998, 38–51 (finding that Irish who return home tend to have higher educations than those who remain abroad).

13. See Gaillard and Gaillard, *International Migration of the Highly Qualified*, 27, n.30 (noting that large numbers of South Koreans began to return home in the 1980s, and that to the extent there is a "brain drain" of South Koreans today, it mainly involves students, not qualified graduates); Jean M. Johnson and Mark C. Regets, "International Mobility of Scientists and Engineers to the United States—Brain Drain or

Brain Circulation?," *Issue Brief* (National Science Foundation, June 22, 1998), available at http://www.nsf.gov/statistics/issuebrf/ib98316.htm (explaining that "[d]ata on mobility and stay rates of foreign-born [scientists and engineers] working in the United States support the notion of brain circulation" for South Korea). See also United Nations Development Programme, *Human Development Report, 2001: Making New Technologies Work for Human Development* 92 (2001) (reporting that Korea and Taiwan have focused on encouraging their diaspora to return); "Overseas Korean Networks to Power Homeland Economy," *Korea Times*, October 9, 2002 (noting a recent trend for overseas ethnic Koreans to return home); Mario Cervantes and Dominique Guellec, "The Brain Drain: Old Myths, New Realities," *OECD Observer*, January 1, 2002, 40 (reporting that "only 11% of Koreans . . . who earned [science and engineering doctorates] from U.S. universities in 1990–91 were working in the United States in 1995").

14. See Johnson and Regets, "International Mobility of Scientists and Engineers to the United States—Brain Drain or Brain Circulation?," available at http://www.nsf.gov/statistics/issuebrf/ib98316.htm (explaining that "[d]ata on mobility and stay rates of foreign-born [scientists and engineers] working in the United States support the notion of brain circulation" for Taiwan); Louise Kehoe, "Time Spent in California's Technology Hub Has Been Fruitful for Professionals from Asia," *Financial Times*, May 15, 2002, 13 (noting that many Taiwanese had "spent several years in California at established Silicon Valley companies before returning to Taiwan to help build their home country's burgeoning technology industry"); Stan Sesser, "A Brain Drain in Reverse Boosts High-Tech Taiwan," *Wall Street Journal*, December 28, 1999, A13 (stating that Taiwan "is enjoying a reverse brain drain that is fueling high-tech startups"); Ashley Dunn, "Skilled Asians Leaving U.S. for High-Tech Jobs at Home," *New York Times*, February 21, 1995, A1 (reporting on Taiwanese returning home to pursue new business opportunities); Teresa Watanabe, "Taiwanese 'Brains' Leave U.S.: Career Opportunities Help Lure Engineers Trained and Educated in America Back Home," *Los Angeles Times*, December 29, 1989, A1 (reporting reverse migration of skilled engineers and scientists to Taiwan); Gaillard and Gaillard, *International Migration of the Highly Qualified*, 27, n.30 (noting that to the extent there is a "brain drain" of Taiwanese today, it mainly involves students, not qualified graduates).

15. Priya Srinivasan, "Return of the Techie," *Business Today*, October 26, 2003, 70. See also Sadanand Dhume, "Bringing It Home," *Far Eastern Economic Review* 163 (February 2000): 44 (noting that Indians are increasingly returning to Bangalore, India, to pursue careers in its fast-growing information technology industry).

16. Srinivasan, "Return of the Techie," 70. Internet job sites, such as Monsterindia.com, are also attracting an increasing number of resumes from Indian STEP OUT migrants hoping to return to India. Srinivasan, "Return of the Techie," 70.

17. Dhume, "Bringing It Home," 44 (noting that the reverse migration trend represents a sharp increase from 1993 when relatively few persons returned to India). See also Saritha Rai, "Technology: Company Town Keeps Indians at Home," *New York Times*, March 18, 2002, at C3 (quoting a claim by a Bangalore venture capitalist that "half the young engineers I meet talk about their plans to return to India as soon as they have a nest egg of experience and capital").

18. Sadanand Dhume, "Bringing It Home," 44.

19. Keely, "Migration for Professional, Cultural, and Academic Reasons," 103.

20. Hugo, "Circular Migration: Keeping Development Rolling?" at http://www.migrationinformation.org/Feature/display.cfm?ID=129.

21. See, e.g., Grubel, "Reflections on the Present State of the Brain Drain and a Suggested Remedy," 209–10; Johnson, "The Economics of the 'Brain Drain,'" 308. See also Cong. Research Service for the House Subcommittee on National Security Policy and Scientific Developments, 93d Congress, "Brain Drain: A Study of the Persistent Issue of International Scientific Mobility," (U.S. Government Printing Office, 1974), 4–5 (noting "brain drain" statistics were flawed because, among other things, they failed to measure return flows and did not adequately define the category they sought to measure).

22. See chapter 7 (discussing 1965 Act). For a discussion of the impact of the 1965 Immigration Act on food in the United States, see Calvin Trillin, *Feeding a Yen: Savoring Local Specialties from Kansas City to Cuzco* (New York: Random House 2003), 70–74 (explaining that "[t]hanks to the Immigration Act of 1965, Roosevelt Avenue [in Queens, New York] is the sort of place where someone who has just downed some Filipino barbeque may emerge from the restaurant and, in the next block or two, be tempted to follow that up with an Afghan shish kebab, a Mexican torta, an Indian dosa, and a Tibetan momo before making a decision about whether to go with Korean or Uruguayan baked goods").

23. See, e.g., Gaillard and Gaillard, *International Migration of the Highly Qualified*, at 25; Chantal Blayo, "Problems of Measurement," in *The Impact of International Immigration on Developing Countries*, ed. Reginald Appleyard (Paris: Development Centre of the Organisation for Economic Co-operation and Development, 1989); 63, 63 (indicating persistence of measurement problems into the 1980s, author states that necessary information "is seldom available in developing countries"); Jagdish Bhagwati, "The Brain Drain," *International Social Science Journal* 28 (1976): 691, 693–94 (noting that statistical difficulties make analysis of the data difficult); Grubel, "Reflections on the Present State of the Brain Drain and a Suggested Remedy," 209–10 (noting that the early statistics overstated the problems because they did not include information on return migration); Jagdish N. Bhagwati, "The International Brain Drain and Taxation," in *The Brain Drain and Taxation II: Theory and Empirical Analysis*, ed. Jagdish N. Bhagwati (Amsterdam: North-Holland Publishing, 1976): 3, 5 (noting that "the data on immigration of skilled manpower are quite inadequate for a number of analytical purposes").

24. Gaillard and Gaillard, *International Migration of the Highly Qualified*, 25.

25. See, e.g., Johnson, "The Economics of the 'Brain Drain,'" 304; Hla Myint, "The Underdeveloped Countries: A Less Alarmist View," in *The Brain Drain*, ed. Walter Adams (New York: Macmillan Company, 1968): 233 (stating that "it is fair to say we have no reliable statistical information about the total numbers involved in the brain drain from the underdeveloped countries to the advanced countries as a whole").

26. Gaillard and Gaillard, *International Migration of the Highly Qualified*, 26.

27. Grubel, "Reflections on the Present State of the Brain Drain and a Suggested Remedy," 209–10 (footnotes omitted). See also Congressional Research Service for the House Subcommittee on National Security Policy and Scientific Developments,

93rd Congress, *Brain Drain: A Study of the Persistent Issue of International Scientific Mobility* (U.S. Government Printing Office, 1974), 4 (noting "the lack of accurate, comprehensive, and rationally structured statistics on the flow of professional and highly skilled manpower").

28. See chapters 11–14.

29. Concededly, only one of the authors (Pistone) was "born" Italian, but who can say whether she is really more Italian than the other (Hoeffner), who not only was surely "made" at least somewhat Italian through his marriage (to Pistone), but who also has had Italianness repeatedly "thrust upon" him in the form of multitudinous meals of pasta throughout fifteen years of courtship and marriage. Indeed, if you are what you eat, Hoeffner is by now as Italian as they come.

30. We refer, of course, to that part of Italy that is shaped like a boot—plus Sicily, of course.

31. Admittedly, our metaphor is stretched a bit here; given the billions and billions served unhealthy food—at their own request—it perhaps would not be entirely accurate to assert that only a "few" of them are indifferent to their food's nutritional quality. The general categories proposed by the metaphor match the research reality, however, even if the numbers in any particular category do not.

32. Grubel, "Reflections on the Present State of the Brain Drain and a Suggested Remedy," 220 (stating that "poor countries have every incentive to exaggerate and none to understate the seriousness of the problem of the brain drain"). See also Alan Dowty, *Closed Borders* (New Haven: Yale University Press, 1987), 164. Asking why, given the paucity of solid evidence demonstrating the harm of "brain drain" to developing countries, "the matter [has] created such a stir." Dowty notes that "the brain drain enables Third-World governments to take advantage of tensions between north and south" in order to "gain recognition for the responsibility of industrialized nations to assist the less developed." Dowty, *Closed Borders*, 164.

33. 509 U.S. 579 (1993).

34. 526 U.S. 137 (1999). Daubert and Kumho complicated the trial court's obligation to ensure the reliability of expert testimony, and, consequently, complicated the responsibilities of attorneys, by holding that the admission or exclusion of expert testimony required a detailed exploration of the particular methodologies employed by proposed experts. Previously, most courts applied the common law rule, expounded most famously in *Frye v. United States*, which focused courts' preliminary reliability inquiry on the question of whether the expert's theories and techniques were "generally accepted" in the scientific community. 293 F. 1013, 1014 (D.C. Cir. 1923). In rejecting the Frye test, recent cases of the Supreme Court have clearly established that, in order to ensure the reliability of expert testimony in cases of both "scientific" (Daubert, 509 U.S. at 590 n.8) and "technical or other specialized knowledge" (Kumho, 526 U.S. at 141), trial courts can inquire into not only the general acceptance of an expert's theories and techniques, but also more specifically into the "testimony's factual basis, data, principles, methods, or their application." Kumho, 526 U.S. at 149.

35. See, e.g., In re TMI Litigation Cases Consolidated II, 911 F. Supp. 775 (M.D. Pa. 1996), affirmed in relevant part, 193 F.3d 613, 662 n.85 (3d Cir. 1999). In TMI, after being confronted at a deposition with deficiencies in his analysis, see id. at

789–90 (noting admissions during deposition that the expert being deposed "neglected" to account for some factors and used mistaken figures in calculating others), the expert left a voice-mail message for opposing counsel disavowing that analysis, at 790.

36. See this chapter, at text accompanying note 27.

37. See chapter 2, at note 31.

38. Hugo, "Circular Migration: Keeping Development Rolling?," at http://www.migrationinformation.org/Feature/display.cfm?ID=129.

39. O'Neil, "Using Remittances and Circular Migration to Drive Development," http://www.migrationinformation.org/Feature/display.cfm?ID=133.

40. See, e.g., Kathleen Newland, *Migration as a Factor in Development and Poverty Reduction*, at http://www.migrationinformation.org/Feature/display.cfm?ID=136 (stating that "the absence of data, frequently inaccurate data, and a lack of comparable data" conspire to frustrate understanding of the effect of migration on development); Carrington and Enrica Detragiache, "How Extensive is the Brain Drain?," 46. Among other things, Carrington and Detragiache note that: (1) "there is no uniform system of statistics on the number and characteristics of international migrants", (2) "source countries typically do not keep track of emigrants' characteristics", (3) only some of the receiving countries track such data, and (4) even among countries that do attempt to compile such data, comparisons are difficult because "definitions of immigration differ."

41. See this chapter, at text accompanying note 27.

42. Gaillard and Gaillard, *International Migration of the Highly Qualified*, 27.

43. Gaillard and Gaillard, *International Migration of the Highly Qualified*, 28–29.

44. Jagdish Bhagwati, "Borders Beyond Control," *Foreign Affairs* 82 (Jan./Feb. 2003): 98, 99.

45. Gaillard and Gaillard, *International Migration of the Highly Qualified*, 28.

46. Gaillard and Gaillard, *International Migration of the Highly Qualified*, 28.

47. O'Neil, "Using Remittances and Circular Migration to Drive Development," at http://www.migrationinformation.org/Feature/display.cfm?ID=133; Hugo, "Circular Migration: Keeping Development Rolling?," at http://www.migrationinformation.org/Feature/display.cfm?ID=129; B. Lindsay Lowell, at http://www.migrationinformation.org/Feature/display.cfm?ID=135; Sharon Stanton Russell, "Migration and Development: Reframing the International Policy Agenda", Migration Information Source (Migration Policy Institute, June 1, 2003), at http://www.migrationinformation.org/Feature/display.cfm?ID=126; Carrington and Enrica Detragiache, "How Extensive is the Brain Drain?," 46.

Chapter Eleven

The Importance of Modern Technology and Globalization

Recent developments in technology and the economy, including globalization, have changed the contextual framework appropriate to a fair analysis of the costs and benefits of STEP OUT migration. The evidence that emerges from this new context undermines Catholic social teaching's opposition to STEP OUT migration. Revealed as particularly vulnerable is the foundational belief that a STEP OUT migrant can no longer contribute to her home country, and therefore harms it, by leaving.

Under this now anachronistic view, the prevailing assumption was that the physical separation inherent in the migrant's lot necessarily isolated the migrant from his home community. This governing assumption certainly was an accurate one for most of history. Indeed, it was perhaps largely accurate even when the Church first spoke out on STEP OUT migration. However, it is no longer well founded. As detailed in the first part of this chapter, technological advances have greatly facilitated international communications and travel, thereby substantially ameliorating the migrant's isolation. Moreover, as is explained generally in this chapter's second half, and illustrated with specific examples in chapters 12, 13, and 14, these new technologies have combined with the development of the globalized economy to position STEP OUT migrants not only to contribute to their home country's development from abroad, but also to make vital and unique contributions that would not be possible *but for* the fact that they had migrated. Catholic social teaching must take note of these mutually reinforcing developments,[1] which collectively rebut the idea that STEP OUT migrants are unable to render assistance to their home countries to help them develop.

Indeed, eight years ago, Anne Marie Gaillard and Jacques Gaillard concluded in their comprehensive review of the literature on "brain drain" that "[t]here almost seem[ed] to be a consensus about" the great potential for STEP OUT migration, via the diaspora model, to benefit developing countries.[2] If

115

those scholars wrote today, they might appropriately remove the "almost" from their conclusion. As the advance of technology and globalization continues into even the most remote areas of the world, there can be little doubt that the diaspora model, which is buoyed by technology and globalization, and particularly by their convergence, will be deemed an even more attractive model eight years hence. There is no turning back the clock. We might and should debate the merits of particular technologies and the shape of globalization in the years to come, but the existential facts of technology and globalization cannot be denied. Even those who lament many of the consequences of these developments, such as Eduardo Galeano, the prominent Uruguayan social critic, know that the world we live in is one of "mandatory globalization."[3] As Gaillard and Gaillard note, "It is significant that people who long rode the nationalistic [anti-migration] wave now recognize the advantages, for the home country, that can be derived from the external migration of the elite."[4] Indeed, the developing countries—for so long stridently anti–STEP OUT migration—themselves have increasingly come around to this view.[5] Catholic social teaching must consider objectively the import of all these developments. When it does, it is likely to and should conclude, as many others already have done, that a previously established position against STEP OUT migration can no longer be maintained. Discussed below and in the next three chapters are some of the most important reasons such a reconsideration is warranted: technology, globalization, and especially the combination of the two.

THE STATE OF ISOLATION FORMERLY EXPERIENCED BY MIGRANTS HAS BEEN SUBSTANTIALLY AMELIORATED BY TECHNOLOGICAL ADVANCES THAT AID INTERNATIONAL COMMUNICATIONS IN NEW, COST-EFFICIENT WAYS

At the time that the Catholic Church developed its position opposing STEP OUT migration, international travel and communications were—by the standards of today—slow, prohibitively costly, and often unreliable. The Internet, fax machines, and e-mail were, of course, entirely unknown. As a consequence, the physical distance between migrants and sending countries created insurmountable obstacles even for migrants determined to make meaningful contributions to their home communities.

In recent years, however, modern transportation and communications technologies have greatly reduced the "friction of distance"[6] between sending and receiving countries. In ways large and small, technological advances have removed barriers to international communications. Because of these advances, communications that were prohibitively expensive or impossible in the past are widely available to educated migrants today. Some of the technological improvements differ in kind from anything that existed before: instant communication technologies such as the Internet, fax machines, and e-mail. Other improvements represent a change in degree, such as more affordable international air travel, express mail services, and telephone rates. These developments all have one thing in common—they make international communication much more common by making it in some way more practical or useful.[7]

It is easy to underestimate or forget how much communications have improved in just the last two decades. By way of personal example, when one of us was a college student in 1985, she studied in Japan for six months. During that period, her only options for communicating with her family in New York were telephone calls and so-called "snail" mail. Because international phone calls were prohibitively expensive for a student of modest means, she telephoned only once. Instead, she sent letters through the postal service. A round-trip exchange of letters typically took at least three weeks, making the speed of international mail delivery between two industrialized nations in 1985 only slightly *less* rapid than similar exchanges via Pony Express mail deliveries between St. Joseph, Missouri, and San Francisco, California, before the Civil War.[8]

Many migrants no doubt found similar, if not worse, barriers to international communication. Until recently, these barriers have inhibited communication by STEP OUT migrants to people in their home countries. Many STEP OUT migrants surely had little money available to spend on expensive overseas telephone calls, even assuming that their home countries had reliable telephone systems.[9] And the postal systems in their home countries may have been—in fact, probably were—less reliable than those of the United States and Japan. Until the advent of cost effective and (at least for businesses and governments) near ubiquitous telecommunications systems, many migrants would have been deterred from communicating with people in their home country on anything other than an occasional basis.

To a very significant degree, things now have changed. Indeed, the same co-author's experience providing legal representation to asylum seekers over the past fifteen years has demonstrated concretely the ever-increasing reach of modern communications technology. In the course of representing clients from all social strata—from professor to "slave"—she has had the occasion, together with her students, to send faxes to Ethiopia and Indonesia and e-mails to Guinea and Belarus, and to communicate by telephone with people in Azerbaijan and Sierra Leone.[10] It is not always easy to establish such contacts, but it usually is possible,[11] and of course should similarly be possible for STEP OUT migrants, who today are normally quite familiar with the basic tools of the communications revolution.

Moreover, it usually *is* easy for STEP OUT migrants to keep in touch with at least some members of their home societies. Most scholars, scientists, and researchers can maintain ties with like-minded individuals in their respective fields of study, for example, by maintaining membership on one of the many e-mail list-serves that distribute information and provide for regular exchanges with colleagues around the world.[12] Using this technology, people can pose questions about almost anything and receive answers within minutes, all at marginal cost. The ability to transmit documents, including text, music, photos, video, and even x-rays, which would have taken weeks to transport internationally a few years ago, now can be sent instantaneously through the Internet, again at marginal cost. As a result of these and other technological advances, such as speedier and less expensive air travel, STEP OUT migrants not only can regularly interact in real time with people across borders, but they can also more frequently travel to their home countries and meet in person with friends, family, and colleagues from the private and public sectors.[13]

In sum, while it was generally true that the physical separation between STEP OUT migrants and their home communities may have made it extremely difficult for the migrants to contribute to sending countries in the past, it generally is not true today. With recent technological advances, the physical separation between STEP OUT migrants and sending countries no longer stands as an insurmountable obstacle deterring the migrants from contributing to their home countries. Now, almost anyone who wants to maintain ties with his home country can do so with little effort and at minimal cost. In many respects, there has been an annihilation of distance—the globe has shrunk. As a result, STEP OUT migrants are able to maintain closer and more intimate connections with and make more meaningful contributions to their home countries than were possible as recently as ten years ago. These developments accordingly undercut the notion—upon which the Church's opposition to STEP OUT migration is based—that STEP OUT migrants are unable to contribute in meaningful ways to their home countries when they are living outside the country.

GLOBALIZATION AND OTHER NEW ECONOMIC AND POLITICAL REALITIES PROVIDE NEW WAYS FOR STEP OUT MIGRANTS TO CONTRIBUTE TO THEIR HOME COUNTRIES WHILE ABROAD

In addition to technology's obliteration of the isolation formerly experienced by STEP OUT migrants, recent developments in globalization similarly have undercut the assumption that STEP OUT migrants need to be physically in a country to contribute to its development. Given the global nature of the world today,

STEP OUT migrants can make contributions to their home countries while they are living abroad. Indeed, in some ways they are able to contribute only *because* they emigrated. Thus, in today's global world, more than ever before, the act of emigrating may be a plus for the home country, rather than a minus.

Globalization is "a new phenomenon that has become almost a buzz-word."[14] Because the phenomenon "is very complex, multidimensional and is generated by multifarious factors," it is "impossible to find one generally accepted understanding or definition."[15] The economic, technological, and communications dimensions of the phenomenon that are crucial for our purposes, however, are fairly captured by Thomas Friedman's statement that globalization is the "inexorable integration of markets, nation-states and technologies to a degree never witnessed before—in a way that is enabling individuals, corporations and nation-states to reach around the world farther, faster, deeper and cheaper than ever before."[16] The "reality of economic globalization has forced states to learn how to be more multilateral."[17] As a result of this higher interdependence between nations, globalization "pushes local systems to open up"[18] to new ideas and viewpoints about issues that impact development and foster democracy.[19] And STEP OUT migrants are uniquely positioned to serve as transnational messengers in that process.

WHICH GLOBALIZATION?

Perhaps the best answer to the question "what is globalization?" is another question: "Which globalization do you mean?" In fact, there are at least four types of globalization: (1) an economic globalization; (2) a globalization in communications; (3) a cultural globalization; and (4) an ideological globalization.

This book focuses mainly on the implications of the economic and communications aspects of globalization. Economic globalization is manifested by the development of global markets for goods, services, and labor. Economic globalization advances the communications globalization, even as the communications globalization enables the economic one.

Economic globalization and the communications revolution of satellites, cell phones, cable, and the Internet permit and promote the exchange of ideas and the transfer of knowledge between people who, until recently, had to travel great distances or use other expensive methods to communicate. Cultural consequences spring from these developments to such a significant extent that one may appropriately speak of a cultural globalization.

One of the most interesting aspects of all these globalizations is that while each may at first appear to be defined by a single particular characteristic— economic globalization = efficiency; communications globalization = speed;

(*continued*)

cultural globalization = standardization—they each might also appropriately be
defined by an "opposite" quality. Thus, while an ever-increasing demand for
efficiency seems to characterize economic globalization, the "Long Tail" of the
internet allows producers of "inefficiently" produced products, such as hand-
crafted greeting cards and artisan cheeses, to survive and perhaps prosper by
gaining a critical mass of customers over a widely-dispersed geographical area.
Similarly, while one undoubted affect of today's cultural globalization is to expand the reach of the world's dominant cultures, the revolution in communications also allows smaller cultures to find new audiences and to penetrate into
new areas. In this sense, the creators of the steel drum music of Trinidad and
the fado music of Portugal have much in common with "inefficient" makers of
greeting cards and cheeses. Moreover, advances in communications also make
it easier for different cultures to flourish by making it easier for migrants to remain in contact with the people and cultures of their homelands.

The globalization of communications likewise is characterized by more than
advances in the speed of communications. The "weight" or "depth" of the information that can be communicated also is enhanced by communications advances. In this case, faster does not necessarily mean more superficial.

Ideological globalization, too, is distinguished by different and in some
sense opposing characteristics. The fundamental question here is what is the
ideology of ideological globalization? Is it the ideology of liberal human rights
groups? Or is it the ideology of capitalism? Or is it the ideology of a religious
group? In truth, using the tools of the communications revolution, all these ide-
ologies now compete on the global stage in a way they never have before.

In sum, broadly speaking, globalization is a fact of life. Which globalization
will predominate, however, and which aspects of each type of globalization
will turn out to be the most important, remains to be determined.

When they travel, STEP OUT migrants both "project [their home country's] system outward and bring variety back into [their home country's] system."[20] They serve as the conduit for the cross-border information exchanges
that drive "the export and import of variety and know-how,"[21] which is ever
more important in the new knowledge-based economy.[22] And because of their
familiarity with the traditions of their home countries, they can contribute insights into "how to integrate that variety and make something new"[23] at
home. By making new transnational connections, STEP OUT migrants facilitated the integration of "nations into an international system, and now [facil-
itate] an international system into a global one."[24] All of this enhances the
processes of development and, as some commentators posit, democratization.[25] Indeed, it increasingly has come to be understood that, in the pursuit
of development, there needs to be "inclusion of the world's populations into

global democratic institutions and political processes on a foundation of an expanded normative system of rights."[26] STEP OUT migrants play an important role in the evolution of that process.

The next three chapters add detail to the case for STEP OUT migration. They discuss specific contributions that STEP OUT migrants—because they have migrated—can and have made to their home countries. Some of the contributions noted may have been possible in years past, but all have been made easier, sometimes substantially so, by globalization and recent technological developments. On a practical level, that means that such contributions are made much more often now than ever before.

NOTES

1. See Pope John Paul II, *Sollicitudo Rei Socialis* (1987), sec. 3 (stating that "teaching in the social sphere . . . is ever new, because it is subject to the necessary and opportune adaptations suggested by the changes in historical conditions and by the unceasing flow of the events which are the setting of the life of people and society"). See also Congregation for the Doctrine of the Faith, "The Participation of Catholics in Political Life," (November 24, 2002), Part IV, sec. 7 (noting that it is an error to adhere to "a rigid framework" in addressing the issues of society because social and political conditions are "susceptible to rapid change"), available at http://www.vatican.va; W. J. Smith, "Interpreting Papal Documents," in *The Church and Social Progress*, ed. Benjamin L. Masse (Milwaukee: Bruce Publishing Company, 1966), 28, 31 (noting the recognition by the Church that the truth of the "assertions, directives, or proposals [of Catholic social thought] directly based on the findings of scientific investigations in the fields of economics, politics, and sociology have a direct relation to the validity or adequacy of the investigations themselves, or of the interpretation of their findings"). "[T]he highest level of church teaching" acknowledges that, in light of new circumstances, "Catholic doctrine can develop, can change." David Hollenbach, *Justice, Peace, & Human Rights: American Catholic Social Ethics in a Pluralistic Context* (New York: Crossroad, 1988), 88. Since the 1960s, many new developments, which could not have been anticipated at that time, have occurred. Significant technological and economic changes are among those developments. Current policy should take note of these changes, just as prior teachings "of course, were put forward in response to significant social and political events" and "shaped" by them. David Hollenbach, *Claims in Conflict: Retrieving and Renewing the Catholic Human Rights Tradition* (New York: Paulist Press, 1979), 42; see, e.g., Hollenbach, *Claims in Conflict*, 70 (explaining that Pope John XXIII's *Mater et Magistra* was stimulated by a complex interdependence of social, technological, economic, and political developments); Pope John XXIII, *Mater et Magistra* (1961) (noting that Vatican II's *Gaudium et Spes* was developed with a clear reference to its time); Marvin L. Krier Mich, *Catholic Social Teaching and Movements* (Mystic:

Twenty-Third Publications, 1998), 159 (explaining that Pope Paul VI applied the Church's teachings to "today's situation" in drafting *Populorum Progressio*); Mich, *Catholic Social Teaching and Movements*, 185 (referencing *Octogesima Adveniens'* discernment of the "signs of the times"); National Conference of Catholic Bishops, *Economic Justice for All: Pastoral Letter on Catholic Social Teaching and the U.S. Economy* (Washington, D.C.: U.S. Catholic Conference, 1986), par. 135 (in which the U.S. bishops acknowledge that "[o]ur judgments and recommendations on specific economic issues . . . are related to circumstances that can change").

2. Anne Marie Gaillard and Jacques Gaillard, *International Migration of the Highly Qualified: A Bibliographic and Conceptual Itinerary* (Staten Island: Center for Migration Studies, 1998), 28. See National Intelligence Council, "Report of the National Intelligence Council's 2020 Project: The Contradictions of Globalization" (2004) (noting that the greatest benefits of globalization will be enjoyed by nations that best access new technologies, and that "the growing two-way flow of high-tech brain power between developing countries and Western countries" is a key driver in this process).

3. Eduardo Galeano, "Globalization's Discontents," *Los Angeles Times*, May 23, 1999, 4. Galeano is an essayist, journalist, and historian. He has written several books on social conditions in Latin America. See, e.g., Eduardo Galeano, *Memory of Fire*, trans. Cedric Belfrage (New York: Pantheon Books, 1985); Eduardo Galeano, *Open Veins of Latin America: Five Centuries of the Pillage of a Continent*, trans. Cedric Belfrage (New York: Monthly Review Press, 1973).

4. Gaillard and Gaillard, *International Migration of the Highly Qualified*, 28. The U.N. Development Programme, for example, has noted that the "global dispersal [of scientists and technologists from developing countries] creates diaspora that can become valuable networks of finance, business contacts and skill transfer for their home country"). United Nations Development Programme, "Human Development Report, 2001: Making New Technologies Work for Human Development" (2001), 31 [hereinafter UNDP, Making New Technologies Work].

5. Gaillard and Gaillard, *International Migration of the Highly Qualified*, 28. The Gaillards note the conclusion of Jagdish Bhagwati in 1994 "that the developing countries had changed their opinion. They increasingly view the emigration of their most talented nationals as an opportunity for them (the nationals) to gain distinction and contribute to the glory of their home country. . . . These countries hope to profit from the talents of their overseas nationals. In short, what appeared as a brain drain is now seen as the diaspora." Gaillard and Gaillard, *International Migration of the Highly Qualified*, 28; see Philip Martin, "Copenhagen Consensus: Challenge Paper on Population and Migration" (2004), 46. (stating that "[t]here has been a sea-change in attitudes of governments toward migrants, with some that once saw migrants as 'traitors' now considering them key engines of development"); World Bank, *Global Economic Prospects, 2006: Economic Implications of Remittances and Migration* (Washington, D.C.: World Bank, 2006), 68 (noting favorable view of some developing country governments toward STEP OUT migration). Cf. Jagdish Bhagwati, "The Global Age: From a Skeptical South to a Fearful North," in *A Stream of Windows* (Cambridge: The MIT Press, 1998), 29, 36-37 (noting the change to a "warm embrace of the Global Age by the policymakers in a large number of the developing countries").

6. Graeme Hugo, "Circular Migration: Keeping Development Rolling?" *Migration Information Source* (Washington, D.C.: Migration Policy Institute, June 1, 2003), at http://www.migrationinformation.org./Feature/display.cfm?ID=129.

7. See UNDP, *Making New Technologies Work*, 30 (noting that technological changes "radically alter access to information and the structure of communication—extending the networked reach to all corners of the world").

8. See Pony Express Home Page, at http://www.xphomestation.com/ (explaining that the trip from St. Joseph, Missouri, to San Francisco, California, initially took ten days, but later trips were made in as little as eight days). Cf. Grzegorz W. Kolodko, "Working Paper No. 176: Globalisation and Transformation: Illusions and Reality," (May 2001), 11-12, available at http://www.oecd.org/dataoecd/60/30/1899735.pdf (noting that in 1860 it cost the equivalent of $40 to send just two words across the Atlantic, the price of transporting the entire Library of Congress today).

9. In India, for example, until recently only a small percentage of the population could be reached by telephone. In 1980, there was barely a telephone for every 300 people, and most of the telephones were in large urban areas. Moreover, "[t]he telephones that existed were not dependable." Gurcharan Das, *India Unbound* (New York: Alfred A. Knopf, 2001), 208. See also Monique Maddy, *Learning to Love Africa: My Journey from Africa to Harvard Business School and Back* (New York: HarperBusiness, 2004), 279 (noting that Tanzania "had less than a 1 percent telephone penetration-density" in the 1990s).

10. Professor Pistone has worked with asylum seekers for sixteen years, the last ten while teaching law students in law school clinical courses at Villanova and Georgetown Universities, and has had the opportunity to represent more than one hundred asylum seekers in their immigration proceedings before the Executive Office for Immigration Review and the Department of Homeland Security (DHS), formerly the Immigration and Naturalization Service (INS). Her clients have come from many countries around the world, including Azerbaijan, Belarus, Burma (Myanmar), China, Colombia, Congo, Ethiopia, Indonesia, Iraq, Jordan, Laos, Liberia, Mauritania, Mexico, Sierra Leone, and Somalia.

11. Abundant statistical evidence supports these anecdotal observations. Thus, while few telephones, relatively speaking, were available in India in 1980, especially in rural villages (see this chapter note 9), by 1995 20 percent of India's 500,000 villages had telephone service, and by 2000, 75 percent had such service. Das, *India Unbound*, 209. The trend has continued; thus, the number of mobile phone subscribers in India almost tripled from 2003 to December 2005, and almost doubled again—to approximately 150,000,000—from 2005 to 2006. See Ray Marcelo, "India Telecoms 'Set to Invest $12bn in Network,'" *Financial Times*, December 30, 2003, 7; John Ribeiro, "India nearly doubles mobile phone use in 2006," IDG News Service, Jan. 16, 2007.

12. This ease of personal communication is evident from, among other things, the "increasingly collaborative" nature of scientific research between researchers living in different countries. UNDP, "Making Technologies Work," 31 (noting that "[f]rom 1995-97, scientists in the United States co-authored articles with scientists from 173 other countries; scientists in Brazil with 114, in Kenya with 81, in Algeria 59"). Moreover, beyond person-to-person communications, maintenance of ties with one's

homeland is easier today due to advances in mass communication, such as satellite television and various portable transfer services. For descriptions of the latter, see Elizabeth Corcoran, "Shifting Places," *Forbes*, September 6, 2004, 150 (describing technology allowing video to be redirected to remote places via wireless Internet connections); and 'May Wong, "TiVo Unveils Portable Transfer Service," Associated Press wire story, January 3, 2005 (discussing various technologies allowing television to be seen "where you want it").

13. See UNDP, "Making New Technologies Work," 29 (explaining that recent technological developments such as the fax "opened up communications, reducing isolation and enabling people to be better informed and to participate in decisions that affect their lives").

14. Louis Henkin, "That S Word: Sovereignty and Globalization and Human Rights, Et Cetera," *Fordham Law Review* 68 (1999): 1, 5-6. See also Janusz Symonides, "Globalization and Human Rights," *Mediterranean Journal of Human Rights* 4 (2000): 145, 145 ("At the dawn of the XXIst century, the term 'globalization' is one of the most used, analyzed, referred to and quoted"); Mark Tushnet, "1999-2000 Supreme Court Review: Globalization and Federalism in a Post-Prinz World," *Tulsa Law Review* 36 (2000): 11 (noting "globalization" has become a buzzword); Henry Tuene, "Global Democracy," *Annals* 581 (2002): 22, 23 (explaining that "[g]lobalization exploded in the 1990s," and that the "era of globalization began in the middle of the 1970s"). One might quibble, of course, over whether globalization is a "new" phenomenon. Certainly, globalization is not an entirely new phenomenon; however, "[t]hat globalization has accelerated is hard to dispute," Bhagwati, "The Global Age: From a Skeptical South to a Fearful North," 38, and today's accelerated globalization may appropriately be considered a new phenomenon.

15. Symonides, "Globalization and Human Rights," 145; see Michael Novak, *Three in One: Essays in Democratic Capitalism, 1976-2000* (Lanham: Rowman & Littlefield Publishers, 2001): 299 (stating that "most attempts to define globalization fail" because "globalization . . . has an interior dimension" that is often ignored, as it requires those operating in it to think about the entire world).

16. Thomas L. Friedman, *The Lexus and the Olive Tree* (New York: Farrar, Straus, and Giroux, 1999), 7-8. See also Lester Thurow, "Globalization: The Product of a Knowledge-Based Economy," *Annals* 570 (2000): 19, 20-21 (listing examples of economic "globalization").

17. Saskia Sassen, "Regulating Immigration in a Global Age: A New Policy Landscape," *Annals* 570 (2000): 65, 66.

18. Tuene, "Global Democracy," 24.

19. See generally Tuene, "Global Democracy," 24-25 (asserting that "both globalization and democratization are manifestations of the integration of diversity into systems of greater scale"); Doron M. Kalir, "Taking Globalization Seriously: Toward General Jurisprudence," *Columbia Journal of Transnational Law* 39 (2001): 785, 816 (asserting that "[c]losely linked to the market-oriented part of globalization . . . one can find the tendency toward democratization").

20. See Tuene, "Global Democracy," 24.

21. See Tuene, "Global Democracy," 24

22. See generally Thurow, "Globalization: The Product of a Knowledge-Based Economy," 20 (noting how technological advances are "producing a knowledge-based economy that is systematically changing how all people conduct their economic and social lives").

23. See Tuene, "Global Democracy," 24.

24. See Tuene, "Global Democracy," 24

25. Tuene, "Global Democracy," 24; Benjamin M. Friedman, *The Moral Consequences of Economic Growth* (New York: Alfred A. Knopf, 2005), 10 (stating that, "taken as a whole, the experience of the developing world during the last two decades, indeed since World War II, is clearly more consistent with a positive connection between economic growth and democratization than with the opposite"): Helen Milner & Keiko Kubota, "Why the Rush to Free Trade? Democracy and Trade Policy in the Developing Countries" Jan. 23, 2003, at http://www.poli.duke.edu/resources/workshop/keohane/LDCdem.pdf (providing empirical support for the claim that the trends toward globalization and democratization are related). See also Kalir, "Taking Globalization Seriously" 816-17 (quoting economists who link globalization with democratization). Cf. Jagdish Bhagwati, "Democracy and Development: New Thinking on an Old Question," *A Stream of Windows*, 379, 391, 406 n.39 (citing, among others, economists Mancur Olson and Surjit Bhalla, Bhagwati notes that democracy can promote economic growth for developing countries).

26. Tuene, "Global Democracy," 23. See John B. Taylor, "Economic Freedom and the Millennium Challenge Account," July 15, 2002, available at http://www.ustreas.gov/press/releases/js1787.htm (speech by the U.S. Treasury Department's Under Secretary for International Affairs discussing reports showing strong correlations between economic rights and freedoms and economic growth); Das, *India Unbound*, 354 (noting that "[t]oday, virtually all countries have embraced or are trying to adopt liberal institutions of democracy and market-oriented institutions of capitalism as they integrate themselves into the global economy"); Bhagwati, "The Global Age: From a Skeptical South to a Fearful North," 33 ("the notion that democracy is fine for the developed countries but that development requires authoritarian structures of governance is no longer considered plausible"). A World Bank report on development has explained the connection between development and democracy as follows:

> The checks and balances of participatory democratic regimes—and the procedures for consensus building—limit the scope for rent seeking and drastic policy reversals, offering a much more reliable and sustainable path to development. Participatory political regimes are associated with more stable growth—very important for poverty reduction, given the highly adverse effects that shocks have on poor people. . . .

World Bank, "World Development Report 2000/2001: Attacking Poverty: Opportunity, Empowerment, and Security," (2000), 113 (footnotes omitted). Even analysts ambivalent about the effects of globalization have concluded that "[h]uman rights and democracy are not only moral and legal values; they also constitute the very process of development and are instrumental for economic and social welfare." E.g., Nsongurua J. Udombana, "How Should We Then Live? Globalization and the New Partnership for Africa's Development," *Boston University International Law Journal* 20 (2002): 293, 339–340.

Part Five

THE CONTRIBUTIONS OF STEP OUT MIGRANTS

Chapter Twelve

International Knowledge Transfers

The transnational exchange of information, knowledge, and ideas constitutes one of the greatest contributions made by STEP OUT migrants. These exchanges add value and diversity to both sending and receiving countries. Migrants are among the primary vehicles that transport and exchange ideas, practices, and knowledge around the world. Aided by today's technology, past and present citizens of developing countries form diasporas, with the original home country at the center. Members of the diasporas bridge the gap between sending and receiving countries and become the cross-border conduits through which information and ideas can be exchanged.

When STEP OUT migrants initially emigrate, they bring knowledge, practices, techniques, and ideas from their countries of origin to the receiving country. While they are living abroad as STEP OUT migrants, they share ideas from the receiving country with their colleagues at home and vice versa. And, if they return (a phenomenon which is becoming more common among STEP OUT migrant groups),[1] they bring ideas, practices, and knowledge gained while living abroad back to sending countries.

The substance of this knowledge is not limited to cutting-edge technology, but can take varied forms, including "in relatively low-technology service industries, such as food services and hotels."[2] In these areas and across the board, simple incremental advances can be of huge practical importance. For example, in every industry, "[u]seful knowledge about how to produce things at low cost . . . is hard to keep a secret. People have a high incentive to observe what [low cost producers] are doing" and then to replicate it elsewhere—in other words, especially in a world of modern communications technology, knowledge "leaks."[3]

Knowledge transfers also are not limited to information of the type most directly useful to businesses and business efficiency. Important transfers also include information about political and business systems, as well as information about culture and customs. Indeed, globalization is not merely an economic process. Rather, as the United Nations recognizes, the phenomenon also encompasses "social, political, environmental, cultural and legal dimensions which have an impact on the full enjoyment of all human rights."[4] And knowledge about all of these processes is exchanged across borders through STEP OUT migration.[5]

The increasing and increasingly rapid exchanges of knowledge between diasporas and their home countries are becoming more relevant for development policy. Commentators have come to recognize that knowledge transfers are among the primary ingredients of innovation and development in both sending and receiving countries and can yield significant economic benefits to them.[6] In fact, "[m]any students of migration agree that . . . transnational networks are today the most important developmental resource associated with international migration."[7] The introduction of the telling term "political and social remittances"[8]—used to describe the benefits to sending countries of international knowledge transfers—underscores the perceived importance of these networks. The remainder of this chapter provides some specific examples of political and social remittances to both the private sector, including through academic exchanges, and to government agencies.

KNOWLEDGE TRANSFERS BY STEP OUT MIGRANTS TO PRIVATE SECTOR AND ACADEMIC COLLEAGUES IN THEIR HOME COUNTRIES

Knowledge transfers are most evident between STEP OUT migrants and business and academic colleagues who remain in their home countries.[9] Through transnational organizations, list-serves, conferences, and related activities, members of various communities living abroad are now connected with their counterparts who remain in the sending countries in ways that were not common a few decades ago.[10] For example, numerous professional associations have been created whose primary mission is to promote technology and information transfers between the United States and sending countries. In addition to providing support to newly arriving STEP OUT migrants,[11] these organizations "have become global institutions that connect new immigrants with their counterparts at home. These new transnational communities provide the shared information, contacts, and trust that allow local producers to participate in an increasingly global economy."[12] In fact, one study reports that 82 percent of highly skilled immigrants living in the United States share information about technology with colleagues back in their home countries.[13]

Such transnational contacts are likely to expand with time; indeed, it has been reported that in India there recently has been a "more fluid exchange between the research establishment, drug companies, financiers and overseas Indians."[14]

STEP OUT migrants in the United States are also well suited to create links between U.S. companies and economic centers in their countries of origin. Building on their shared language and cultural backgrounds, STEP OUT migrants are positioned to partner with foreign companies without having to scale, with respect to business customs and cultures, the learning curve that non-natives face. Indeed, many highly skilled immigrants living in developed countries tend to form business relationships with natives of their home countries.[15] A recent survey reports that "[h]alf of Silicon Valley's foreign-born professionals report traveling to their native country for business at least yearly, and five percent of those surveyed make the trip five times or more per year."[16] Many also help to arrange business contacts[17] or serve as advisors or consultants for companies in their home countries.[18] Further, contact with STEP OUT migrants can provide the additional advantage of helping to develop some of the softer skills "needed to flourish in a global business setting," such as "how to address colleagues."[19]

The investment in knowledge that resulted from a business relationship between Desh Garments, Ltd., headquartered in Bangladesh, and Daewoo Corporation of South Korea illustrates the vast benefits that a society can reap from knowledge transfers.[20] In 1979 the two companies entered into an agreement whereby Daewoo, intending to avoid U.S.–Korea garment import quotas, would bring 130 Desh employees to South Korea to train them about Daewoo's operations.[21] Over many years, Daewoo had developed techniques for manufacturing textiles at low costs and had learned how to sell those textiles on the world market. They also had developed innovative financing schemes. The agreement called for the Desh employees to be taught this information in South Korea, and then bring it back to Bangladesh so that they could manufacture textiles there, giving Daewoo a percentage of its sales.

After learning about Daewoo's operations, the Desh employees returned to Bangladesh. They adapted what they had learned to their own experience, culture, and local conditions. Desh's business flourished, as it went from manufacturing 43,000 shirts in 1980 to 2.3 million in 1987.[22]

Soon thereafter, however, the knowledge about how to develop a flourishing business in the garment industry leaked out of Desh to benefit the larger society. Within a few years of the exchange, an amazing 115 of the 130 Desh employees trained by Daewoo left Desh to start their own garment manufacturing and export companies.[23] This was the start of what is now a more than $2 billion garment sales industry in Bangladesh, which amounts to 54 percent

of all its exports, much of which has its roots in the Desh/Daewoo exchange.[24]
Desh is a very striking example of a very broad global phenomenon, which
sees employees at many levels going out on their own.[25]

KNOWLEDGE TRANSFERS BY STEP OUT MIGRANTS
TO THEIR HOME COUNTRIES' GOVERNMENTS

In addition to creating partnerships or associations with the private and academic sectors back home, STEP OUT migrants also share information and
knowledge with government officials. One study shows that 30 percent of the
STEP OUT migrants interviewed meet frequently with home-country government officials in order to share information.[26]

The messages being communicated typically relate to regulatory systems
and the government's role in economic and development affairs. A STEP
OUT migrant might, for example, productively talk about the importance of
property rights, as recent studies have recognized "*secure* and *transferable*
property rights [as] the key to economic efficiency and wealth."[27] Such messages could be communicated through general discussion about what one has
learned about politics and development while living abroad. They also could
be communicated through specific negotiations with government officials regarding investment of capital in the home country. In both such cases, a native of a country may bring more credibility to a discussion with government
officials from his or her home country than would someone who is considered
an outsider.[28] As a result, the message may be more easily welcomed and embraced.

Moreover, STEP OUT migrants are also well suited to act as ambassadors,
in the informal sense of the word, for sending countries in the migrants' countries of residence. As they straddle two cultures, STEP OUT migrants are able
to communicate the unique concerns of their native countries to the politicians and governments of the countries in which the migrants reside. Indeed,
Jagdish Bhagwati contends that "India's increasing friendship with the United
States and the economic and diplomatic rewards that come with it owe largely
to the Indians who have come to the United States and work there."[29]

NOTES

1. See chapter 10, notes 5–18 and accompanying text.
2. World Bank, *World Bank Development Report, 1998/99: Knowledge for Development* (Washington, D.C.: World Bank, 1999), 8.

3. William Easterly, *The Elusive Quest for Growth: Economic Adventures and Misadventures in the Tropics* (Cambridge: MIT Press, 2001), 145–46, 150.

4. *Globalization and Its Impact on the Full Enjoyment of All Human Rights*, General Assembly Resolution 55/102, U.N. GAOR 3rd Committee, 55th Session, 81st plen. mtg. at 2, U.N. Doc. A/RES/55/102 (2001).

5. Knowledge about political systems includes a host of matters, from how specific political systems operate with respect to specific matters, such as how regulations are implemented, or how the hurdles of dealing with a bureaucracy are overcome, to the broader values of the rule of law and of respect for human rights. Business system information includes matters such as how to manufacture, market, sell, distribute, and advertise; how to start a business; and with whom to enter a joint venture. Customs and culture include how to negotiate with a certain official or business, the possible unanticipated consequences of certain actions, and the receptiveness of a community to a new idea.

6. See generally Kevin O'Neil, "Using Remittances and Circular Migration to Drive Development," *Migration Information Source* (Washington, D.C.: Migration Policy Institute, June 1, 2003), at http://www.migrationinformation.org/Feature/display.cfm?ID=133 (discussing the positive impact of circular migration on development). See also B. Lindsay Lowell, *International Migration Papers 46: Some Developmental Effects of the International Migration of Highly Skilled Persons* 22 (Geneva: International Labour Office, 2002) (noting that migration of highly skilled can "yield a flow back of new technologies that can boost" the growth of the sending country); Julian Simon, *The Economic Consequences of Migration*, 166 (Washington, D.C.: CATO Institute, 1989) (same). In April 2003, the University of California, San Diego, Center for Comparative Immigration Studies and the Migration Policy Institute hosted a two day meeting entitled "Using Remittances and Circular Migration as Drivers of Development," Kevin O'Neil, *at* http://www.migrationinformation.org/Feature/display.cfm?ID=133.

7. Kathleen Newland, "Migration as a Factor in Development and Poverty Reduction," *Migration Information Source* (Washington, D.C.: Migration Policy Institute, June 1, 2003), at http://www.migrationinformation.org/Feature/display.cfm?ID=136.

8. Kevin O'Neil, "Using Remittances and Circular Migration to Drive Development," *Migration Information Source* (Washington, D.C.: Migration Policy Institute, June 1, 2003,) at http://www.migrationinformation.org/Feature/display.cfm?ID=133.

9. B. Lindsay Lowell, *International Migration Papers* 46, at 22 (explaining that "especially in developing countries, expatriates themselves organize networks that stimulate return flows of knowledge and lead to collaborative ventures between home-country academics and expatriate researchers"); Mercy Brown, "*Using the Intellectual Diaspora to Reverse the Brain Drain: Some Useful Examples*," University of Cape Town, South Africa (2000), at http://www.uneca.org/eca_resources/Conference_Reports_and_Other_Documents/brain_drain/word_documents/brown.doc (explaining that the Internet has become a forum for list-serves and discussion groups between those in the sending country and their expatriate communities); David E. Kaplan, "Reversing the Brain Drain: The Case for Utilizing South Africa's Unique Intellectual Diaspora," *Science, Technology, and Society* 2 (1997): 387–406 (explaining

that expatriate researchers often network and collaborate with their home country's academics in order to stimulate the flow of knowledge between the sending and receiving countries).

10. *See* AnnaLee Saxenian, *Silicon Valley's New Immigrant Entrepreneurs* (San Francisco: Public Policy Institute of California, 1999), 29–30, Table 3.1 (listing professional associations that were developed for expatriate communities living in the United States beginning in the 1980s); Melanie Warner, "The Indians of Silicon Valley," *Fortune* (May 15, 2000), 357, 372 (explaining that Indian nationals living in the United States began to network formally in the early 1990s).

11. *See generally* AnnaLee Saxenian, "Brain Circulation: How High-Skill Immigration Makes Everyone Better Off," *Brookings Review*, Winter 2002: 28, 29; Saxenian, *Silicon Valley's New Immigrant Entrepreneurs*, at 29–30, Table 3.1. Many organizations "offer first-generation immigrants professional contacts and networks within the local technology community. They serve as recruitment channels and provide role models of successful immigrant entrepreneurs and managers. They sponsor regular speakers and conferences whose subjects range from specialized technical and market information to how to write a business plan or manage a business." Saxenian, "Brain Circulation: How High-Skill Immigration Makes Everyone Better Off," at 30.

12. AnnaLee Saxenian, "Brain Circulation: How High-Skill Immigration Makes Everyone Better Off," at 30. Examples of such associations include the Ghana Association of Distance Learning, established by Ghanaians in the diaspora to advance education; the South African Network of Skills Abroad (SANSA), which seeks to connect migrants from South Africa to scientific and technological projects in their home country, (*see* http://sansa.nrf.ac.za/); the Monte Jade Science and Technology Association, which promotes the cooperation and flow of technology between the United States and Taiwan, (*see* http://www.montejade.org); the North American Chinese Semiconductor Association, which facilitates interaction between individuals in the United States and China, (*see* http://www.nacsa.com); the North American Taiwanese Engineers Association (NATEA), which promotes the exchange of scientific and technological information between the United States and Taiwan, (*see* http://www.natea.org); the Silicon Valley Chinese Engineers Association, which promotes entrepreneurship and the establishment of business ties to China, (*see* http://www.scea.org); the Silicon Valley Indian Professionals Association, which helps to facilitate knowledge transfers and professional, career, and business development for its South Asian members working in the United States, (*see* http://www.sipa.org); and the IndUS Entrepreneurs ("TiE"), which is a global, not-for-profit organization created for the advancement of entrepreneurship among Indians, (*see* http://www.tie.org). TiE is particularly interesting because of the scope of its international presence; as of December 2004, it had forty-two chapters in nine countries. Robert D. Hof, "India and Silicon Valley: Now the R&D Flows Both Ways," *Business Week*, December 8, 2003, 74.

13. AnnaLee Saxenian, *Local and Global Networks of Immigrant Professionals in Silicon Valley* (San Francisco: Public Policy Institute of California, 2002), 25 (the study found that of the group of individuals sharing information with colleagues from

their home countries, 28 percent did so on a regular basis); Saxenian, *Silicon Valley's New Immigrant Entrepreneurs*, 35 (noting that the Chinese Institute of Engineers, a Silicon Valley–based professional business association, "plays a central role in promoting collaboration between Chinese-American engineers and their counterparts in Asia"). Networking is also prominent among migrant communities in receiving countries. See, e.g., Melanie Warner, "The Indians of Silicon Valley," *Fortune* (May 15, 2000): 357, 372 (explaining the origins and mission of The IndUS Entrepreneurs ("TiE"), a global, not-for-profit organization created for the advancement of Indian entrepreneurship, that was founded by senior professionals and corporate executives with roots in the Indus Valley, in India.)

14. Geoff Dyer and Khozem Merchant, "The Birth of a Biotech Cluster: Hyderabad Is Witnessing a Gathering of the Elements to Create a Life Sciences Hotspot to Match Its IT Industry," *Financial Times*, August 14, 2003, 10.

15. Saxenian, "Brain Circulation: How High-Skilled Immigration Makes Everyone Better Off," 30 (explaining how "transnational communities provide the shared information, contacts and trust that allow local producers to participate in an increasingly global economy"). The phenomenon is not limited to U.S. immigration. For example, the Colombian capacity for robotics technology was jump-started by ties with Colombian STEP OUT migrants living in France. Adrienne Roberts, "Can S.A. Recycle Lost Resources," *Financial Mail*, November 19, 1999, 16 (noting, in addition, the importance of the Colombian Network of Scientists and Engineers (Caldas) in generating interactions between STEP OUT migrants and their colleagues back home).

16. Saxenian, *Local and Global Networks of Immigrant Professionals*, 25.

17. Saxenian, *Local and Global Networks of Immigrant Professionals*, 28 (reporting the results of a survey that found that 40 percent of highly skilled immigrants in the United States arrange business contracts in their home countries).

18. Saxenian, *Local and Global Networks of Immigrant Professionals*, 26–27 (reporting that 27 percent of a focus group of highly skilled immigrants in the United States served as consultants or advisors to companies in their native countries). See, e.g., Gurcharan Das, *India Unbound* (New York: Alfred A. Knopf, 2001), 335 (noting such efforts by the Indus Entrepreneurs, a network of Silicon Valley entrepreneurs formed in 1992, "for the purpose of fostering entrepreneurship" in India).

19. Saritha Rai, "Indian Tech Workers Learning U.S. Social Codes," *International Herald Tribune*, the *IHP Hotline*, August 20, 2003 (noting the importance of developing soft skills as well as the need to rely on "programmers, returning from abroad" for the information necessary to develop them).

20. Easterly, *The Elusive Quest for Growth*, 147–152.

21. Easterly, *The Elusive Quest for Growth*, 147.

22. Easterly, *The Elusive Quest for Growth*, 147.

23. Easterly, *The Elusive Quest for Growth*, 147–48.

24. Easterly, *The Elusive Quest for Growth*, 147–48.

25. Das, *India Unbound*, 252–53, 331 (citing examples, including an Indian engineer who worked sixteen years at Intel, and the former head of GE Capital's outsourcing

center in India); *World Development Report, 1998/99*, at 8. The World Bank's World
Development Report 1998/99 notes that

> Valuable knowledge spillovers can occur through the training of local staff and through
> contacts with domestic suppliers and subcontractors. Both are evident in Malaysia, where
> the local plant of the U.S. firm Intel Corporation now subcontracts a growing part of its
> production to new firms set up by former Intel engineers.

26. Saxenian, *Local and Global Networks of Immigrant Professionals*, 29 (reporting that 30 percent of highly skilled immigrants in the United States meet frequently
with officials of the governments in their home countries).

27. Bernhard Heitger, "Property Rights and the Wealth of Nations: A Cross-Coun-
try Study," *Cato Journal* 23, Winter 2004: 381, 385, 399–400. See Hernando De Soto,
*The Mystery of Capital: Why Capitalism Triumphs in the West and Fails Everywhere
Else* (New York: Basic Books, 2000), 224–25 (stating that "few are aware of the
tremendous edge that formal property systems have given Western societies"); see
also Michael Novak, *Free Persons and the Common Good* (Lanham: Madison Books,
1989), 118–19 (noting that "many educated persons in the Third World hardly know
of liberal ideas and institutions. . . . They do not recognize that the liberal order begins *from the bottom up*, that is, from universal property ownership, [among other
things]") (emphasis in original).

28. See, e.g., Warner, "The Indians of Silicon Valley," 357, 372 (explaining that
Kanwal Rekhi, a prominent Indian-born entrepreneur from Silicon Valley, California,
meets regularly with the Indian Prime Minister and cabinet members to discuss economic reform in India); Jagdish Bhagwati, "The Poverty of Protectionism," in *A
Stream of Windows: Unsettling Reflections on Trade, Immigration, and Democracy*
(Cambridge: the MIT Press, 1998): 75, 81 (in which the author, an internationally
prominent economist who migrated to the United States from India, discusses meet-
ings he has had with Indian policymakers to explain the benefits to India of its adoption of intellectual property protection laws).

29. Jagdish Bhagwati, *In Defense of Globalization* (New York: Oxford University
Press, 2004), 215. The 2004 U.S. presidential election provides a specific example of
this phenomenon at work as, in that election, Indian-American political groups advanced a pro-outsourcing message—one thought advantageous to India—in a domestic political environment that was generally hostile to that view. See Joshua
Kurlantzick, "Vote Getters," *The New Republic Online* (May 26, 2004), available at
http://tnr.com/doc.mhtml?i=express&s=kurlantzick052604.

Chapter Thirteen

Monetary Transfers

Monetary transfers are the contribution that historically has received the most attention from commentators, particularly the calculation of the amount of remittances, which "are defined as the quantity of currency that migrants earn abroad and then send home to their families and communities."[1] Today, remittances are much greater than ever before, clearly in absolute terms, but also as a percentage of the GDP of the developing countries which receive them. Moreover, remittances are not the only source of financial contributions by STEP OUT migrants to home countries. Increasingly, foreign direct investment is proving an attractive additional means of supporting one's home community. Foreign direct investment and remittances by STEP OUT migrants—as well as other less substantial contributions[2]—can provide jobs, economic growth, educational opportunities, and necessary living expenses. Indeed, a few very successful STEP OUT migrants can provide—and have provided—for the education of thousands of people from their homelands.[3]

FOREIGN DIRECT INVESTMENT

Apart from the phenomenon of remittances, STEP OUT migrants living in the United States can directly invest more formally in their home countries. Many migrants have set up businesses in their native countries to gain access both to lower-cost labor and to their home countries' markets. These new businesses stimulate growth and development by creating new jobs and wealth for sending countries. STEP OUT migrants also have been instrumental in educating the companies in which they work about business opportunities in the migrants' home countries.

Indeed, when AnnaLee Saxenian, a prominent migration researcher, conducted surveys of foreign-born entrepreneurs in California's Silicon Valley, she found that half of the entrepreneurs had "set up subsidiaries, joint ventures, subcontracting or other business opportunities"[4] in their home countries, and that 18 percent had invested in either start-up businesses or venture capital funds in those countries.[5] STEP OUT migrants who work for U.S.–based companies also have become "instrumental in convincing senior management in their firms to source software or establish operations" in their home countries.[6] Government officials in developing countries are well aware of this advantage of STEP OUT migration and have even actively lobbied their STEP OUT emigrants to influence their employers to invest in the developing countries.[7]

Several countries have prospered from these investments. In India, for example, in large part due to foreign direct investment, the information technology business has blossomed in the last decade: India exported $6 billion in software in the year 2000, and more than $15 billion by 2004, 100 times more than the $150 million in software exported yearly at the start of the 1990s.[8] Significantly, and not coincidentally, "60 percent of [India's] software exports [go] to the United States."[9]

Clearly, India's information technology industry would not have developed as quickly or as significantly if it were not helped and supported by Indians living in the United States, who gave India "the edge [needed]" to become a global center for high technology.[10] Indeed, as "Indian professionals in the U.S. have been the primary drivers of knowledge and capital flows to India," they appear at the heart of such advances as Bangalore's development into the fourth largest technology hub in the world.[11] Today, in recognition of that development, many foreign-based companies, including cutting-edge technology companies like Google, Microsoft, and Oracle,[12] are shifting or adding operations to Bangalore and other cities in India,[13] and many of the jobs are high-end positions previously rarely offered overseas.[14] Other types of U.S.–based companies are following suit by moving some of their own higher-paying positions abroad. Morgan Stanley, for example, recently opened an operation in India in which they plan to employ "50 research-related employees . . . only a few of [whom] are expected to be junior analysts."[15]

ONE SMALL EXAMPLE OF A LARGE PHENOMENON

When STEP OUT migrants start businesses, benefits often accrue to both the migrants' original and adopted homelands. The mutually beneficial process can be illustrated by the example of Sabinsa Corporation. Sabinsa was founded by Dr. Muhammed Majeed, who came to the United States from India for his post-graduate education. After obtaining a Ph.D. at St. John's University in New York and working, among other places, at Pfizer, the world's largest pharmaceutical company, Dr. Majeed decided to combine his knowledge of Ayurveda, the traditional Indian medical and health system, with his knowledge of modern laboratory methods to form a new company. Incorporated in New Jersey in 1988, Sabinsa's 120 Ayurveda-based products include anti-inflammatories and digestive aids. Sabinsa and its affiliates now employ 55 employees in the United States and 750 in India, including more than 100 Ph.D. researchers. Moreover, Sabinsa and its affiliate Sami Labs indirectly employ more than 5,000 farmers in India, through contracts to supply the natural products that constitute the raw materials of the companies' laboratory work.

Dr. Majeed's success provides a good example of the win-win nature of much of the foreign direct investment by STEP OUT migrants. Had Dr. Majeed not emigrated, the jobs of his company's 55 U.S.–based employees probably would not exist—it is unlikely that anyone but an Indian would have had the knowledge and desire to form a modern company based on India's ancient health system. Nor would the jobs of his 750 employees in India likely exist—not to mention some of the jobs of the 5,000 farmer-suppliers—for only a person with knowledge of and experience in the United States or another developed country is likely to have correctly anticipated and assessed the undeveloped market opportunity that existed in providing Ayurveda-based products to the developed world. Many thousands of customers who rely on Sabinsa's products also have gained from Dr. Majeed's migration, as those products evidently are perceived by the customers to offer more help than any competing alternatives. Finally, by helping to create a market for and educate the developed world about Ayurveda and Ayurveda-based products, Dr. Majeed has provided a service for an untold number of future Indian scientists and entrepreneurs. Any place in which there is knowledge about and acceptance of Ayurveda and Ayurveda-based products is a place in which Indians, to some extent, have a natural competitive advantage for, generally speaking, no one knows more than they about Ayurveda. By establishing a foothold for Ayurveda in the developed world, efforts like Dr. Majeed's increase the likelihood that the future market potential of Ayurveda will be fully exploited, and exploited by Indians.

The example of Sabinsa illustrates how a process that starts with what is certainly in some sense an immediate loss—the departure of a talented national—can in the end redound to the benefit of the original homeland, as well as benefit the new home, and, indeed, the world. And it is a process that is by no means rare. Thousands of other examples could be used to make the same points. Cumulatively, these examples suggest that STEP OUT migration plays a unique and irreplaceable role in stimulating development of the underdeveloped nations of the world.

Further, besides off-shoring their own jobs, U.S. companies are also hiring overseas companies to perform a host of tasks, including research and development, evaluation of insurance health claims, preparation of U.S. tax returns, and analysis of financial data.[16] More particularly, Bank of America uses 250 engineers from the Indian company Infosys Technologies to develop new information technology applications;[17] Indian radiologists interpret thirty CT scans a day for Massachusetts General Hospital; and Ph.D.s in molecular biology conduct scientific research for Western pharmaceutical companies.[18]

It should be noted that there are some concomitant benefits to direct investment. For instance, it can accelerate the phenomenon of brain return, even as the desire to return can motivate direct investment. General Electric (GE), for example, has been investing in India for many years.[19] It operates a call center and back-office business that employs 11,000 people; additionally, "more than 7,000 people at Indian software firms work on GE projects."[20] Most recently, GE invested more than $80 million to create a research center in Bangalore, India, making it GE's largest research center outside the United States.[21] The new center will employ 1,600 employees.

One of the principal reasons that GE chose to invest in India was the large "number of Indians already doing research for GE in the U.S."[22] Before this center opened, some of GE's Indian employees had wanted to return home but could not find jobs in India at the level of sophistication that would challenge them.[23] Tapping into this talent pool, GE decided to lure them back to India to work for GE there by offering high-level and sophisticated work.[24] Similarly, when the computer software company Oracle hired 1,000 people in India, "10 per cent were professionals who had returned from overseas."[25]

These hiring trends appear likely to continue. Thus, a report by McKinsey and Company predicts that in the next few years "India's [information technology] industry could generate $87 billion in annual revenues, $225 billion in market value, and 2.2 million jobs,"[26] and a similar report concerning the financial industry predicts that by 2008, "financial companies will move 1 million jobs" to India.[27]

Among the many other countries benefiting from foreign direct investment, Taiwan is also particularly noteworthy. Taiwan has experienced recent growth in its technology sector in part because of the ties it shares with the Taiwanese diaspora living and working abroad. Indeed, individuals who had worked and/or studied in the United States started 40 percent of the technology companies located in the Hsinchu Science Park near Taipei.[28] In sum, as these examples show, STEP OUT migration may not be a necessary condition for foreign direct investment, but it is very likely to accelerate and multiply the phenomenon.[29]

Moreover, foreign direct investment by or because of STEP OUT migrants generally can be expected to be far superior in effectiveness than government-to-government aid in triggering and sustaining economic growth.[30] There are two main reasons for this.

First, direct investment by private parties has the advantage in almost all cases of actually having the primary aim of creating positive economic effects. Indeed, because the resources of STEP OUT migrants and even the resources of their companies are limited, rational investors must have this aim if they hope to continue investing. Thus, those prospective investments subjectively deemed least likely to attain positive economic ends will, for the most part, remain unfunded by STEP OUT migrants. The same cannot be said, however, of government-to-government aid which, even when it is ostensibly economic in nature, may carry little or no expectation of achieving positive economic ends. This is not necessarily a criticism of those who would authorize such aid. Larger concerns may make a wasteful decision from the perspective of fostering growth in a recipient country a very appropriate decision from, for example, the broader perspective of the national security of the nation giving the aid. However, it should be understood that, from an economic perspective, aid given with such motives in mind not only may be inefficient relative to direct investment by businesses, it may actually be worse than useless. This is because the provision of such aid provides an enhanced opportunity for corruption, as all parties know that the provider is not primarily concerned with economic outcomes, and hence the recipient may more freely direct the aid toward other goals, which might include punishing severely one's political opponents, rewarding lavishly one's political friends, and avoiding political and economic reforms that might hamper one's ability to so reward friends and punish enemies. All three of these activities, of course, directly or indirectly, are likely to suppress economic growth, and possibly political freedom as well.[31]

Second, even with the best of motives, government aid will almost inevitably be distributed less efficiently than private investment, perhaps especially if the former is distributed through a multi-national organization. A large literature on bureaucracy demonstrates that "[b]ureaucracy works best where there is high feedback from beneficiaries, high incentives for the bureaucracy to respond to such feedback, easily observable outcomes, high probability that bureaucratic effort will translate into favorable outcomes, and competitive pressure from other bureaucracies and agencies."[32] The incentive structure for the foreign direct investment of private businesses, who face elimination if they do not efficiently deploy their capital while satisfying the needs of their customers, ensures the presence of these conditions to a high degree in projects financed by foreign direct investment; however, "[a]ll of these conditions are unfavorable in foreign aid."[33] Accordingly, the provision of foreign aid by multi-national organizations, such as the World Bank, stands almost as a caricature of bureaucratic inefficiency. To make a very long story very short, it is enough merely to note that, at the end of the aid process, money requested by a national government from large development agencies such as the World Bank will require distribution "in accordance with the NDP, ADLI, CRSP, MTEF, CDF, PRGF, PRSC, and PRSP," many of which will have been prepared specifically for the particular request.[34] Requirements of this type cause Tanzania, for example, "to produce more than 2400 reports a year for the donors," who themselves generate numerous internal reports on each aid request.[35] The required reports can be substantial; for instance, "Niger's recently completed [Poverty Reduction Strategy Paper] is 187 pages long [and] took 15 months to prepare."[36] The national governments that theoretically can exercise political control over the multi-national agencies are, in practical terms, incapable of doing so, due to differences among the governments that can be exploited by the aid agencies and the difficulty of effective monitoring of the agencies' performances.[37] Indeed, to the extent that the national governments have worked together, they have actually made things worse, "by themselves imposing conditions on the multilaterals" in order to satisfy national objectives other than the reduction of poverty.[38] In addition, even if the distribution of aid suffers from none of these problems, because money is fungible, recipient governments can and often do undercut the effectiveness of a particular grant by diverting other funds under government control away from the targets of aid, thereby ensuring that the grant will accomplish nothing more than maintaining the presumably unsatisfactory status quo.

This is not to say that foreign aid, as traditionally distributed, might not sometimes be the most effective mechanism, e.g., in emergency situations or in addressing broad impediments to foreign direct investment, such as a broken administrative capability.[39] It is not even to say that foreign aid currently is too large, or should be reduced; given the dire circumstances of so many persons in so many corners of the world, one might contend that to focus on waste is about as useful as demanding that the fire department be called upon to account for each drop of water used in fighting a horrible blaze.[40] Indeed, one might recognize foreign aid's undeniable relative inefficiencies, and yet persuasively conclude, as did the recent Report of the Commission for Africa, that aid should be substantially increased—in all events, the issue is complex, subject to serious dispute,[41] and ultimately far beyond the scope of this work. For our limited discussion here, the matter is not decisive. Our point is that given the almost unimaginable need that exists for economic development and the necessarily limited (and practically, very limited) supply of funding, it is incumbent upon all interested parties not to advocate policies that, even indirectly, discourage the types of investment that can most efficiently lift people out of poverty. On this point, it is extremely important to underscore that the comparative deficiencies in the quality of government aid vis-à-vis foreign direct investment are not aberrations, but instead are inherent in the nature and the sources of the aid. No government is *ever* going to make economic aid decisions with no regard for how those decisions will impact priorities other than economic growth.[42] Indeed, governments giving aid have every incentive to characterize decisions made for other reasons as actually being motivated by benevolent humanitarian and economic growth concerns. Similarly, government and multi-national organization bureaucracies will only rarely deploy capital as efficiently as private businesses. This is not, as James Q. Wilson has persuasively explained, due to the dullness or laziness of public agency bureaucrats; rather, it is that public bureaucracies generally need to respond to the efficiency-insensitive demands of rule following, consensus development, and perceived fairness to a much greater degree than private actors do.[43]

The net effect of all these considerations is to suggest that foreign direct investment by STEP OUT migrants is much more important vis-à-vis government foreign aid than the raw numbers would indicate. Additionally, it is a mistake to believe that the advantages of foreign direct investment over government and multi-national organization aid are accidents of history, rather than attributable to irreducible institutional factors. Besides, even in a fantasy land where all moneys currently given in foreign aid could, without any diminution from administrative costs or corruption, be directly transferred to that portion of the world's population that lives on less than $365 per year, the poorest of the poor would be better off by a grand total of less than fifteen cents a day. Put in this context, no rational assessment of the world as it exists and as it is likely to exist could deny that the foreign direct investment of STEP OUT migrants provides a needed mechanism to help some of the hundreds of millions of people who otherwise would not ever be helped by any other source.

REMITTANCES

Remittances that STEP OUT migrants send to friends, relatives, and communities of origin in their home countries constitute another direct financial benefit that sending countries derive from migration. According to the Migration Policy Institute, a prominent Washington, D.C., think tank, the "most often cited support for the positive side of [migration] is the observation that remittances from international migrants play an extraordinary role in the economic accounts of many developing countries, far more important than official development assistance."[44] Notably, the role of remittances has expanded greatly in recent years, in both absolute and relative terms. Thus, "[t]he remittance flow has doubled in the last decade, reaching $216 billion in 2004, with $150 billion going to developing countries."[45] Meanwhile, relative to international development aid, which has stagnated, remittances have grown from being about 75 percent of aid amounts during the 1980s to being more than twice as large today.[46] Further, trends indicate that total remittances will continue to grow at an impressive rate.[47]

Even now, of course, remittances represent significant monetary flows into countries.[48] From 1999 to 2000, remittances to India exceeded $20 billion.[49] In 2002, Mexico received $10.5 billion in remittance flows;[50] Brazil received 4.6 billion;[51] and Colombians living abroad remitted $2.4 billion to their communities of origin.[52] Significantly, subsequent years saw substantial increases in all these amounts.[53]

In many countries, remittances constitute one of the largest sources of income for the local economy. For example, in 2001 Jordan received more than $2 billion in remittances, which constituted 22.8 percent of its gross domestic product (GDP).[54] Similarly, remittances sent to Yemen, El Salvador, and Bosnia and Herzogovina also constituted a significant portion of each country's GDP at 15.7, 14, and 18 percent, respectively.[55] The volume of remittances in El Salvador has risen above the amount of income from exports in recent years.[56] And even back in 1995, remittances to Mexico amounted to 57 percent of the "foreign exchange available through foreign direct investment."[57]

Until recently, policymakers and economists failed to fully appreciate the importance of remittances and the positive role they can play in developing countries.[58] In the last few years, however, that failure has been remedied, as more "international organizations, national governments, universities, foundations, and financial institutions . . . 'discover[ed] remittances.'"[59] Research by these bodies has explored the number of ways in which remittances can stimulate sending countries' development and economic growth.

First, some of the money that is sent back home is used for consumption of local goods and services, thus growing the economies of the sending countries.[60] This creates local demand, increases employment, and leads to business development. "In sub-Saharan Africa remittances are invested in education or in agricultural equipment, such as water pumps, irrigation equipment, and tractors. Remittances may also enable migrants' families to employ labour in their fields, while they themselves develop activities in urban settings."[61] As a result, for each dollar sent to their home communities, there is a "multiplier effect of three to four dollars of economic growth"[62] because each transaction has a series of secondary consequences: salaries are paid, new raw materials are bought, new orders are placed, new loans are made, new investments are made, new capital improvements are made, and on and on. In Mexico, "[s]tatistical analysis finds that each $1 remitted to Mexico produces an increase of $2.90 in the GDP and an increase of $3.20 in economic output, which leads to an increase in national income and production of billions of dollars each year."[63]

Additionally, remittances that are not spent on goods and services can be and are saved or invested.[64] The savings are then available for banks, insurance companies, and other lending institutions to finance loans that in turn lead to economic development and growth. In fact, a recent study shows that "27 percent of the capital invested in micro-enterprise in Mexico" is attributable to remittances.[65] In sum, remittances have a positive effect on development. As the Philippines Minister of Labor aptly commented, "overseas employment has built more homes, sent more children of the poor to college and established more business enterprises than all the other programmes of the government put together."[66] Indeed, although questions remain as to the extent of remittances' impact, "[t]he link between remittances and development is growing stronger."[67] Moreover, on "a macroeconomic level, remittances often provide a significant source of foreign currency, increase national income, finance imports, and contribute to the balance of payments."[68]

NOTES

1. Rodolfo O. de la Garza and Manual Orozco, "Binational Impact of Latino Remittances," in *Sending Money Home: Hispanic Remittances and Community Development*, ed. Rodolfo O. de la Garza and Briant Lindsay Lowell (Lanham: Rowman & Littlefield Publishers, Inc., 2002): 29 (internal quotation marks omitted).

2. Other types of contributions include the sending of consumer goods to the country of origin, the purchase of products from the country of origin that are imported into the receiving country, and visits to the home country. See Inter-American Development Bank, Multilateral Investment Fund, *Sending Money Home: Remittance to Latin America and the Caribbean* (2004), 15.

3. Gurcharan Das, *India Unbound* (New York: Alfred A. Knopf, 2001), 335. See Thomas L. Friedman, "Making India Shine," *New York Times*, May 20, 2004, A27 (noting the founding of the Shanti Bhavan school in India by "one of those brainy Indians who made it big in high-tech America": the privately financed Shanti Bhavan school, located an hour's drive from Bangalore, is particularly noteworthy because its 160 students are all, in the language of India's caste system, "untouchables"). See also Monique Maddy, *Learning to Love Africa: My Journey from Africa to Harvard Business School and Back* (New York: HarperBusiness, 2004), 333–34 (discussing plan to finance school in Kenya).

4. AnnaLee Saxenian, *Local and Global Networks of Immigrant Professionals in Silicon Valley* (San Francisco: Public Policy Institute of California, 2002), 37 (stating that her survey also reported that most of the other respondents "would consider establishing such operations in the future").

5. Saxenian, *Local and Global Networks of Immigrant Professionals in Silicon Valley*, 29. For example, "Chinese graduates of U.S. business and engineering schools are getting work experience in the United States and then going back home to launch companies, lured by China's strong economy." Matt Marshall, "China Ventures Reaping Dividends," *San Jose Mercury News*, February 17, 2002, 1F.

6. See AnnaLee Saxenian, "The Bangalore Boom: From Brain Drain to Brain Circulation," *IT Experience in India: Bridging the Digital Divide*, eds. Kenneth Keniston and Deepak Kumar (New Delhi: Sage Publications, 2004): 169, 177 (describing Indian nationals who work in Silicon Valley–based companies).

7. Geoff Dyer and Khozem Merchant, "The Birth of a Biotech Cluster: Hyderabad Is Witnessing a Gathering of the Elements to Create a Life Sciences Hotspot to Match Its IT Industry," *Financial Times*, August 14, 2003, 10 (noting that officials from Indian government and industry have nurtured their ties to STEP OUT emigrants working for major international pharmaceutical companies abroad, hoping that the emigrants will influence their employers to invest in its burgeoning biotechnology industry).

8. Saritha Rai, "Technology: Company Town Keeps Indians at Home," *New York Times*, March 18, 2002, C3; Khozem Merchant, "India Attacks U.S. on Plan to Ban Outsourcing," *Financial Times*, January 25, 2004, 6. Software exports by India are expected to rise still further to $50 billion by 2008. Das, *India Unbound*, 326.

9. Saritha Rai, "Chinese Race to Supplant India in Software," *New York Times*, January 5, 2002, B1, B3.

10. Sadanand Dhume, "Bringing It Home," *Far Eastern Economic Review* 163 (February 2000), 44 (explaining that "the returnees are often familiar with the latest trends and standards in America. They have networks of friends and contacts in Silicon Valley" and other high-technology centers).

11. Mario Cervantes and Dominique Guellec, "The Brain Drain: Old Myths, New Realities," *OECD Observer*, January 1, 2002, 40; see "Software Exports Record 25 P.C. Growth," *The Hindu*, Global News Wire–Asia Africa Intelligence Wire, April 24, 2003 (mentioning Bangalore's status as a major technology hub in report noting a 25 percent growth in software exports despite a global recession).

12. Dominic Basulto, "Whither Innovation?" Tech Central Station, January 6, 2004, at http://www.techcentralstation.com/010604D.html. E.g., Saritha Rai, "Microsoft Joins Industry Trend of Investing Heavily in India," *New York Times*, December 8, 2005, C2 (noting Microsoft's plans to hire an additional 3,000 employees at its research facility in India).

13. Pete Engardio et al., "The New Global Job Shift," *Business Week*, February 3, 2003, 50. At the start of 2004, "[t]he five Indian cities of Bangalore, Delhi, Mumbai, Chennai and Hyderabad . . . account[ed] for more than 300,000 IT-related jobs—including as many as 40,000 R&D jobs." Basulto, "Whither Innovation?" at http://www.techcentralstation.com/010604D.html.

14. Robert D. Hof, "India and Silicon Valley: Now the R&D Flows Both Ways," *Business Week*, December 8, 2003, 74 (stating the hiring of Indians by U.S. companies has gone "far beyond the 'body shopping' of the 1990s, when U.S. companies mainly wanted low-wage software-code writers"); Basulto, "Whither Innovation?" at

http://www.techcentralstation.com/010604D.html (noting that the jobs being added are no longer only "low end" but now include many "high-end R&D jobs").

15. Rob Stewart and Sam Nagarajan, "India Graduates from the Back Office," *International Herald Tribune*, the IHT Online, August 7, 2003, athttp://www.iht.com/articles/105542.html. The newly hired Indian researchers will do "company research, complementing work by its analysts in six to eight industries globally. The bank is also hiring people to do financial modeling, compiling company data and analyzing spreadsheets, and others with the computer and technical skills they need to support the division." Stewart and Nagarajan, "India Graduates from the Back Office." It should be noted, however, that outsourcing of back office jobs will continue to be a source of job growth for India. See Rob Stewart, "Bank of America Joins Exodus to China," *International Herald Tribune*, the IHT Online, August 19, 2003, at http://www.iht.com/articles/106894.html (noting that U.S. and European financial companies will alone move two million jobs "offshore by 2008," with "[h]alf of that number . . . shift[ing] to India").

16. Amy Waldman, "More 'Can I Help You?' Jobs Migrate from U.S. to India," *New York Times*, May 11, 2003, A4. Technology and globalization have combined to shift more mundane tasks across borders as well, such as transcription of doctors' medical notes. Waldman, "More 'Can I Help You?'" See also Nigel Harris, *Thinking the Unthinkable: The Immigration Myth Exposed* (London: I.B. Tauris, 2002), 113 (noting that "three million criminal records for England and Wales were loaded and processed by 200 typists in Manila through an Australian contractor"); Das, *India Unbound*, 251, 336–37 (noting other examples of outsourcing of remote data processing tasks).

17. Engardio et al., "The New Global Job Shift," 50. Infosys is the most successful of Bangalore's 325 software companies. See Das, *India Unbound*, xiv–xv, 246–47.

18. Engardio et al., "The New Global Job Shift," 50. Some analysts predict that by the year 2015, "3.3 million white collar jobs and $136 billion in wages will shift from the U.S. to low-cost countries." Engardio et al., "The New Global Job Shift,"

19. Joanna Slater, "GE Takes Advantage of India's Talented Research Pool," *Wall Street Journal*, March 26, 2003, A10.

20. Joanna Slater, "GE Takes Advantage of India's Talented Research Pool," A10.

21. Joanna Slater, "GE Takes Advantage of India's Talented Research Pool," A10

22. Joanna Slater, "GE Takes Advantage of India's Talented Research Pool," A10

23. Joanna Slater, "GE Takes Advantage of India's Talented Research Pool," A10

24. Joanna Slater, "GE Takes Advantage of India's Talented Research Pool." Based in part on GE's success, General Motors decided to open a $21 million research and engineering center in Bangalore. The center will be the company's first outside the United States. Joanna Slater, "GE Takes Advantage of India's Talented Research Pool," A10.

25. Priya Srinivasan, "Return of the Techie," *Business Today*, October 26, 2003, 70.

26. AnnaLee Saxenian, *The Bangalore Boom: From Brain Drain to Brain Circulation*, 180.

27. Rob Stewart and Sam Nagarajan, "India Graduates from the Back Office," *International Herald Tribune*, the IHT Online, August 7, 2003, at http://www.iht.com/articles/105542.html (discussing a report by Deloitte Research).

28. See Christopher Parkes, "California Urged to Raise a Cheer for Asian Immigrants: Indians and Chinese Are Playing an Invaluable Role in Helping to Create

High-Tech Growth," *Financial Times*, July 3, 1999, 3 (noting that 40 percent of the companies in the Hsinchu Science Park were started by individuals who had returned after living in the United States).

29. Significant direct investment is not limited to what one might term the usual suspects of China, Taiwan, India, South Korea, etc. For example, to take one unusual case, in the aftermath of the overthrow of Saddam Hussein, Iraq has seen an influx of investment from its own STEP OUT migrants. See Ellen McCarthy, "Iraqis Try to Build Nation and Fortune," *Washington Post*, July 7, 2004, E01, available at http://www.arcadd.com/WP_Story-7-7-04.htm (noting that "Iraqis living outside of Iraq are pouring $5 million a day into private enterprises in the country"). Moreover, even given the containing violence in Iraq, the effect of this investment cannot be dismissed. See Silvia Spring, "Blood and Money," *Newsweek International*, Dec. 25, 2006–Jan. 1, 2007 (stating that "[i]n what might be called the mother of all surprises, Iraq's economy is growing strong, even booming in places")

30. See generally Fredrik Segerfeldt, *Companies Are the Solution, Not the Problem: Businesses and the Fight Against Poverty* (Confederation of Swedish Enterprise, April 2003), at http://www.iedm.org/uploaded/pdf/fredriksegerfeldt.pdf (concluding foreign business investment is more effective at building economic growth in developing countries than foreign aid); cf. William Easterly, "Working Paper No. 65, Reliving the '50s: the Big Push, Poverty Traps, and Takeoffs in Economic Development," (Washington, D.C.: Center for Global Development, August 2005), 8 (noting that donors gave twenty-two African countries $187 billion in aid from 1970 to 1994, and that the "increase in productivity, measured as per capita growth over this period, was zero"); Nsongurua J. Udombana, "How Should We Then Live? Globalization and the New Partnership for Africa's Development," *Boston University International Law Journal* 20 (2002): 293, 325 (noting that Africa, the only continent to lose economic ground over the last forty years, "has had an extraordinary share in terms of foreign aid, compared to other regions and even to African economic aggregates").

31. Indeed, a tremendous danger of anti-growth corruption exists even when aid clearly is intended to assist the receiving nation's poor. Thus, in Zimbabwe, allies of President Robert Mugabe—a leader who has for several decades enriched his friends while impoverishing his country and persecuting his enemies—managed to skim off almost all of a European Union aid package of several hundred million dollars. See David Bamber, "Mugabe's Friends Siphon Off Nine-Tenths of EU's Aid to Zimbabwe's Poor," *Daily Telegraph*, February 29, 2004, available at http://www.telegraph.co.uk/news/main.jhtml;jsessionid=JVZ30NJ2GYYEXQFIQMGCNAGAVCBQUJVC?xml= /news/2004/02/29/wzim29.xml. Such corruption, with its baneful economic effects, is so pervasive in many countries that Nobel Peace prize winner, Shirin Ebadi, has argued that financial aid to undemocratic governments should be halted because it only works to prop up repressive regimes. Stephanie Ho, "Non-Democratic Governments Should Not Receive Assistance, Says Iranian Nobel Laureate Shirin Ebadi," *Payvand's Iran News*, May 4, 2004, available at http://www.payvand.com/news/04/may/1023.html (discussing speech given at the Washington, D.C., headquarters of the World Bank). See also Michael Novak, *The Catholic Ethic and the Spirit of Capitalism* (New York: Free Press, 1993), 153 (noting that many scholars "are particularly

opposed to foreign aid granted by one government to another, on the grounds that the corruption of political elites in Third World countries is virtually uncontrollable"); William Easterly, *The Elusive Quest for Growth: Economists' Adventures and Misadventures in the Tropics* (Cambridge: the MIT Press, 2001), 116–17 (detailing how the presence of motives other than development can distort oversight and inadvertently reduce incentives to adopt necessary political and economic reforms); Richard Tren, "Aiding and Abetting Poverty," Tech Central Station, February 26, 2004, available at http://www.techcentralstation.com/022604C.html (arguing that aid transfers have the perverse effects of prolonging bad economic policies within a recipient country and encouraging political unresponsiveness and even oppression).

32. William Easterly, "The Cartel of Good Intentions: The Problem of Bureaucracy in Foreign Aid," *Journal of Policy Reform* 5 (2003): 223, 226, n.3.

33. Easterly, "The Cartel of Good Intentions: The Problem of Bureaucracy in Foreign Aid," 226. For an even more critical view of the incentive structure in foreign aid bureaucracies, see Monique Maddy, *Learning to Love Africa*. Maddy asserts that there is "little or no incentive to bring a project to fruition," and that, indeed, to the contrary, aid agency bureaucrats and developing nation government officials often "connive" to extend failed programs for selfish reasons of their own. Monique Maddy, *Learning to Love Africa*, 50–54, 253–57.

34. Easterly, "The Cartel of Good Intentions: The Problem of Bureaucracy in Foreign Aid," 223–24 (outlining the complete approval process). The acronyms mentioned above stand for the national development program, the Agricultural Development Led Industrialization strategy, the Civil Service Reform Program, the medium-term expenditure framework, the Comprehensive Development Framework, the Poverty Reduction and Growth Facility, the poverty reduction support credit, and the poverty reduction strategy paper.

35. Easterly, "The Cartel of Good Intentions: The Problem of Bureaucracy in Foreign Aid," 223, 242 (stating that, to approve a poverty reduction support credit, the internal steps followed by the World Bank "include the preparation of a Country Assistance Strategy (CAS), a pre-appraisal mission, an appraisal mission, negotiations, and Board approval," and noting that Tanzania receives a thousand "missions," i.e., visits of aid agency staff, each year).

36. William Easterly, "The Cartel of Good Intentions," *Foreign Policy* 131 (July–August 2002): 40.

37. Easterly, "The Cartel of Good Intentions: The Problem of Bureaucracy in Foreign Aid," 244–46.

38. Easterly, "The Cartel of Good Intentions: The Problem of Bureaucracy in Foreign Aid," 230 n.8.

39. See, e.g., The World Bank Group, Annual Report 2002 (noting in report overview that assistance was given in Afghanistan to support "key public administration" functions).

40. Catholic social teaching has strongly and consistently favored the provision of foreign aid to poor countries. E.g., Pope Paul VI, *Populorum Progressio* (1967), par. 44 (emphasizing the importance of "the aid that the rich nations must give to developing countries"); Pope John XXIII, *Pacem in Terris* (1963), par. 121 (noting *Mater*

et Magistra's appeal "to economically developed nations to come to the aid of those which were in the process of development"). However, Pope John Paul II did offer a mild and gingerly phrased criticism in *Centesimus Annus*. See Pope John Paul II, *Centesimus Annus* (1991), sec. 21 (noting that "the overall balance of the various policies of aid for development has not always been positive").

41. Compare "Our Common Interest: Report of the Commission for Africa (2005)," 14 (stating that aid should be increased between 25 and 50 billion dollars a year) with id. at 54 (acknowledging that aid to Africa is "haphazard, uncoordinated, and unfocused," that "[r]ich countries pursue their own fixations" and wrongly insist on requiring "demanding, cumbersome, time-consuming accounting and monitoring systems," that the grant of aid is "insufficiently flexible" and too often tied to reciprocal purchases of particular goods, and that, as a consequence, aid sometimes "undermine[s] the long-term development prospects of those [it is] supposed to be helping"). Compare also Harold J. Brumm, "Aid, Policies, and Growth: Bauer Was Right," *Cato Journal* 23 (2003): 167, 168 (concluding that "foreign aid has a negative growth effect even where economic policy is sound"), to Craig Burnside and David Dollar, "Aid, Policies, and Growth," *American Economic Review* 90 (2000): 847, 847 (concluding "that aid has a positive impact on growth in developing countries with good fiscal, monetary, and trade policies but has little effect in the presence of poor policies"). For a passionate—though perhaps overstated—indictment of foreign aid, see Michael Maren, *The Road to Hell: The Ravaging Effects of Foreign Aid and International Charity* (New York: The Free Press, 1999). See also Fredrik Erixon, *Aid and Development: Will It Work This Time?* (London: International Policy Network, 2005), 3, at http://www.policynetwork.net/uploaded/pdf/Aid_&_Development_final.pdf (concluding that "over the past fifty years, [foreign aid has] largely been counterproductive"); Nicolas van de Walle, "Aid's Crisis of Legitimacy: Current Proposals and Future Prospects," *African Affairs* 98 (1999): 337. Many other analysts, of course, adhere to the overall belief that "aid is good," even though they, as did the Commission for Africa, increasingly recognize foreign aid's shortcomings. Udombana "How Should We Then Live," 325 (stating that "there appears to be a 'crisis of legitimacy' in aid that so regularly disappoints the expectations vested in it" and concluding that "the effectiveness of the renewed emphasis put by some donors on the use of aid directly to relieve poverty is very doubtful").

42. Indeed, even believers in the efficacy of foreign aid admit this deficiency. See, e.g., Harsh Sethi, "What Price Hubris?," the Hindu, June 20, 2003, at http://www.the-hindu.com/2003/06/20/stories/2003062000191000.htm (conceding that "whatever the humanitarian impulse behind giving aid, it is difficult to deny that it comes at a price, tied in myriad ways to the interests of the donor country").

43. James Q. Wilson, *Bureaucracy: What Government Agencies Do and Why They Do It* (New York: Basic Books, 1989), 131–32. See generally Easterly, "The Cartel of Good Intentions: The Problem of Bureaucracy in Foreign Aid," at passim (discussing the causes and extent of inefficiency by foreign aid agencies).

44. Kathleen Newland, *Migration as a Factor in Development and Poverty Reduction*, Migration Information Source (Washington, D.C.: Migration Policy Institute, June 1, 2003), at http://www.migrationinformation.org/Feature/display.cfm?ID=136

(noting that worldwide remittances exceeded $100 billion per year whereas development assistance from the Organization for Economic Cooperation and Development (OECD) was $54 billion in the year 2000); see Inter-American Development Bank, Multilateral Investment Fund, *Sending Money Home: Remittance to Latin America and the Caribbean* (2004), 11 (stating that, "[i]n 2003, remittances flows exceeded all combined Foreign Direct Investment (FDI) and Official Development Assistance to" Latin America and the Caribbean).

45. Çağlar Özden and Maurice Schiff, "Overview," *International Migration, Remittances, & the Brain Drain*, eds. Çağlar Özden and Maurice Schiff 1 (Washington, D.C.: World Bank, 2006). Remittances to a particular country are usually generated from a combination of countries, rather than from a single country. Manuel Orozco, *Worker Remittances in an International Scope* (Multilateral Investment Fund of the Inter-American Development Bank, Working Paper, 2003), 4.

46. World Bank, *Global Economic Prospects, 2006: Economic Implications of Remittances and Migration* (Washington, D.C.: World Bank 2006), xi; Kenneth Hermele, "The Discourse on Migration and Development," *International Migration, Immobility and Development*, eds. Tomas Hammar, Grete Brochmann, Kristof Tamas and Thomas Faist (Oxford: Berg, 1997): 133, 139; Newland, *Migration as a Factor in Development and Poverty Reduction*, at http://www.migrationinformation.org/Feature/display.cfm?ID=136.

47. World Bank, *Global Economic Prospects, 2006*, 92–93 (stating that "[t]he surge in remittances is likely to continue in the medium term"). See Orozco, *Worker Remittances in an International Scope*, 1. For example, the World Bank has estimated that "recorded remittances sent home by migrants from developing countries . . . reach[ed] $199 billion in 2006," a figure "more than double level in 2001." World Bank, Development Prospects Group, Migration and Remittances Team, "Migration and Development Brief 2: Remittance Trends 2006," at 1 (2006). Further, "remittance payments to Latin America and the Caribbean topped $32 billion in 2002, up from $23 billion in 2001 and a 60% increase since 2000." Joel Millman, "Latin Americans Boost Home Coffers: Emigrant Workers Increase Remittances, Matching Direct Foreign Investment," *Wall Street Journal*, March 17, 2003, A2. Moreover, 2003 saw a similar increase in remittances to the same region. Inter-American Development Bank, Multilateral Investment Fund, *Sending Money Home* (2004), 11 (noting increase in remittances to $38 billion for Latin American and Caribbean countries alone). Indeed, officially recorded remittances multiplied several times from the 1980s to 1997. Briant Lindsay Lowell and Rodolfo O. de la Garza, "A New Phase in the Story of Remittances," *Sending Money Home* (2002): 3, 3–4; see also Susan Martin, *Remittance Flows and Impact*, Remarks at Remittances as a Development Tool: A Regional Conference Organized by the Multilateral Investment Fund, Inter-American Development Bank, May, 17, 2001, at http://www.iadb.org/mif/v2/files%5Csusanmartin.doc (predicting that remittances will continue to grow).

48. Most calculations of "remittances are based on the balance of payments statistics reported to the International Monetary Fund (IMF) by the central banks of the recipient countries." Deborah Waller Meyers, "Migrant Remittances to Latin America: Reviewing the Literature," *Sending Money Home* (2002): 53, 57. It bears noting that

many of these estimates are generally considered to understate the actual monetary value of remittances, and that the actual value may be 50 percent or more higher than the estimates. World Bank, *Global Economic Prospects 2006: Economic Implications of Remittances, and Migration* (Washington, D.C.: World Bank, 2006), 85. That is because each central bank uses a different formula to calculate remittances and "only a certain percentage of remittances flow through a country's official banking system." World Bank, *Global Economic Prospects 2006*, 85. There are numerous reasons that the central bank may not generate data on all remittances. First, many migrants deposit remittances directly in bank accounts in their home countries while they are living abroad. But, because they are similar to all other deposits, "[c]entral banks do not register these transfers as remittances even though immediate relatives are the main beneficiaries of those accounts." Orozco, *Worker Remittances in an International Scope*, 3. Second, "because remittances are private transfers" (Alexander O'Neill, "Note, Emigrant Remittances: Policies to Increase Inflows and Maximize Benefits," *Indiana Journal of Global Legal Studies* 9 (2001): 345, 351), some "remittances are not reported at all." Orozco, *Worker Remittances in an International Scope*, 1. For example, official estimates of remittances do not include payments made "outside the official banking system (legal and illegal)." Harris, *Thinking the Unthinkable*, 86. Transfers outside the formal banking system are common, for example, among migrants from the Middle East and the Indian subcontinent, who use informal "hawala" and "hundi" transactions to send remittances to members of their family through intermediaries who advance the money and receive a promise from the migrant to pay in the future. See Richard Black, "Soaring Remittances Raise New Issues," *Migration Information Source* (Washington, D.C.: Migration Policy Institute, June 1, 2003), at http://www.migrationinformation.org/Feature/display.cfm?ID=127. Other migrants send cash remittances to relatives by hand delivery through individuals who are traveling back to the migrants' home communities. Manuel Orozco, "From Family Ties to Transnational Linkages: The Impact of Family Remittances in Latin America," *Latin American Politics and Society* 44 (2002): 41, 54. Third, estimates of remittances do not include "payments made in the form of goods sent or carried by returning workers or through trade." Harris, *Thinking the Unthinkable*, 86.

   49. *Balance of Payment Statistics Yearbook, Part 2: World and Regional Tables*, International Monetary Fund (2001), 54 (statistics for the year 1999–2000). India is the "world's largest remittance recipient country." Orozco, *Worker Remittances in an International Scope*, 3.

   50. Millman, "Latin Americans Boost Home Coffers," A2. Remittances from abroad are now Mexico's second largest source of foreign revenue, behind only oil exports. See Inter-American Development Bank, Multilateral Investment Fund, *Sending Money Home* (2004), 11 (noting that, in 2003, remittances to Mexico "were more than the country's total tourism revenues, more than two-thirds of the value of petroleum exports, and 180% of the country's agricultural exports); Graham Gori, "A Card Allows U.S. Banks to Aid Mexican Immigrants," *New York Times*, July 6, 2002, at C3 (noting that, in 2002, remittances were third as a source of foreign revenue, behind oil exports and, just barely, tourism).

   51. Millman, "Latin Americans Boost Home Coffers," A2.

52. Millman, "Latin Americans Boost Home Coffers," A2.

53. Editorial, "When Cash Crosses Over," *L.A. Times*, May 21, 2005, B18 and accompanying box (providing remittance amounts for 2004 indicating increases in remittances of 20 per cent or more to Mexico, Colombia, and Brazil between 2002 and 2004).

54. MPI Staff, "Remittance Data," Migration Information Source (June 1, 2003), at http://www.migrationinformation.org/Feature/display.cfm?ID=137.

55. MPI Staff, "Remittance Data," Migration Information Source. Moreover, in 2003, remittances "account[ed] for at least 10% of gross domestic product (GDP) in . . . Haiti, Nicaragua, . . . Jamaica, the Dominican Republic, and Guyana." Inter-American Development Bank, Multilateral Investment Fund, *Sending Money Home* (2004), 11. Further, remittances through official channels to Bangladesh reached nearly $2 billion in 2001, becoming the country's second largest source of foreign revenue after garment exports. Somini Sengupta, "Money from Kin Abroad Helps Bengalis Get By," *New York Times*, June 24, 2002, A3. And in the Philippines, remittances, which amounted to $6 billion in 2001 or approximately 8.9 percent of GDP, constituted the second largest source of foreign revenue, just behind electronic exports. Jane Perlez, "Educated Filipinos, Disillusioned at Home, Look Abroad for a Better Life," *New York Times*, April 8, 2002, A13.

56. Lowell and de la Garza, "A New Phase in the Story of Remittances," 4. The U.S. government recognizes the impact of remittances on the economy of El Salvador and on occasion has adjusted its immigration policies to ensure that Salvadorans are able to work legally in the United States. See Editorial Desk, "Contributing to the Old Country," *New York Times*, June 1, 2001, A18 (explaining that the Bush administration allowed Salvadoran nationals to apply for eighteen-month work permits so that remittances could be sent home to help the country recover from devastating earthquakes).

57. U.S. Commission on Immigration Reform and Mexican Department of External Relations, "Binational Study on Migration between Mexico and the United States" (1997), 36, available at http://www.utexas.edu/lbj/uscir/binational.html.

58. Inter-American Development Bank, Multilateral Investment Fund, *Sending Money Home* (2004), 7; Susan Martin, at http://www.iadb.org/mif/v2/files%5Csusan-martin.doc.

59. Inter-American Development Bank, Multilateral Investment Fund, *Sending Money Home* (2004), 7. See World Bank, Development Prospects Group, Migration and Remittances Team, 2 (noting that "with increasing awareness of the size, magnitude and development impact of remittances, authorities in many . . . developing countries are now pro-actively trying to attract remittances").

60. U.S. Commission on Immigration Reform and Mexican Department of External Relations, 37, available at http://www.utexas.edu/lbj/uscir/binational.html.

61. Hermele, "The Discourse on Migration and Development," 139 (citation omitted). However, researchers in some countries have found that remittances are spent on "imported consumer goods, rather than locally produced ones, decreasing the potential multiplier effect of the money." Meyers, "Migrant Remittances to Latin America," 64.

62. Press Release, Inter-American Development Bank, "Emigrants from Latin America Hailed as Major Force for Economic and Social Development," May 18,

2001, available at http://www.iadb.org/NEWS/DISPLAY/PRView.cfm?PR_Num=84/01&Language=English (citing Susan Martin).

63. Meyers, "Migrant Remittances to Latin America," 63.

64. Manuel Orozco, "Remittances, the Rural Sector, and Policy Options in Latin America," *Migration Information Source* (Washington, D.C.: Migration Policy Institute, June 1, 2003), at http://www.migrationinformation.org/Feature/display.cfm?ID=128.

65. Manuel Orozco, "Remittances, the Rural Sector, and Policy Options in Latin America."

66. Harris, *Thinking the Unthinkable*, 89 (internal quotation marks omitted).

67. Manuel Orozco, "Remittances, the Rural Sector, and Policy Options in Latin America," at http://www.migrationinformation.org/Feature/display.cfm?ID=128.

68. Meyers, "Migrant Remittances to Latin America," 63. Indeed, "[r]emittances are the largest source of external financing in many developing countries"; additionally, remittances are "less volatile than other sources of foreign exchange earnings." World Bank, Development Prospects Group, Migration and Remittances Team, 1.

Chapter Fourteen

Technology Development and Transfer

This chapter discusses particular ways in which STEP OUT migrants can contribute to sending countries through the development of new technologies. First, however, we think it will prove productive to examine briefly the theoretical basis for *heightened* immigrant creativity. Doing so will add weight to the particular examples that follow, by placing them in the context of a broader phenomenon caused by circumstances that reasonably can be expected to occur over and over and over again.

What accounts for the creativity and inventiveness of immigrants? A noncontroversial answer might be a certain level of training and intelligence placed in an environment conducive to invention; in other words, exactly the same elements that account for the inventiveness of the native born. These facts alone might be enough to justify a characterization of STEP OUT migration as a benevolent phenomenon, for a certain number of inventions attributable to STEP OUT migrants that redound to the benefit of the home country almost certainly would not have been created in the home environment—due to a failure of technological resources, or a failure of high-level collaborators, or both.

On top of this argument, however, may be added a profound truth that explains why immigrants, as a group, are in some respects likely to be objectively *more* creative than the native born. Creativity and inventiveness demand the ability to see what others cannot: "the essence of invention consists of an act . . . by which . . . elements are wrenched out of their accepted frameworks and put together in new combinations."[1] Consider that point in connection with the following insight by Henry David Thoreau:

A man receives only what he is ready to receive, whether physically or intellectually or morally. . . . We hear and we apprehend only what we already half

155

know. Every man thus *tracks himself* through life, in all his hearing and reading and observation and travelling. His observations make a chain. The phenomenon or fact that cannot in any wise be linked with the rest, which he has observed, he does not observe.[2]

The implication of this, for our purposes, is that immigrants, having trodden down different paths for portions of their lives, may be able to make links between phenomena that others cannot and, to that extent, will be able to observe (and therefore be creative about) what others, having a different background, simply cannot see. The further implication of this insight is that STEP OUT migration's cost-benefit calculation again must be adjusted in favor of the phenomenon's benefits. Indeed, not only is the benefit side of the ledger augmented by the heightened creativity of the STEP OUT migrant—which creativity will, as shown below, bring benefits to his home nation and the world—but also the cost is less than would otherwise be expected because the "immigrant" who never migrates loses the comparative creativity advantage the novelty of his insights would otherwise provide, even if everything else remained the same.

A recent article by University of Chicago sociologist Robert S. Burt on the social origins of good ideas fleshes out the particular creativity advantages held by "[p]eople familiar with activities in two groups." First, such people "are more able than people confined within either group to see how a belief or practice in one group could create value in the other." Second, they "make people on both sides . . . aware of interests and difficulties in the other group." And third, "people familiar with activities in two groups are more likely to see new beliefs or behaviors that combine elements from both groups."[3] Professor Burt concludes that

> [such people] are critical to learning and creativity. People whose networks span [several groups] have early access to diverse, often contradictory, ideas. People connected to groups beyond their own can expect to find themselves delivering valuable ideas, seeming to be gifted with creativity. This is not creativity born of deep intellectual ability. It is creativity as an import-export business. An idea mundane in one group can be a valuable insight in another.[4]

Professor Burt found this conclusion buttressed by study of American business. In terms of immigrants, one might look for additional confirmation in a big-picture view of history, which time and time again has shown that powerful nations who exclude the insights of outsiders—China, Japan, Spain, Portugal, North Korea, and much of the Arab world, for instance—simultaneously sow the seeds of previously unimaginable decline.[5] Conversely, the influential work of the late economist Mancur Olson highlights, among many other things, the constructive role immigrants can play in helping to avoid the institutionalized sclerosis identified by Olson as a major cause of national decline.[6] Additional lessons writ in the hand of broad historical events might be found in the study of military organizations across the centuries. These organizations are famous for "always fighting the last war," an overstatement, to be sure, but one that contains more than a kernel of truth. And this should surprise no one. For the reasons suggested by Professor Burt, optimal creativity may require substantial disclosure to outsiders, but no organization has a better reason for keeping outsiders away than a military force whose success may well depend on maintaining order in its ranks and keeping secret its capability and planned operations.[7] The dilemma the military by necessity finds itself on the horns of, however, is not one that most other parts of society should, in general, volunteer to face. To the extent they do, they too will too often find themselves fighting the last war.

THE PRICE OF ISOLATION

In his book, *The Wealth and Poverty of Nations*, Harvard University Professor David S. Landes notes a theme repeated throughout history: the temptation for powerful nations to preserve their power by isolating their societies from other peoples. As Landes demonstrates, acting on that temptation is self-defeating behavior of the most consequential kind. Historical examples are numerous and compelling. Thus, before China's decline from the most technologically advanced nation on earth, and related to that decline, the Ming rulers of the Celestial Empire not only prevented the travel of their own subjects to other lands, but also "quarantin[ed]" visitors "like an infection," confining them "to some peripheral point like Macao"—all this as part of a larger policy of "rejection of the foreign," including "imported knowledge and ideas." Similarly, Japan also engaged, to its detriment, in "a deliberate exclusion of foreign things and knowledge," including a ban on foreign travel and the confinement of foreign traders to isolated areas. The Arab world also exacerbated its own decline through its rejection of foreign ideas and innovations, including, most disastrously, the printing press. In the West, Spain and Portugal suffered the same fate, for the same general reason:

> In the centuries before the Reformation, southern Europe was a center of learning and intellectual inquiry . . . because [it was] on the frontier of Christian and Islamic civilization and had the benefit of Jewish intermediaries . . . .. Spain and Portugal lost out early, because religious passion and military crusade drove away the outsiders (Jews and then the conversos) and discouraged the pursuit of the strange and potentially heretical. . . .

(continued)

In the era of Inquisition, the expulsion of Jews may be the most prominent example of Spain's determination to free itself of the influences of outsiders, but many other examples might be cited as well, ranging from the introduction of the death penalty for importing foreign books without permission and the introduction of the same penalty for unlicensed printing, to a drastic reduction in the number of Spaniards allowed to study abroad. Portugal followed a similar policy of closure and censure, with similar results. Finally, in the paradigmatic modern case of North Korea, the completeness of the Hermit Kingdom's isolation is matched only by the dreadfulness of its economic performance.

Source: David S. Landes, *The Wealth and Poverty of Nations: Why Some Are So Rich and Some So Poor* 96, 133-36, 179-80, 336-37, 351, 356, 358, 401-02, 410 (1998).

The remainder of this chapter illustrates how the creative force that, in its presence and absence, has so clearly shown its influence on large-scale historical events also can be seen operating today at the level of technology development. Detailed below are stories of success on many fronts, with the twin focus on the many benefits inventions and discoveries made in receiving countries can bring to sending countries, and the contributions of STEP OUT migrants to those inventions and discoveries.

TECHNOLOGY OPTIMIZATION

STEP OUT migrants contribute to their native communities through pursuing and realizing discoveries that can be of particular benefit to sending countries. It is a fair assumption to grant STEP OUT migrants a special desire to make such discoveries—indeed, "as India's high-tech dynamos," including its STEP OUT migrants, "turn more attention to the needs of the nation's countless poor," this desire has found expression to such an extent that, one analyst has proffered, "'India could lead the world in . . . teach[ing] . . . how to use technology for the common good.'"[8] To this desire, STEP OUT migrants add a uniquely deep knowledge of their culture, with all its attendant problems and strengths. As a result, migrants from developing countries are in a position to influence research and development agendas in the receiving countries so as to encourage the creation of products and services that may be uniquely or atypically useful to individuals in their home countries. Moreover, absent interactions between STEP OUT migrants and scientists in developed countries, such scientists may not comprehend how their work can or would be used in other countries and by other cultures.

The work of STEP OUT migrant Dr. Keerti Rathore, an Indian-born scientist, illustrates many of the possibilities.[9] Dr. Rathore is the leader of a research team at Texas A&M University. Dr. Rathore's research has focused on goals uniquely important to his home community and similar developing countries, namely, the improvement of vital crops, such as cotton, soybeans, and rice, by enhancing their nutritional quality and disease, drought and insect resistance. Most recently, Dr. Rathore has used the advanced resources and techniques available in the United States to genetically modify cottonseeds to make them safely edible for humans. The techniques pioneered by Dr. Rathore to make the usually toxic cottonseed fit for human consumption holds great promise for relieving hunger and malnutrition in the developing world, both directly and indirectly, through the application of Dr. Rathore's methods to other potential food sources.[10] Other STEP OUT migrants, such as Dr. Maurice Iwu, a Nigerian who worked at the Walter Reed Army Institute of Research in Washington, D.C., have used leads from traditional medicine to conduct research to help their home countries that no scientist from the developed world is likely to do and no developing world scientist likely could ever do except by migrating to a technologically developed nation.[11]

Dr. Iwu also contributes to development through international knowledge transfers. In this case, he has helped transfer knowledge and ideas about, among other things, traditional African healing remedies and approaches. Between the United States and Nigeria, and across the globe, he has accomplished this through various positions, including a term as president of the International Society of Ethnobiology and frequent consulting assignments "on technology management and establishment of strategic alliances and multinational cooperative R&D projects for international agencies . . . and national agencies in Africa, Asia, and South America."[12]

Similarly, Dr. Florence Wambugu's work on sustainable agriculture offers another striking example of how research by STEP OUT migrants abroad benefits their home communities. Dr. Wambugu, a STEP OUT migrant from Kenya, studied at the University of Nairobi before pursuing a Ph.D. at the University of Bath in England.[13] Then, the "U.S. Department of Agriculture offered her a grant to study transgenetics in St. Louis in collaboration with Washington University and Monsanto," at the time primarily a U.S.–based drug company.[14] For more than seven years Dr. Wambugu worked to create and test a genetically modified sweet potato that would resist infestation by worms common to the fields of sub-Saharan Africa.

"On a continent where population growth outstrips food supply growth by 1% a year, Wambugu's modified sweet potato offers tangible hope" for those suffering poverty, hunger, and malnutrition.[15] The sweet potato is a staple crop for farmers in Africa. According to Dr. Wambugu, "The sweet potato is a woman's crop, a security crop."[16] And Dr. Wambugu's version yields more than double the crop of the normal sweet potato plant, and the "[p]otatoes are bigger and richer in color, indicating they've retained more nutritional value."[17] Since creating the African sweet potato, Dr. Wambugu has returned to Africa where she remains active in efforts to ensure sustainable agriculture development.[18] Moreover, Dr. Wambugu also is active in spreading her knowledge throughout the world, especially in Africa and developing countries.[19]

The ultimate fruits of efforts like those of Drs. Rathore, Iwu and Wambugu are beyond anyone's imagination. And that is exactly the point and exactly the reason why such efforts, and the STEP OUT migration that propels them, is crucial. Citizens of the developed world certainly are not aware of all of the needs of developing countries. Scientists from a developing country, for example, may develop a vaccine for a disease prominent in a developed country and consider their work complete, without fully realizing that developing countries may have problems delivering those vaccines to the people who most need them. Indeed, because of this relative ignorance, the developed world's scientists might not even try to develop a universally effective delivery system. In such cases, it may take someone familiar with the problems of developing countries, through upbringing or travel, to extend the research in ways that are most useful to poorer communities—who is most likely, to take one actual example, to tackle the difficult job of solving the vaccine delivery problem by developing edible vaccines that can be incorporated into vegetables and fruits?[20] These types of edible vaccines are designed principally for citizens of the developing world who do not have ready access to refrigeration, and as a result cannot store or readily transport vaccines. The problem is tremendous: "UNICEF estimates that 30 million infants go without basic immunizations every year. Three million die from preventable diseases."[21] The development of vaccines that do not need to be refrigerated or injected will remedy a tragic situation.

The development of this kind of vaccine would be most beneficial, or perhaps exclusively beneficial, to people in the developing world. Yet, it is a concern that may not have been researched in the developed world but for the influence of scientists familiar with the unique problems of refrigeration, transportation, and cost facing some developing countries.[22]

The ultimate goal, of course, which would multiply by orders of magnitude achievements like those of Drs. Rathore, Iwu and Wambugu, is for developing countries themselves to establish in greater numbers domestic industries able to harness the powers of modern technology in order to solve domestic problems. It is technological development applied to everyday human needs that is responsible for all or almost all the long-term economic growth that has lifted some societies above the level of widespread subsistence living.[23] And it is a relatively rare thing that a society organizes itself in a way that encourages the development of such technological progress.[24] In India, for example, an ancient civilization and a well-established democracy, the "License Raj" of the government until relatively recently *actively discouraged* such progress, unless it took place within certain narrow, pre-approved channels[25]—which is but a minor qualification given that technological progress is an unwieldy, unpredictable thing that at its most innovative creates entirely new channels.

Ironically, STEP OUT migrants—for so long criticized as effectively precluding the development of domestic industries attentive to domestic needs—in fact may prove to be catalysts for exactly such development. To return to the example of India, now that the Indian government has loosened the stranglehold the "License Raj" placed on Indian business,[26] it can hardly be considered a coincidence that India's most promising businesses are emerging in the fields most commonly entered by STEP OUT migrants, that is, high technology and pharmaceuticals. Even more propitiously, these companies are becoming increasingly attentive to the particular needs of India as a developing country, and to developing technologies particularly suited to satisfying those needs.

Thus, for example, Indian researchers are making strides toward using new technologies to provide affordable access to the Internet, video on demand, and interactive media to large (and largely poor) segments of the Indian population.[27] Providing a vivid example is the work of Midas Communications Technologies (Midas), a technology company in Madras, India, whose ranks are filled with former STEP OUT migrants who have returned to India after studying and working abroad.[28] Recognizing that many existing telecommunications technologies were not designed to reach most Indians, the founders of Midas were intent on developing telecommunications products for the Indian market.[29]

In collaboration with a U.S.–based partner, Midas has created "a low-cost Internet access system" that can be used to reach low-income populations in India who do not have access to the costly landline telephone or cable lines that at best reach only 2 to 3 percent of the Indian population.[30] The system "needs no modem and eliminates expensive copper [telephone] lines" so that Indians who do not have telephone access can nevertheless access the Internet.[31] The technology has made Internet access affordable and available to low-income communities throughout India[32] and other developing countries, from "Fiji and Yemen to Nigeria and Tunisia."[33] Similarly, Praveen Bhagwat, a former STEP OUT migrant who worked at IBM and Bell Labs, developed upon his return to India a substantially improved wireless standard for rural use.[34]

Research of the type of these examples will open—indeed, already has opened—many avenues of development to the populations that benefit, and thus will enhance and extend future economic growth in the same way that other discoveries can enhance and extend life itself.[35] Similarly, pharmaceutical development in India has focused on the peculiarities of the Indian market, in which cost represents the steepest barrier to pharmaceuticals access, and thus a generic drug industry has sprouted and flourished, particularly in Hyderabad, India, as a way to overcome this domestic barrier.[36]

Developments like these represent technological optimization of a very important sort, because they create deep and broadly based connections to large portions of the developing country's domestic economy. By penetrating more deeply into that economy, these developments are more likely to raise the standard of living throughout the country. Islands of development in poor countries, like Bangalore, for instance, which initially produce products destined mainly for developed nations, are a necessary first step, but the ultimate goal is to create a sea of development, in which places like Bangalore are at the center, different in degree but no longer in kind. While STEP OUT migrants have been demonstrably crucial in forming Bangalore's economic connections to the developed world—as STEP OUT migrants from other nations have elsewhere done—the latter stage of development, connecting industrial centers to the rest of a developing nation, is of even greater long-term importance. As we have seen, STEP OUT migrants play a major role here as well.

Moreover, the logic of technological development in poor countries does not end with the emergence of technological centers directed toward satisfying needs of the domestic market. Rather, as these centers develop, they inevitably will progress toward satisfying—as leaders, not followers—needs of the entire world. Indeed, tangible signs of this happening already have occurred.

For instance, the Indian generic drug industry has laid the groundwork for what is now becoming a biotechnology hub focused on creating new and original cures. Hyderabad, the location of this nascent hub, has the "largest mass of scientific talent in India . . . [including] 40 laboratories, research centers and universities."[37] Moreover, although it is still in the early stages of development, the computer and communications technology being developed in Bangalore clearly has the potential to find a worldwide audience as well, even in the developed countries. By some measures, for example, the technology of Midas, the telecommunications company, makes available Internet access speeds that exceed those of many technologies currently in use in the *developed* world.[38]

Thus, in the future, the cures and technologies developed in India may prove—in fact, are almost certain to prove—to be of benefit to the entire world. In truth, Indian nationals have been making such contributions for years; the difference in the future will be that these worldwide benefits will more often emerge more directly from the Indian nation as well as from its people. And, of course, this is likely to be true of other nations and other peoples as well. Indeed, Singapore, South Korea, Taiwan, and China all are currently trying to establish biotechnology centers of their own.[39]

Not surprisingly, the contributions of STEP OUT migrants to this process are substantial. In Hyderabad, for example, STEP OUT migrants interested in biotechnology and the life sciences "are returning with funds, ideas and entrepreneurship."[40] In fact, according to the head of the panel advising the Indian government on biotechnology, the "network of non-resident Indians is absolutely essential [to development of this new industry]. Otherwise this whole thing would be much slower."[41] Other nations seeking to develop biotechnology centers similarly recognize the crucial role of STEP OUT migrants in generating research ideas, securing funding, and utilizing entrepreneurial skills, as they too have tried to "attract expatriate scientists back from the U.S., where they were trained."[42]

When this process has fully evolved, we will have come full circle, starting from the initial, discrete employments of STEP OUT migrants in developed countries, and progressing to the development of industrial centers like Bangalore—serving at first mainly the technology needs of developed countries, and then serving the needs of the homeland, and then finally serving the needs of the entire world in competition with the current industrialized world. Presently, however, we are somewhere in the middle of this process, and so STEP OUT migrants still are more likely to make cutting-edge contributions to world development while residing away from their homelands. In evaluating the benefits of STEP OUT migration, this fact of world development by emigrants thus is still of considerable importance; accordingly, it will be explored in some detail in the remainder of this chapter.

WORLD DEVELOPMENT

In addition to research focused on issues that primarily impact the developing world, technological developments of more general applicability are also being made by STEP OUT migrants. This latter group of developments directly benefits the entire world in areas ranging from medicine to communications to agriculture. The two biggest developments of the last several decades—the explosive growth of the Internet and the advent of biotechnology together with mapping of the human genome—are prominent among such developments.

No one can dispute that STEP OUT migrants have played a tremendous role in developing Internet and biotechnology breakthroughs. With respect to development of the Internet and modern telecommunications technologies, in Silicon Valley alone, the hub of high technology in the United States, reports show that in 1999 almost 24 percent of Silicon Valley firms were led by Chinese and Indian immigrants, many of whom are STEP OUT migrants;[43] that Indian and Chinese entrepreneurs were responsible for 29 percent of Silicon Valley's new technology businesses;[44] and that "foreign-owned firms accounted for 14 percent of the region's total employment."[45] The involvement of STEP OUT migrants in biotechnology and the mapping of the human genome also is clear. Several of the scientists working on the Human Genome Project for the National Institutes of Health are STEP OUT migrants.[46] And, as the discussion in the prior section indicates, STEP OUT migrants are elsewhere prominent in biotechnology; that is why so many developing countries seeking to establish biotechnology hubs are so earnestly recruiting their former residents.[47] Indeed, even small biotechnology companies in the United States can employ immigrants from more than twenty countries.[48]

Although no one can dispute the contributions of STEP OUT migrants to these landmark technological developments, some might argue that the benefits of the developments are likely to favor disproportionately the developed world, and thus do not represent world development so much as *developed world development*. In truth, Internet penetration *is* many times higher in richer countries than it is in less developed countries, and the cures resulting from biotechnology and genomics in most cases *will* be more available in the developed world.

However, countervailing facts make the world development paradigm an appropriate one. For example, while it is true that the Internet has significantly more penetration in developed countries, it also is true that the comparative change brought about through Internet access in developing countries is more substantial than in developed countries. In the developed world, the Internet makes communications faster, cheaper, and more convenient, but even before the Internet, individuals in developed countries had access to information, libraries, and communications systems.

In the developing world, however, the changes are more dramatic. There, the Internet introduced changes *in kind*, which "break barriers to human development" that previously limited knowledge, participation, and economic opportunity.[49] Indeed, this latest technological revolution offers, "[f]or the first time in history," an "opportunity for bridging the gap between the haves and the have-nots."[50] Before the Internet was introduced, many developing world communities did not have access to extensive knowledge or information. In some countries this was due to the fact that information was controlled by the government, while in other countries individuals did not have access to libraries or library resources were limited.[51] The Internet makes information available on a much larger scale than ever before, even given continuing efforts to control its use. Poor communities have also long been disenfranchised from the political process because of isolation and "lack of means to take collective action"; the Internet and modern telecommunications can help to overcome this barrier.[52] And from the perspective of economic opportunity, the technology and communications industries offer developing countries the opportunity for economic growth by "expand[ing] exports, creat[ing] good jobs and diversify[ing] their economies."[53]

Moreover, while breaking these barriers will require more widespread access to communications technologies by poor communities,[54] many efforts are currently underway to provide just that. Thus, although the Internet, in general, has not yet penetrated deeply into developing countries and remains unavailable to many communities, *at an increasing rate* efforts, like those by Midas discussed earlier in this chapter, are being made to expand access to those who historically have not had access to modern telecommunications technologies.[55] Once access to these new technologies is made available and individuals are educated about how to use them,[56] these technological breakthroughs will be especially meaningful to developing countries because the Internet and modern telecommunications technologies offer striking changes in the kind of communications and information systems available in those countries, which in turn will break barriers to knowledge, participation, and economic opportunity for the poor.[57]

Similarly, mapping of the human genome promises to alter the way medical science and biotechnology develop over the coming years in ways very favorable to developing countries. Indeed, the possibilities of "[d]esigning new drugs and treatments based on genomics and related technologies offer potential for tackling the major health challenges facing poor countries and people—possibly leading, for example, to vaccines for malaria and HIV/AIDS."[58] Moreover, one great discovery of human genome research has already provided great benefit to people from developing countries, disproportionately so, in fact. Analysis of the genome has essentially provided biological refutations of the various notions of racism that are found in the world.[59] This conclusion is particularly beneficial to communities who are more likely to be targets of racist views, which communities are often found in developing countries.

In addition to medical breakthroughs, the possibilities for advances in agriculture through the use of biotechnology are substantial. For example, as noted previously in the discussion of Dr. Wambugu's efforts, "[g]enomics can speed up plant breeding and drive the development of new crop varieties with greater drought and disease resistance, less environmental stress and more nutritional value."[60] Indeed, according to the United Nations Development Programme, "biotechnology offers the only or the best 'tool of choice' for marginal ecological zones—left behind by the green revolution but home to more than half of the world's poorest people, dependent on agriculture and livestock."[61]

Discoveries by STEP OUT migrants in other areas also positively impact world development. The work of STEP OUT migrant Alexander Gorlov, a Russian emigrant, provides an example.[62] Mr. Gorlov invented a turbine that uses "the power of moving water to generate electricity."[63] The turbine has produced electricity at reduced costs for towns from Maine to South Korea, including villages along the Amazon River, all with little harm to the environment.

Mr. Gorlov is just one of the many STEP OUT migrants whose work has improved living conditions of individuals worldwide. For example, a recent study shows that about twenty percent of all patents granted in the United States were granted to immigrants.[64] Immigrants are also prevalent among Nobel Prize winners. In the post-war period "50 percent of the Nobel Prizes in physics won by the United States went to naturalized" citizens of the United States[65] and almost half of the U.S.–based recipients of the Nobel Prize in the year 2000 were immigrant scientists to the United States.[66] When these and other scientists doing research in physics, chemistry, biology, or economics make key discoveries of great value to a society it does not matter where they are living. As the United Nations Development Programme recognizes, "such advances have a global reach: a breakthrough in one country can be used around the world."[67]

Finally, two more points favor the concept of world development. First, because STEP OUT migrants working in the United States and other developed countries often have equipment and financial support not available in their home countries, the likelihood is greater that such discoveries will be made by STEP OUT migrants in receiving countries.[68] This is especially true given that many migrants come from countries that, in one way or another, stifle human creativity.[69] Second, such developments are especially useful today, when modern communications technologies make it much more likely that people in developing countries will learn of discoveries that could make huge differences in their lives.[70] It thus remains generally true that great scientific discoveries do have worldwide benefit, and that, as was said almost forty years ago, "if an Indian scientist discovers the cure for cancer at Berkeley, his countrymen are certain to benefit as much as if he had discovered it in Bombay."[71]

* * *

In sum, until recently, it was customary among migration commentators "to underline the negative impact of migration on emigration countries."[72] As a result, many of the benefits that sending countries derive from STEP OUT migration were overlooked and underappreciated, particularly by critics of the phenomenon. An underappreciation of these benefits, especially among migration researchers, contributed to the negative view of the phenomenon that was prevalent when the Catholic Church developed its policy disfavoring STEP OUT migration. However, as the "brain drain" phenomenon regains prominence, many have begun to properly value the developmental benefits—large and small—that result from STEP OUT migration.[73] Chapters 11, 12, 13, and 14 have surveyed some of those benefits.

NOTES

1. Martin van Creveld, *Technology and War: From 2000 B.C. to the Present* (New York: the Free Press, 1989), 219.

2. Robert D. Richardson, Jr., "Introduction: Thoreau's Broken Task," in Henry David Thoreau, *Faith in a Seed*, ed. Bradley P. Dean (1993), 12 (quoting Thoreau's journal; underscoring in original journal). Thoreau thought enough of this insight to end his most famous work, Walden, with another version of it: "Only that day dawns to which we are awake. There is more day to dawn. The sun is but a morning star." Henry David Thoreau, *Walden*, in *Walden and Other Writings by Henry David Thoreau*, ed. Joseph Wood Krutch (New York: Bantam Books, 1962), 351. The Zen aphorism, "When the student is ready, the teacher will appear," rests on the same understanding.

3. Robert S. Burt, "Structural Holes and Good Ideas," *American Journal of Sociology* 110 (2004): 349, 355.

4. Burt, "Structural Holes and Good Ideas," 355. See also Gnanaraj Chellaraj, Keith E. Maskus & Aaditya Mattoo, The Contribution of Skilled Immigration and International Graduate Students to U.S. Innovation, World Bank Policy Research Working Paper 3588, at 3, 4, 24 (May 2005), available at http://search.ssrn.com/5013/papers.cfm?abstract_id=744625 (concluding that the "immigration of skilled workers has a strong and positive impact on the development of ideas in the United States," the authors suggest that the impact is due in significant part to the fact that the skills of such workers are "complementary to local skills, rather than substitutes for them").

5. See, e.g., David S. Landes, *The Wealth and Poverty of Nations: Why Some Are So Rich and Some So Poor* (New York: W. W. Norton & Company, 1998), 96, 133–36, 179–80, 336–37, 351, 356, 358, 401–2, 410.

6. See Mancur Olson, *The Rise and Decline of Nations: Economic Growth, Stagflation, and Social Rigidities* (New Haven: Yale University Press, 1982), 130, 135 (noting that immigration helps to prevent the establishment of, or ameliorate the effect of, entrenched inefficiencies which otherwise might cause substantial societal damage).

7. See van Creveld, *Technology and War*, 220 (noting reasons that "military organizations have tended to be even less flexible than most large bureaucratic structures").

8. Manjeet Kripalani, "The Digital Village," *Business Week Online*, June 28, 2004, available at http://www.businessweek.com:/print/magazine/content/04_26/b3889003. htm?mz (quoting Professor Kenneth Keniston, of the Massachusetts Institute of Technology).

9. See Subhra Priyadarshini, "Dining Out? Try Cottonseeds," The Telegraph (India), Dec. 4, 2006, at http://www.telegraphindia.com/1061204/asp/others/print.html; "Gene Tweak Makes Cottonseed Edible," Nov. 20, 2006, at http://health.yahoo.com/ news/169042.

10. Priyadarshini, "Dining Out? Try Cottonseeds," at http://www.telegraphindia. com/1061204/asp/others/print.html. See Biographical Information for Keerti S. Rathore, at http://ipgb.tamu.edu/bios/keerti_rathore.html.

11. "Ancient Plant Could Cure Modern Ailments," *Diversity*, Vol. 15., No. 2 (1999): 3; "Scientists Say W. African Plant May Be Ebola Cure," Reuters Limited, August 4, 1999. See "Success Story: Maurice Iwu," *Partners of the Heart: A Viewer's Guide*, 38, at http://www.pbs.org/wgbh/amex/partners/today/partners_guide.pdf. Professor Iwu was born into a family of traditional healers and applied his unique cultural understandings and background to his work in pharmacology. Id. Indeed, he was led to the plant that his research indicated could be used to cure the deadly Ebola virus by traditional healers. See "Scientists Say W. African Plant May Be Ebola Cure."

12. See "Success Story" at http://www.pbs.org/wgbh/amex/partners/today/partners_guide.pdf.

13. Lynn J. Cook, "Millions Served," *Forbes*, December 23, 2002, 302.

14. Cook, "Millions Served," 304.

15. Cook, "Millions Served," 304.

16. Cook, "Millions Served," 302.

17. Cook, "Millions Served," 302.

18. Cook, "Millions Served," 304. Dr. Wambugu currently resides in Nairobi, Kenya. She recently facilitated the "successful transfer of tissue culture from South Africa to smallholder farmers in Kenya and Tanzania, for which she won the World Bank Global Development Network Award." See http://www.ahbfi.org/florence.htm.

19. Dr. Wambugu founded and directs a not-for-profit organization through which she educates Africans and their governments about sustainable agricultural development and its positive impact on development of the African continent. The organization is called Africa Harvest Biotech Foundation International (AHBFI). See http://www.ahbfi.org/index.htm.

20. Ron Wheery, "Planting Hope," *Fortune*, January 20, 2003, 109, 111.

21. Ron Wheery, "Planting Hope," 111.

22. The first plant biologist to work on the project, Charles Arntzen, became aware of the problem while traveling in Thailand and seeing a mother feed her child a banana. As he watched, he thought: "Wouldn't it be great if that banana could shield the child from disease?" Ron Wheery, "Planting Hope." One of Dr. Arntzen's colleagues, STEP migrant Dr. Yasmin Thanavala, recently successfully concluded a test of a "potato vaccine" against hepatitis B, a disease that kills approximately one million people each year.

23. William Easterly, *The Elusive Quest for Growth: Economists' Adventures and Misadventures in the Tropics* (Cambridge: MIT Press, 2001), 51–53 ("In the

long run, all growth of production per worker has to be labor-saving technical change").

24. James S. Shikwati, "Invisible Wealth," *Tech Central Station*, March 4, 2004, at http://www.techcentralstation.com/030404B.html (noting that, rather than encourage technological progess, "[m]ost Third World countries" focus on "visible wealth" (such as land and natural resources) and "tribal organization," focuses which, "instead of fostering wealth, promote war over resources").

25. Gurcharan Das, *India Unbound* (New York: Alfred A. Knopf, 2001), 93–95, 169–71, 196–200, 226 (describing how India's notoriously anti-market "License Raj" destroyed incentives for innovation and growth). The legal foundation for the License Raj was "the Industries (Development and Regulation) Act of 1951, which required an entrepreneur to get a license to set up a new unit, to expand it, or to change the product mix." Das, *India Unbound*, 93. India's licensing regime "result[ed] in enormous delays, sometimes lasting years, with staggering opportunities for corruption," and thus "discouraged the entry of efficient and honest entrants." Das, *India Unbound*, 94–95. Bureaucrats would make decisions as basic as "the choice of technology" to be used by companies. Das, *India Unbound*, 95. In 1969, this "unmitigated disaster" of a system was made even worse by the passage of "the Monopolies and Restrictive Trade Practice (MRTP) Act . . . which crippled private industry for a generation." Das, *India Unbound*, 95, 168. The MRTP effectively barred any business group with assets over $26.7 million from expanding its business, and placed companies with as little as $1.3 million in assets under "antimonopolistic supervision and control." Das, *India Unbound*, 169–70. Other laws completely barred large and medium sized companies from entering over 800 industries, thus removing most of "the incentive [for small firms] to improve their products, update production techniques, reduce costs, and introduce new technology or new designs." Das, *India Unbound*, 171. In sum, until the reforms of 1991 (Das, *India Unbound*, 200, 213–21), India's "Kafkaesque bureaucratic controls" (Das, *India Unbound*, x), discouraged innovation by both new and established businesses by restricting the fields they could enter (see Das, *India Unbound*, 93–95, 168–70 (describing various laws)); discouraged innovation by established businesses by restricting output (Das, *India Unbound*, 94, 175 (noting that because "[i]t was an offense punishable under the law to manufacture beyond the capacity granted by [a] license," a producer of needed medical products would fear exceeding authorized limits even during an epidemic)); and in general diverted enormous entrepreneurial energies away from innovation and growth, and toward development of the ability to jump through onerous bureaucratic hoops, see Das, *India Unbound*, 94, 115–17 (noting manipulation of the license application process and extensive efforts to escape price controls by reclassifying modern drugs as ancient Ayurvedic cures). See also Jagdish Bhagwati, "A Machine for Going Backwards," *A Stream of Windows* (Cambridge: MIT Press, 1998): 507, 510 (stating that the Indian bureaucracy "killed off the possibility of entrepreneurial efficiency and innovation and produced irresistible incentives for . . . corruption"). But see Vijay Dandapani, "The Consumer as Sovereign," *Tech Central Station*, March 11, 2004, at http://www.techcentralstation.com/031104A.html (providing evidence that the "License Raj" has been loosened but not yet removed, the author notes that India

still "reserve[s] over 675 items for exclusive manufacture in the small scale sector," including pickles, chutney, cricket balls, and pencils).

26. See Das, *India Unbound*, 200, 213–21, 264 (describing the Indian economic reforms of the early 1990's, which inter alia, reintroduced the right "to expand existing businesses or start new ones without government approval"). But see Dandapani, "The Consumer as Sovereign," at http://www.techcentralstation.com/031104A.html (noting that many restrictive entry requirements and price controls remain in India).

27. AnnaLee Saxenian, "The Bangalore Boom: From Brain Drain to Brain Circulation," *IT Experience in India: Bridging the Digital Divide*, eds. Kenneth Keniston and Deepak Kumar (New Delhi: Sage Publications, 2004): 169, 180.

28. United Nations Development Programme, "Human Development Report 2001: Making New Technologies Work for Human Development," 98 (2001) [hereinafter UNDP, "Making New Technologies Work"]. See also Midas Communications Technologies website, at http://www.midascomm.com.

29. Midas Communications Technologies website, at http://www.midascomm.com.

30. UNDP, "Making New Technologies Work," at 98.

31. UNDP, "Making New Technologies Work," at 98. The wireless technology is also useful in remote areas where the installation of landline wires is prohibitively costly or impossible. For example, the technology is being used in Kuppam, a remote town in India in which the surrounding rocky terrain has prevented the national telephone company from installing sufficient landline wires, to "hook up a local school, a public call center and a handful of government offices." S. Srinivansan, "'Box' May Propel Communications in Developing Countries," Associated Press, October 29, 2001.

32. The cost of Internet access using Midas technology is "about a third of the cost of a traditional copper-wire landline connection." Srinivansan, "'Box' May Propel Communications in Developing Countries."

33. UNDP, "Making New Technologies Work," at 98.

34. Kripalani, "The Digital Village," available at http://www.businessweek.com:/print/magazine/content/04_26/b3889003.htm?mz

35. For example, the MS Swaminathan Research Foundation has begun to provide Internet access using solar power to individuals from "assetless households." See UNDP, "Making New Technologies Work," at 33. This provision of Internet access has resulted in a marked increase in the productivity of the rural poor and their participation in the domestic and international community. Using the technology, rural farmers can check market prices before negotiating with intermediaries, and fishermen can "download satellite images that indicate where fish shoals are. Internet connections with other villages have encouraged local dialogue on farming techniques, microcredit management, business and education opportunities, traditional medicine and religious events." See UNDP, "Making New Technologies Work," 32–33; see also Amy Waldman, "Internet Transforms Farming in India," *International Herald Tribune*, January 2, 2004, 2 (noting that by bringing the Internet to Indian farmers through the use of satellites and solar panels, an Indian company has provided the means for farmers to increase their productivity and improve their market knowledge).

36. Geoff Dyer and Khozem Merchant, "The Birth of a Biotech Cluster: Hyderabad Is Witnessing a Gathering of the Elements to Create a Life Sciences Hotspot to

Match Its IT Industry," *Financial Times*, August 14, 2003, 10. The generic drug industry in India began to flourish in the 1990s, after the reforms of 1991, and now boasts numerous successful companies. Das, *India Unbound*, 258. One of the leading companies is Shantha Biotechnics, which is located in Hyderabad. "In the 1990s, Shantha launched a Hepatitis B vaccine, the first drug made in India involving the manipulation of genes [and] it was a huge success, slashing the retail cost of a drug only available previously from abroad." Dyer and Merchant, "The Birth of a Biotech Cluster," 10. Another leading company is Ranbaxy, which now sells its products in forty-five countries. Das, *India Unbound*, 275. See Donald McNeil, Jr., "Selling Cheap Generic Drugs, India's Copycats Irk Industry," *New York Times*, December 1, 2000, 1.

37. Dyer and Merchant, "The Birth of a Biotech Cluster," 10.

38. Midas Communications Technologies website, at http://www.midascomm.com.

39. Dyer and Merchant, "The Birth of a Biotech Cluster," 10.

40. Dyer and Merchant, "The Birth of a Biotech Cluster," 10.

41. Dyer and Merchant, "The Birth of a Biotech Cluster," 10.

42. Dyer and Merchant, "The Birth of a Biotech Cluster," 10.

43. See AnnaLee Saxenian, *Silicon Valley's New Immigrant Entrepreneurs* (San Francisco: Public Policy Institute of California, 1999), 23.

44. Karen Breslau, "Tomorrowland, Today," *Newsweek*, September 18, 2000, 52.

45. AnnaLee Saxenian, *Local and Global Networks of Immigrant Professionals in Silicon Valley* (San Francisco: Public Policy Institute of California, 2002), iii.

46. Four of the thirty-seven scientists who worked on the project for the National Institutes of Health were STEP OUT migrants. Drs. Pu Paul Liu and Yingzi Yang, two of the doctors on the National Institutes of Health team working on the human genome, migrated to the United States from China. After receiving a medical degree from the Capital Institute of Medicine in Beijing, Dr. Liu pursued a Ph.D. at the University of Texas before working at NIH, see http://www.genome.gov/10000358, while Dr. Yang migrated to the United States to attend graduate school at Cornell University and remained in the United States after she graduated. See http://www.genome.gov/10000366. Similarly, Kyungjae Myung, Ph.D., an investigator working on the NIH Human Genome Project and head of its Genome Instability Section, is from South Korea. See http://www.genome.gov/10004700 Finally, Settara C. Chandrasekharappa, Ph.D., an associate investigator on the project, is from India. He received a Ph.D. from the Indian Institute of Science before migrating to the United States. See http://www.genome.gov/10000442

47. See this chapter, at text accompanying notes 37–42.

48. Maxygen, Inc., "2001 Annual Report" (2002).

49. UNDP, "Making New Technologies Work," at 35.

50. Das, *India Unbound*, 325.

51. Das, *India Unbound*, 342 (noting the Internet's power to "liberate millions" by "diminish[ing] the importance of . . . political, economic, and social [hierarchies]—for example, government officials—[that] maintain their dominance by controlling access to information").

52. UNDP, "Making New Technologies Work," at 35–36.

53. UNDP, "Making New Technologies Work," at 35–36.

54. Access to the Internet has "grown exponentially, from 16 million users in 1995 to more than 400 million in 2000—and to an expected 1 billion users in 2005." UNDP, "Making New Technologies Work," at 35–36. However, the increase has occurred mainly in developed countries. The rate of penetration is much slower in the developing world. In Latin America, for example, "only 12% of individuals will be connected by 2005." UNDP, "Making New Technologies Work," at 35–36. But, even in those parts of the world in which "diffusion of technology is slow and incomplete," efforts are underway to use new technologies and improve skill levels. UNDP, "Making New Technologies Work," 47.

55. See Kripalani, "The Digital Village," available at http://www.businessweek.com:/print/magazine/content/04_26/b3889003.htm?mz (discussing the increasing number of efforts to bring the benefits of technology to India's rural poor, through initiatives like Internet kiosks, "smart chip" payment cards, and $200 portable medical diagnostic kits that "can be plugged into kiosk computers to transfer diagnostic information to a city hospital," as well as the increased attention given to the issue at conferences and by entrepreneurs). The effort to bring low-cost communications technologies to poor communities is being duplicated around the world. For example, a Brazilian team of researchers has also built a low-cost computer (it sells for around $300), which the Brazilian government is seeking to install in "public schools to reach 7 million children" and to sell "on credit to low-wage earners." UNDP, "Making New Technologies Work," at 98, Box 5.2. The Brazilian effort is an important one because the high cost of computers makes access to the Internet prohibitively expensive for people in many communities. Another attempt to minimize the cost barrier is being made by "academics at the Indian Institute of Sciences and engineers at [a] Bangalore-based design company [who] designed a handheld Internet appliance" at a cost of 18 percent of the cheapest computer. The first version of the device will provide Internet and e-mail access in local Indian languages, "with touch-screen functions and microbanking applications. Future versions promise speech recognition and text-to-speech software for illiterate users UNDP, "Making New Technologies Work," 35, Box 2.3 (2001).

56. In addition to the development of technologies that make it easier for poor people to obtain access to the Internet, efforts are also underway to educate poor communities about the use of information technology. For example, one of the goals of the U.N. Development Programme is to narrow the digital divide by increasing literacy in information technology. For one of its projects, it has teamed with the Thailand branch of Cisco Systems to offer training courses in information technology to rural communities in Thailand. "United Nations, Cisco Gets Serious over Rural Net," *The Nation* (Thailand), August 18, 2003. See generally United Nations Development Programme, Information, and Communications Technologies for Development, at http://sdnhq.undp.org/it4dev/docs/global.html

57. See e.g., Das, *India Unbound*, 325 ("Although it is not a panacea for all our developmental problems, [the Internet] can be a powerful vehicle to transform the lives of ordinary people, both socially and economically").

58. UNDP, "Making New Technologies Work," 35. See National Intelligence Council, "Report of the National Intelligence Council's 2020 Project, "The Contradictions of Globalization" (2004) (stating that "biotechnology could be a 'leveling' agent between developed and developing nations, spreading dramatic economic and

healthcare enhancements to the neediest areas of the world," including "[p]ossible breakthroughs . . . such as an antiviral barrier [that] will reduce the spread of HIV/AIDS").

59. "Most biologists believe today's common rules of thumb for race—white, black, and yellow—are meaningless as science. . . ." David Berreby, *Us and Them: Understanding Your Tribal Mind* (New York: Little, Brown and Co., 2005), 79. Thus, "[a]t the genetic level, most African Americans have European ancestors as well as African ones; genetically, almost all variations in human DNA are found in all races." Berreby, *Us and Them*, 85. There are genetic differences, but our conceptions of race are too subjective to have scientific validity. In the United States today, race is "defined first and foremost by the amount of melanin in people's skin." Berreby, *Us and Them*, 83. But the few categories this division yields are not scientifically but culturally determined. Other cultures have made different determinations. Accordingly, "[r]ace doesn't . . . mean the same thing today, from country to country," nor did it ever mean the same thing. Berreby, *Us and Them*, 84. Indeed, "[c]ensus figures are hard to compare among nations because their racial categories don't line up." Berreby, *Us and Them*, 84. Moreover, our racial categories are not only too subjective, but are also far too crude to be scientifically meaningful. Take, for example, the view that particular races—as we define them— are naturally advantaged at certain sports. In fact, "[t]he cultural races we can see at the Olympics . . . do not match the patterns in the genes. At the level of genes and haplotypes, scientists sort human beings into hundreds of populations and subpopulations." Berreby, *Us and Them*, 308–9. Rather than members of one of the handful of races we recognize dominating at certain events, geneticists would see "descendents of particular populations, each one too localized to match our idea of races." Berreby, *Us and Them*, 309.

60. UNDP, "Making New Technologies Work," at 35.

61. UNDP, "Making New Technologies Work," at 35.

62. See Wendy Williams, "Harvesting the River's Energy without a Dam," the *Boston Globe*, May 27, 2003, E1. Mr. Gorlov was awarded the 2001 Thomas A. Edison Patent Award from the American Society of Mechanical Engineers.

63. Williams, "Harvesting the River's Energy without a Dam." The invention is viewed by some as revolutionary because it creates "an environmentally less-damaging alternative to damming streams." Similarly, MIT Professor of mechanical engineering Ernesto Blanco, a Cuban emigrant, created "a mechanical arm that automatically turns the page of a music manuscript." The device can be used by musicians and the disabled, and is available for just $150. "Neurosurgeon Dissects Wife's Brain," *Design Engineering*, July 1999, 5.

64. Philip Peters, "Invented in the USA: Immigrants, Patents and Jobs" (Arlington: Alexis de Tocqueville Institution, 1996), 1, available at http://www.adti.net/imm/immpat.html.

65. Jagdish Bhagwati, "The U.S. Brain Gain—At the Expense of Blacks?" *A Stream of Windows* (1998): 353, 356. Professor Bhagwati also notes that a "significant proportion of university faculty in science and engineering are foreign born: 50 percent of the assistant professors in science and engineering hired in 1992 were foreign-born."

66. See American Immigration Law Foundation, "Immigrant Scientists among the World's Best: American Scientists Win 2000 Nobel Prizes," *Immigration Policy Reports*, available at www.ailf.org/ipc/policy_reports_2000_pr0014.htm.

67. UNDP, "Making New Technologies Work," at 95.

68. See Herbert G. Grubel, "The Reduction of the Brain Drain: Problems and Policies," *Minerva* 6 (1968): 541, 546 (explaining that the resources available to scientists in developed countries make it "misleading to point to highly successful, foreign-born scientists in these countries as men who necessarily would have produced the same findings in their native countries"). A Nobel Prize winner in chemistry, Professor Ahmed Zewail, offers an example of the value of a supporting research atmosphere to STEP OUT migrants. See "Ahmed Zewail—Autobiography, Nobel e-Museum," at www.nobel.se/chemistry/laureates/1999/zewail-autobio.html. Born in Egypt, and a graduate of Alexandria University in Egypt, Professor Zewail pursued advanced education in the United States and decided to stay after graduating. His work was influenced significantly by the community of scientists with which he worked in the United States: "My science family came from all over the world, and members were of varied backgrounds, cultures, and abilities. The diversity in this 'small world' I worked in daily provided the most stimulating environment, with many challenges and much optimism. . . . Working with such minds in a village of science has been the most rewarding experience." See "Ahmed Zewail."

69. Michael Novak, *The Catholic Ethic and the Spirit of Capitalism* (New York: Free Press, 1993), 235–37. Michael Novak has further stated that, for poor nations, "[u]nleashing the creative energies of the people is the single most important key, not only to respect for their individual human dignity, but to economic progress as well." Michael Novak, *Catholic Social Thought & Liberal Institutions: Freedom with Justice*, 2nd edition (New Brunswick: Transaction, 1989), 82.

70. Learning about a discovery and being able to utilize it are, of course, quite distinct things. Nonetheless, the learning is a prerequisite for utilization, and thus communications developments that increase awareness of useful discoveries are valuable in their own right, and can reasonably be expected to directly or indirectly increase utilization. Moreover, the gap between the dissemination of knowledge and its utilization is sometimes not so large; for example, "[k]nowledge about how to treat such a simple ailment as diarrhea has existed for centuries—but millions of children continue to die from it because their parents do not know how to save them." World Bank, "World Bank Development Report 1998/99: Knowledge for Development" (1999), 1.

71. See Grubel, "The Reduction of the Brain Drain," 545.

72. Kenneth Hermele, "The Discourse on Migration and Development," *International Migration, Immobility and Development*, eds. Tomas Hammer, et. al (1997), 134.

73. Kevin O'Neil, *Using Remittances and Circular Migration to Drive Development* (Washington, D.C.: Migration Policy Institute, June 1, 2003), at http://www.migrationinformation.org/Feature/display.cfm?ID=133 (noting that recently "concepts like 'circularity' and 'transnationalism' have drawn attention to more ways that developing countries benefit from migration").

Part Six

THE ENCYCLICALS OF POPE JOHN PAUL II AND THEIR IMPLICATIONS

Chapter Fifteen

Work in Catholic Social Thought

The previous four chapters discussed the myriad ways in which migrants, despite the impediment of distance, can and do fulfill their duties to their homelands. The widespread existence of this capability undermines Catholic social teaching's contention that STEP OUT migration should be discouraged because it harms the common good of sending countries.

A reassessment of human dignity's place in the analysis of STEP OUT migration also is in order. As seen previously, Catholic social teaching has been silent on the *specific* matter of how or if human dignity is advanced by a policy opposing STEP OUT migration.[1] In our view, the message of that silence—combined with references to STEP OUT migrants' "greed"[2]—is unmistakable. If human dignity concerns need not be invoked in any way to justify opposition to STEP OUT migration, it must be because, as applied to the elite in the particular context of STEP OUT migration, no affront to human dignity worth mentioning arises merely from the existence of a particular economic structure in a society. How else can silence on the bedrock principle of Catholic social thought be explained?

In light of trends in Catholic social thought that postdate the formation of the Church's opposition to STEP OUT migration, it has become increasingly untenable to so discount the possibility of affronts to the human dignity of elite members of a society arising from economic circumstances. The two main developments that challenge the old view are (1) a deepened understanding of work as a fundamental right, and (2) an increased recognition that certain structural preconditions may be necessary to an adequate realization of that right. These two developments are discussed below.

WORK AND THE RIGHT TO ECONOMIC INITIATIVE

As the U.S. Conference of Catholic Bishops has recently stated, "Work has a special place in Catholic social thought: work is more than just a job; it is a reflection of our human dignity, and a way to contribute to the common good."[3] No reasonable argument can be made that this statement does not accurately summarize longstanding Catholic social teaching on the matter of work. Indeed, from *Rerum Novarum* on, most of the social encyclicals are explicit in asserting and explaining work's special importance.[4]

Nonetheless, it also is plain that the encyclicals of Pope John Paul II gave a heightened emphasis to certain aspects of the nature and purpose of work and, more explicitly than ever before, placed the right to pursue freely work of one's choosing high among the hierarchy of fundamental rights. Pope John Paul II's desire to elevate the subject of work in Catholic social thought is evident even from the title of his first encyclical, *Laborem Exercens*, or *On Human Work*, which was published in 1981. The evidence of this desire begins but does not end with the decision to devote an entire encyclical to "work." Indeed, while acknowledging his adherence to the writings of his predecessors,[5] the Pope forthrightly declared that he intended as well to break new ground,[6] and not merely "gather together and repeat what is already contained in the church's teaching."[7] In particular, in this "painstaking and profound reflection on the nature of human work,"[8] the Pope expressly noted an intention "to highlight—perhaps more than has been done before—the fact that human work is a key, probably the essential key, to the whole social question."[9]

Laborem Exercens' relatively more systematic and much more extensive treatment of work[10] identifies three benefits of work: (1) through work, one "achieves fulfillment as a human being"; (2) work "constitutes a foundation for the formation of family life"; and (3) work contributes to the common good.[11] (Ten years later, these three benefits were emphasized anew, albeit in more summary fashion, in Pope John Paul II's *Centesimus Annus*).[12] For our purposes, the identification of these three functions of work is most important for the light it sheds on a phrase—"the right of economic initiative"—introduced by Pope John Paul II in his next social encyclical, *Sollicitudo Rei Socialis*, or *On Social Concern*.[13] According to Pope John Paul II, the right of economic initiative is denied when a "bureaucratic apparatus" saps the creativity of the citizenry in the economic sphere.[14]

Sollicitudo Rei Socialis makes plain that denial of the right to economic initiative, as an offense against human dignity, has consequences beyond the mere economic. As denial of the right "destroys the spirit of initiative, that is to say *the creative subjectivity of the citizen*," it simultaneously engenders "passivity, dependence and submission."[15] Pope John Paul II lavished particular attention on the effect, at an individual level, of the denial of the right, noting that such a denial "provokes a sense of frustration or desperation and predisposes people to opt out of national life, impelling many to emigrate and also favoring a form of 'psychological' emigration."[16]

Curtailment of the right to economic initiative, in other words and among other things, has the effect of diminishing to a very great extent the first benefit of work identified by *Laborem Exercens*, that is, to enable one to "achieve fulfillment as a human being." The undermining of the first of the three benefits of work noted in *Laborem Exercens* is no minor point; it essentially amounts to a sawing off of one of the legs of a three-legged stool upon which sits "probably the essential key to the whole social question."[17] Who could comfortably rest their future on such an unstable apparatus?

The poor obviously cannot but, Pope John Paul II indicated, neither can relatively better-off persons either:

> [I]n today's world there are many other *forms of poverty* [beyond that caused by a lack of material wealth]. For are there not certain privations or deprivations which deserve this name? The denial or the limitation of human rights—as for example the right to religious freedom . . . or to take initiatives in economic matters—do these not impoverish the human person as much as, if not more than, the deprivation of material goods?[18]

Lest there be any doubt that the Pope intended his rhetorical question to be answered in the affirmative, later in the same encyclical he again emphasized the seriousness of the harm caused by deprivations of the right to economic initiative, and the fact that the harm is not coexistent with traditional conceptions of poverty: "One must not overlook that *special form of poverty* which consists in being deprived of fundamental human rights, in particular the right to religious freedom and also the right of economic initiative."[19]

Having twice identified the right to economic initiative with the most fundamental rights of humankind, and twice identified deprivation of the right as a phenomenon distinct from material poverty, Pope John Paul II clearly signaled the importance and distinctness of his concern. What remains is to flesh out the contours of the right.

Sollicitudo Rei Socialis begins this process, by noting the importance of replacing "corrupt, dictatorial, and authoritarian forms of government [with] *democratic and participatory* ones" respectful of the rule of law and human rights.[20] But a detailed statement of what offends the right to economic initiative and what appropriately fosters it would have to await the publication of Pope John Paul II's next social encyclical, the landmark *Centesimus Annus*.

THE STRUCTURAL PRECONDITIONS NECESSARY
TO EFFECTIVE EXERCISE OF THE RIGHT TO
ECONOMIC INITIATIVE

Centesimus Annus, published in 1991 to mark the 100th anniversary of *Rerum Novarum*, is full of reflections upon (to speak at once both literally and metaphorically) the fall of the Berlin Wall two years before. The encyclical is regarded in many circles as a controversial document. In some instances, it has been said to be the cause of "gloating by neo-conservatives who hailed it"[21] as "a shift away from centralized planning within the Catholic tradition, and a reversal of [a] left-wing trend."[22] Conversely, many Catholics oriented toward the left-wing of the economics continuum experienced *Centesimus Annus* with "disappointment, if not dismay."[23] The "most controversial" portions of the encyclical concerned its various and pointed criticisms of the welfare or "social assistance" state.[24] For example, after noting that "[m]alfunctions and defects in the social assistance state are the result of an inadequate understanding of the tasks proper to the state," *Centesimus Annus* states that

> by intervening directly and depriving society of its responsibility, the social assistance state leads to a loss of human energies and an inordinate increase of public agencies, which are dominated more by bureaucratic ways of thinking than by a concern for serving their clients, and which are accompanied by an enormous increase in spending. In fact, it would appear that needs are best understood and satisfied by people who are closest to them and who act as neighbors to those in need.[25]

Some regard criticisms such as these as implicitly and intentionally rebuffing *Economic Justice for All*, the U.S. bishops' 1986 statement on the U.S. economy,[26] which statement received much criticism for its allegedly too comfortable embrace of the welfare state.[27]

All such disputes notwithstanding, the particular use of *Centesimus Annus* employed here should not be controversial. Whether *Centesimus Annus* "assimilated American ideas of economic liberty"[28] or whether it constituted "a major challenge to . . . U.S. economic and social policy"[29]—and, if it did either, whether that would be a good or bad thing—are not issues upon which our thesis depends. Some portions of *Centesimus Annus* may be influenced by U.S. developments, but for much of the world, the "welfare state" debate is, at present, a purely academic one. The practical reality is that the gulf between what U.S. economic liberals, on the one hand, and economic conservatives, on the other, want in and for the United States is dwarfed by the gulf between what either wants and the dismal conditions of too many poor nations. Much of *Centesimus Annus* is directed at issues and decisions facing the latter group of nations, and not—at least directly—the developed countries of the world.[30]

Thus, when *Centesimus Annus* states that the right of economic initiative cannot be practiced absent "sure guarantees of individual freedom and private property, as well as a stable currency and efficient public services,"[31] who but a few in the developed world would quarrel? When Pope John Paul II asserted that "[t]here is certainly a legitimate sphere of autonomy in economic life which the state should not enter,"[32] who could disagree? When he indicated that such a sphere of autonomy must provide enough "freedom exercised in the economic field" to allow for healthy entrepreneurial initiatives, who would argue?[33] It was not Pope John Paul II's words on behalf of trade unions or the legitimate role of profit and appropriately harnessed self-interest in the interest of economic efficiency that generated the storm of controversy about *Centesimus Annus*.[34] It was not the Pope's call for the rule of law rather than arbitrariness.[35]

Indeed, statements and positions such as these, which fill in the content and contours of the right of economic initiative, may sound so uncontroversial to "Western" ears that one might wonder why the Pope bothered to articulate them. After all, "[t]he experience of a broad range of countries around the world . . . demonstrates the *economic* importance of generally respected property rights . . . and the *economically* depressing effects of crime and government corruption."[36] A second of reflection, however, answers the question of why the Pope felt compelled to articulate these points—he was writing to the world, and many in that audience live without the rule of law and with arbitrary government, without property protections and with fears of confiscation, without stable currencies and with disincentives rather than incentives to entrepreneurship. Pope John Paul II's insistence that frustration of fundamental rights can result from the absence of the *positive* economic structural preconditions noted above has important implications for Catholic social teaching's analysis of STEP OUT migration, and particularly for the view of human dignity within that analysis. The next chapter discusses these implications.

NOTES

1. See chapter 6.
2. See chapter 6, at note 27.
3. U.S. Conference of Catholic Bishops, Office of Social Development and World Peace, *Minimum Wage* (February 2004), available at http://www.usccb.org/sdwp/national/bkgrd04.htm.
4. See Pope John Paul II, *Laborem Exercens* (1981), sec. 8 (noting that "*Rerum Novarum* and many later documents of the church's magisterium" "cried to heaven" against the view that "human work is solely an instrument of production"). See, e.g.,

182 Chapter Fifteen

Pontifical Council for Justice and Peace, *Compendium of the Social Doctrine of the Church* (Washington, D.C.: United States Conference of Catholic Bishops, 2005): section 268 (stating that "*Rerum Novarum is above all a heartfelt defence of the inalienable dignity of workers*") (emphasis in original).

5. Pope John Paul II, *Laborem Exercens*, sec. 2 (stating that *Laborem Exercens'* "present reflections on work are not intended to follow a different line, but rather to be in organic connection with the whole tradition of [Catholic social] teaching and activity").

6. Pope John Paul II, *Laborem Exercens*, secs. 2, 3.

7. Pope John Paul II, *Laborem Exercens*, sec. 3. Persuasive evidence that the Pope succeeded in this objective might be found in Donal Dorr's observation that "remarkabl[y,] *Laborem Exercens*, which was issued to commemorate the ninetieth anniversary of *Rerum Novarum*, does not have a single footnote reference to that encyclical; and the references to the other social encyclicals are sparse." Donal Dorr, *Option for the Poor: A Hundred Years of Catholic Social Teaching*, revised edition (Maryknoll: Orbis Books, 1992), 289.

8. Dorr, *Option for the Poor*, 288.

9. Pope John Paul II, *Laborem Exercens*, sec. 3.

10. Apropos of the Pope's treatment of issues in *Laborem Exercens*, Donal Dorr has appropriately noted that the Pope's "approach is 'radical' in the literal sense: it goes to the root of issues, rather than simply repeating or adapting traditional formulas." Dorr, *Option for the Poor*, 288.

11. Pope John Paul II, *Laborem Exercens*, at secs. 9, 10. It should be noted that a good part of *Laborem Exercens* develops the idea of "human work as a participation in the creative activity of God," with particular emphasis on the Book of Genesis. David Hollenbach has written insightfully of the matter. See David Hollenbach, *Justice, Peace, & Human Rights: American Catholic Social Ethics in a Pluralistic Context* (New York: Crossroad, 1988), 37-51.

12. Pope John Paul II, *Centesimus Annus* (1991), sec. 6. Specifically, *Centesimus Annus* noted that

> work . . . belongs to the vocation of every person; indeed, man expresses and fulfills himself by working. At the same time, work has a "social" dimension through its intimate relationship not only to the family, but also to the common good . . . . These are themes that I have taken up and developed in my encyclical *Laborem Exercens*.

13. The "'right of economic initiative' [was] hinted at but never fully stated by any previous" pope. Robert Royal, "Reforming International Development," in *Building the Free Society: Democracy, Capitalism, and Catholic Social Teaching*, eds. George Weigel and Robert Royal (Grand Rapids: Eerdmans,1993): 131, 133. Indeed, Pope John Paul II's treatment of the topic has been hailed as a "passage[] of extraordinary originality in papal teaching." Michael Novak, Catholic Social Thought & Liberal Institutes: Freedom with Justice, 2nd edition (New Brunswick: Transaction, 1989), 228.

14. Pope John Paul II, *Sollicitudo Rei Socialis* (1987), sec. 15. According to Michael Novak, *Sollicitudo Rei Socialis* "emphasizes in a new way that 'the right of economic initiative' is the fundamental principle of authentic development. This right

are endowed by God with an inalienable creativity, which serves the common good of all." Novak, *Catholic Social Thought & Liberal Institutions*, 243–44.

15. Pope John Paul II, *Sollicitudo Rei Socialis*, sec. 15 (emphasis in original).

16. Pope John Paul II, *Sollicitudo Rei Socialis*, sec. 15.

17. Pope John Paul II, *Laborem Exercens*, sec. 3.

18. Pope John Paul II, *Sollicitudo Rei Socialis*, sec. 15 (emphasis in original).

19. Pope John Paul II, *Sollicitudo Rei Socialis*, sec. 42 (emphasis in original).

20. Pope John Paul II, *Sollicitudo Rei Socialis*, sec. 44 (emphasis in original).

21. Dorr, *Option for the Poor*, 345.

22. Robert A. Sirico, *Catholicism's Developing Social Teaching* (Grand Rapids: Acton Institute for the Study of Religion and Liberty, 1992), 23.

23. Dorr, *Option for the Poor*, 345.

24. Charles E. Curran, *Catholic Social Teaching, 1891—Present: A Historical, Theological, and Ethical Analysis* (Washington, D.C.: Georgetown University Press 2002), 208.

25. Pope John Paul II, *Centesimus Annus*, at sec. 48.

26. See Sirico, *Catholicism's Developing Social Teaching*, 24-26 (noting "the clear difference in thrust and direction" between *Centesimus Annus* and *Economic Justice for All*); cf. Stephen Bainbridge, *Teluk on John Paul II and Capitalism: Mirror of Justice* (February 17, 2004) (acknowledging that "John Paul II's encyclicals temper much of what was said in the U.S. bishops' pastoral letter on economic justice" even while rejecting contentions that John Paul II "embraces 'free-market capitalism'"), *at* http://www.mirrorofjustice.com/mirrorofjustice/2004/02/teluk_on_john_p.html.

27. See Marvin L. Krier Mich, *Catholic Social Teaching and Movements* (Mystic: Twenty-Third Publications, 1998), 323-24 (listing groups opposed to portions of *Economic Justice for All*, and outlining some of the criticisms, including "a failure to grasp what makes poor nations into developed nations," "deficient understandings of . . . the relative roles of government and the free economy," and an "excessive trust in the state and its officials").

28. Michael Novak, "Tested by Our Own Ideals," in *John Paul II and Moral Theology*, eds. Charles E. Curran and Richard A. McCormick (New York: Paulist Press, 1998), 331, 333

29. David Hollenbach, "The Pope and Capitalism," *America* (New York: America Press, June 1, 1991), 585, 591

30. Cf. Richard T. DeGeorge, "Decoding the Pope's Social Encyclicals," in *John Paul II and Moral Theology*, eds. Charles E. Curran and Richard A. McCormick, 255 (stating that *Laborem Exercens* and *Sollicitudo Rei Socialis* "were not written primarily for or aimed at a U.S. audience").

31. Pope John Paul II, *Centesimus Annus*, sec. 48.

32. Pope John Paul II, *Centesimus Annus*, sec. 15.

33. Pope John Paul II, *Centesimus Annus*, sec. 32.

34. Pope John Paul II, *Centesimus Annus*, secs. 15, 25, 35, and 40.

35. Pope John Paul II, *Centesimus Annus*, sec. 44.

36. Benjamin M. Friedman, *The Moral Consequences of Economic Growth* (New York: Alfred A. Knopf, 2005), 400 (italics in original).

Chapter Sixteen

Human Dignity and
STEP OUT Migration

The group of economic unfortunates who suffer under the conditions *Centesimus Annus* describes as inconsistent with the right of economic initiative include, of course, the bulk of STEP OUT migrants, who have tended to come from areas lacking many of the "prerequisites of a free economy."[1] This irrefutable fact challenges severely the adequacy of prior treatments of STEP OUT migration by Catholic social teaching.

The extent of the challenge might be illustrated by a comparison to the treatment of other fundamental rights. Imagine, for example, the issue is one of freedom of religion, a fair basis for comparison since Pope John Paul II grouped together the "fundamental" rights of religious freedom and economic initiative several times in S*ollicitudo Rei Socialis*, and even once specifically identified only these two rights as bringing about a *"special form of poverty"* when infringed.[2] Catholic social teaching clearly holds that infringements of the fundamental right of religious freedom offend human dignity. Yet, infringements happen. In the face of this inescapable fact, the Church does not hold that adherents of a disfavored religious sect are obligated to stay in their homeland and suffer the consequences. To the contrary, it laments their suffering and encourages other nations to open their doors to the suffering faithful seeking refuge. Indeed, so keenly does the Church feel the offense to human dignity that, in assessing these cases, it typically (and appropriately) finds it unnecessary to make a separate analysis of how the refugees' leaving affects the common good.

Imagine now the same scenario, except the offense to human dignity is an infringement of the right to economic initiative. Heretofore, *in documents dealing specifically with the issue of STEP OUT migrants and STEP OUT migration*, the Church's analysis has been the polar opposite of what was outlined directly above. It typically makes *only* an assessment of the common good, and ignores or even discounts the offense to human dignity. Moreover, rather than encourage other nations to open their doors to the offended, it has in some cases advocated the closure of those doors.[3] A starker contrast could not be drawn.

Based on what we know today, this contrast cannot be justified, but can be explained. One might recall Pope John Paul II's reminder in *Sollicitudo Rei Socialis* that, in the 1960s, "there was a *certain* widespread *optimism* about the possibility of overcoming, without excessive efforts, the economic backwardness of the poorer peoples. . . ."[4] If things will be better tomorrow, the hardships of today seem less imposing, at least for the elite who can safely be assumed to have enough resources to last until tomorrow comes. Hence, especially before Pope John Paul II's fuller articulation of the right to economic initiative, one could understandably reason that discouragement of "elite" migration raised neither serious nor long-lasting human dignity concerns. And once the human dignity concern, in this narrow context, was deemed insubstantial, the subsequent step of focusing on the effect on the common good[5]—a focus itself unfortunately plagued by related economic misunderstandings[6]—also would appear perfectly sensible.

In retrospect, then, the source of the difficulty here—mistaken and incomplete economic understandings—is plain, and knowledge of that source underscores the truth that, in prudential judgments of the sort involved in assessing issues like STEP OUT migration, diligence in fact finding is both an essential and an eternal quest. Pope John Paul II recognized this generally; *Sollicitudo Rei Socialis* notes that the Church's "teaching in the social sphere . . . is ever *new*, because it is subject to the necessary and opportune adaptations suggested by the changes in historical conditions and by the unceasing flow of the events which are the setting of the life of people and society."[7] Now that globalization, widespread technological advances, and more informed economic understandings have taken their place as important parts of "the setting of the life of people and society" today, and the magnitude of the harm suffered by even "elite" citizens when governments unduly burden the right of economic initiative can be more completely appreciated, it is appropriate to consider what "necessary and opportune adaptations [to the Church's STEP OUT migration policies are] suggested by the[se] changes." The next chapter addresses this topic.

NOTES

1. Pope John Paul II, *Centesimus Annus* (1991), sec. 15.

2. Pope John Paul II, *Sollicitudo Rei Socialis* (1987), sec. 42 (emphasis in original); see also Pope John Paul II, *Sollicitudo Rei Socialis*, sec. 15.

3. See chapter 6.
4. Pope John Paul II. *Sollicitudo Rei Socialis*, sec.12. See chapter 7 at notes 41–43 and accompanying text.
5. See chapter 6.
6. See chapters 9–14.
7. Pope John Paul II. *Sollicitudo Rei Socialis*, sec. 3 (emphasis in original).

Part Seven

NEXT STEPS

Chapter Seventeen

Recommendations

The time is ripe for the Church to reevaluate and revise its position on STEP OUT migration. Although that position is understandable given the environment in which it was first formulated, new and important developments make a rigid continuation of the current policy extremely problematic. The better course is for the Church to take note of the new developments and to normalize its treatment of STEP OUT migrants, that is, to neither directly encourage nor discourage the individual decisions of STEP OUT migrants to migrate, as is already the policy for refugees and other non–STEP OUT migrants.

This is not to suggest, however, that the Church should retreat into absolute silence on STEP OUT migration. To the contrary, a new recognition of a real right of migration for STEP OUT migrants could invigorate the Church's advocacy on the issue. A neutral position would of course better align the Church with the signs of *these* times, but more would be accomplished than the substantive policy improvement itself. For example, to the extent that the current position casts a suspicion of selfishness over the STEP OUT migrant, it sets up a roadblock to communication with the very people—STEP OUT migrants— whose assistance is most necessary to improve the economies of lesser developed countries. A more neutral position would eliminate this roadblock.

Additionally, a more neutral policy would produce the concomitant benefit of removing a substantial impediment to the Church's wider international poverty reduction efforts. The economic foundation of the Church's opposition to STEP OUT migration is the belief that by "bleed[ing] a nation . . . of its best citizens," STEP OUT migration "gravely endanger[s] the public good" of "national prosperity." The problem is that the more the Church proclaims this message to a world which increasingly has come to recognize the inevitability of STEP OUT migration, the more it (quite inadvertently) underscores the logical futility of rendering assistance to lesser developed nations, that is, if one believes that

STEP OUT migration is at once a great cause of national poverty in sending countries *and* an enduring feature of the modern world, most steps to alleviate that poverty properly can be regarded as exercises in duty only, accompanied by little expectation of any notably beneficial result. To be sure, calls to action may produce some good even when the hoped-for end result is doubted, but clearly the optimal circumstance for motivating action finds no gap between the action's intended and expected effect. A move toward a more neutral view of STEP OUT migration would help to create an environment closer to this optimal circumstance, and thus make the Church's advocacy on a range of issues related to assisting poor nations all the more likely to be well received.

Finally, a more neutral position on STEP OUT migration, stemming from a deeper recognition of the phenomenon's positive as well as its negative consequences, could allow the Church to develop a more coherent and detailed policy on the phenomenon and, in particular, to introduce an augmented sense of urgency and duty into its discussion of the subject. As it now stands, the current policy engenders a sense of passivity and a disavowing of responsibility because few of us can imagine ourselves capable of halting "brain drain." If STEP OUT migration can be a positive phenomenon for underdeveloped nations, however, it becomes incumbent on us to make it so and *now*, since the need is so great and—as we shall see—many of us are capable of actions that would help tip the scales in a positive direction. By changing the focus from why STEP OUT migration should be minimized to how it best could be utilized, the Church conceivably could provide a unifying framework pursuant to which a number of concrete actions might be urged.

Below we propose ten such actions that the Church might undertake itself and/or urge others to undertake in order to help ensure the maximization of STEP OUT migration's benevolent effects. We also offer this preliminary suggestion. The recent Instruction by the Pontifical Council for the Pastoral Care of Migrants and Itinerant People, *Erga migrantes caritas Christi* (*The Love of Christ towards Migrants*), contains an instruction for dioceses to "fix a date for a 'Day (or Week) of Migrants and Refugees.'"[1] The institution of such a day or week, which is intended "to arouse the awareness of all the faithful to their duty of fraternity and charity towards migrants and to collect the necessary economic aid to fulfill pastoral obligations towards them,"[2] provides an opportune and ready-made occasion for every diocese to emphasize the many ways all persons can help STEP OUT migration succeed in reducing poverty, as well as for reiterating the particular duty of STEP OUT migrants to contribute to the common good of their countries of origin. The paramount goal would be to create or deepen awareness of the duty to help and of the many ways that help can be provided, as well as to ensure the widest possible level of participation.

One final note: if the history of development efforts in the post–World War II era teaches us anything, it is that development is exceedingly difficult and complex. If one were to draw up a comprehensive set of recommendations for ending poverty in underdeveloped countries, there would certainly be less of an emphasis on STEP OUT migrants than is found in the suggestions below. Our aim is a smaller one, however—to ensure that, more and more, STEP OUT migration is seen as and, indeed, becomes, part of the solution to, and not part of the problem of, underdevelopment.

1. EXPLAIN THE CHURCH'S
POSITION ON STEP OUT MIGRATION

Should the Church amend its position on STEP OUT migration, it may additionally prove valuable, either as part of the discussion during its "Day (or Week) of Migrants and Refugees," or at other times, to explain the evolution of the Church's position on STEP OUT migration.

The benefits of doing so would be three-fold. First, to the extent the prior position is known, it would appropriately help to remove a real or perceived stigmatization some STEP OUT migrants might feel, based on the prior view of STEP OUT migration as damaging to countries of origin.

Second, explaining the basis for the change necessarily would require a discussion of the duty of migrants to help their countries of origin, and thereby could inspire migrants to fulfill this duty with greater fervor and diligence. An express articulation of the religious obligation could provide new motivation added to existing motivations of satisfying familial and community duties.

A third benefit would be that it would allow all migrants—as well as other parish members—to see that the Church has expectations of migrants not merely as objects of charity, but also as initiators of it. An African proverb holds that "the hand that gives is always on top." It is not good for either migrants or non-migrants to believe that the hand of a migrant is always on the bottom. Emphasizing the duty of migrants to give back to their homelands and recognizing the contributions that they do make would help to correct this harmful misperception.

2. ADVOCATE FOR HUMAN RIGHTS IN ALL COUNTRIES

As previously noted, Pope John Paul II stated that denial of the right of economic initiative "provokes a sense of frustration or desperation and predisposes people to opt out of national life, impelling many to emigrate and also favoring a form of 'psychological' emigration."[3] One might, with justice, say the same regarding the emigration effect of the denial of other fundamental rights. Elimination of all such denials no doubt drastically would reduce the number of future STEP OUT migrants. It also would hasten the return of current STEP OUT migrants, who upon their return could contribute mightily to the development of their home countries. Indeed, the universal adoption and protection of fundamental human rights almost certainly would curtail STEP OUT migration more than any other single policy change.[4]

To a considerable degree, therefore, STEP OUT migration constitutes a visible sign of a quashing of the human spirit even as, in other cases of STEP OUT migration, more positive motivations obtain. In a sense, then, the best thing that could be done for current and prospective STEP OUT migrants is to remove negative causes of their migration. Indeed, should it move to a more accepting view of STEP OUT migration, more than ever it will behoove the Church to cry out against the violations of human rights that quash the spirit, for that movement will signal a heightened appreciation for the suffering of STEP OUT migrants, including and perhaps especially through denial of the right of economic initiative. The Church will have moved, in other words, from a position of blame (holding that STEP OUT migration prevents development) to one of understanding (holding that unfavorable structural preconditions for development, including the denial of economic rights, cause STEP OUT migration). In this new context, added to the victims of STEP OUT migration are the STEP OUT migrants themselves. As this additional harm caused by the status quo is recognized, the urgency of speaking out against that status quo is correspondingly heightened.

Of course, the Church currently stands as a forthright advocate of human rights, including the right of economic initiative; thus, our recommendation that the Church—as it comes to a new understanding of STEP OUT migration—speak with heightened urgency against the rights denials that cause much of that migration, might be thought akin to recommending to a champion sprinter that he "run faster." Our preferred analogy, however, is to a medical researcher passionately and obsessively searching for a cure to a horrible disease who learns that the disease strikes more people than he previously had thought—should the researcher's subsequent determination to concentrate more than ever on finding a cure strike us as meaningless? We think not, no matter how hard the researcher formerly had worked.

Finally, we note that there is no contradiction between our view that STEP OUT migration can benefit developing countries and our recommendation that the Church advocate policies that, if adopted, would lessen STEP OUT migration. The benefits of STEP OUT migration—money, investment, discoveries, knowledge—are largely the benefits a fully functioning economy produces on its own. Optimally, developing nations will adopt appropriate policies for growth and produce all these benefits on their own, and thus it is right to urge them to adopt appropriate policies that do not offend fundamental rights. When nations do not do this, however, STEP OUT migration becomes the next best way of receiving the benefits and, hopefully, preparing the groundwork for future changes that establish the structural preconditions for growth. Unfortunately, bad governance too often prevails now, but that does not mean there is any inconsistency in simultaneously urging (1) greater acceptance of STEP OUT migration, and (2) the optimal solution of adopting good policies, a consequence of which would be that STEP OUT migration would become relatively less desirable, and thereby less frequent.

3. PROMOTE OPENNESS IN GOVERNMENT

A recent report on poverty in Africa, authored by a commission chaired by the United Kingdom's Prime Minister Tony Blair, states that the key to growth is "good governance."[5] The same report also notes that "[t]he corrosive effect of corruption undermines all efforts to improve governance and foster development."[6]

Corruption also undermines, in particular, the ability of STEP OUT migrants to contribute to their home countries. For example, we earlier identified remittances, personal direct investment, and the ability to influence the direct investment of one's employer as some of the more important potential contributions of STEP OUT migrants. Corruption affects all of these contributions in the same detrimental way, by creating a poor investment climate, which is no more likely to attract investors than a poor meteorological climate is likely to attract retirees. This obviously is true of direct business investment, but also of remittances (although perhaps to a lesser degree), as "remittances represent an investment in the region by its diaspora, and they are governed by similar considerations of risk as other investments."[7] For the same reason, corruption also tends to discourage "brain return," the most direct and increasingly common way that STEP OUT migrants put their skills, knowledge and international experience at the service of the home country.

The Roman Catholic religion understands how corruption can be overcome: the corruption of the Garden of Eden and original sin falls before Jesus, the Light of the World. Light, too, is the greatest disinfectant for corruption of the governmental kind, and there are many actions the Church might promote to increase the light.

For example, most budgetary and spending information should be made public as a matter of course, as an affirmative obligation of government. When dissemination of information of this type becomes more commonplace, the results can be dramatic. In Uganda, for instance, after information about budget allocations for public schools began to receive wide publicity, almost 100 percent of allocated funds were shown to reach the schools — before, less than 30 percent did.[8]

Other types of information may be of the type the government may not be required — in the first instance — to volunteer, but should not, without good reason, decline to produce when asked. The Church should press for light to be shed on this type of information as well, through passage of laws facilitating individuals' access to it. Slightly more than fifty nations, mostly in the developed areas of the world, have already promulgated such laws, which are commonly known as freedom of information laws or acts.[9]

The two suggestions above will require more change from underdeveloped countries than from developed ones. However, defeat of the corruption that keeps some underdeveloped countries from reaping the benefits of their diaspora will require some changes by the developed world as well. For example, international anti-bribery agreements often suffer from inadequate enforcement; this encourages the corrupt practices that the agreements were meant to deter. Accordingly, especially for the benefit of the developing world, the Church should urge all nations to more rigorously enforce international anti-bribery laws. Similarly, the Church should encourage developed nations to accept the U.N. Convention Against Corruption, "the first international legal instrument to recognise the need for all states to commit to asset repatriation."[10] Presently, none of the G-8 nations have done so, even though developed nations—as repositories of large amounts of plundered assets from underdeveloped nations—are crucial to the effective enforcement of the convention.

Finally, the Church should encourage "e-governance" initiatives. Breaking government bureaucrats' monopoly on information by placing it on the Internet reduces opportunities for corruption. In India, such an initiative has limited corruption stemming from exclusive control over land records; in Cameroon, it has reduced corruption in the tax office.[11] As Internet penetration increases in underdeveloped nations, e-governance initiatives will become an ever more important tool for defeating corruption, and for persuading STEP OUT migrants that efforts to help their home countries will not be wasted.

4. RECOGNIZE AND URGE CONTRIBUTIONS BY MIGRANTS TO THEIR HOMELANDS

As the Church emphasizes the duties of migrants to render assistance to their homelands, the Church also can and should identify specific methods and means. Doing so adds concreteness to the Church's invocation of duty, and thus reinforces it. Specific examples also may be used to illustrate the general categories of assistance—direct aid, transfers of knowledge, and the maintenance and spread of culture—which also should be emphasized in order to encourage the creativity of the people and the most widespread level of participation possible. While migrants are living in "another society united by a different culture and very often by a different language,"[12] they still can contribute to their home communities. All such contributions will act to reinforce the migrants' ties to their home communities, to the benefit of both those communities and the migrants themselves.

Moreover, recognizing the specific contributions migrants make as fulfillments of a religious duty not only might inspire some already-contributing migrants to do even more, it also might move to action some not yet involved. Among the contributions the Church could recognize—and encourage—are the following:

Remittances

As remittances are an important development tool for sending countries, the Church could encourage STEP OUT migrants, as well as other migrants, to regularize the practice of sending aid to their home countries in the form of remittances. In addition to providing needed financial support to families, friends, and community, by sending remittances migrants maintain ties with their home communities and its culture and are more likely to feel a sense of ownership and pride in their home countries' growth. Maintaining connections to one's home community will also enrich the emigrant's life abroad—which can often be isolating and lonely—by reinforcing his or her sense of community, culture, and family.

Transnational Knowledge Transfers

Catholic social teaching could highlight the benefits of and encourage continued knowledge transfer and exchanges of diverse viewpoints and ideas. The Church

MANY MESSAGES FOR MANY NATIONS

As virtually all nations are involved in some fashion in STEP OUT migration, the Church in almost every nation might offer suggestions to best utilize STEP OUT migrants. But the message in every nation need not be identical. With respect to remittances, for example, the Church in developed nations might focus on encouraging STEP OUT migrants to send remittances, and on steps government and industry might take to lessen remittance costs, such as by harmonizing regulations, capital requirements, and electronic payment systems. In nations that receive a large amount of remittances, on the other hand, the focus might change to encourage remittance recipients to use the resources responsibly and in ways that further the economic development of the home community. In particular, recipients might be encouraged to direct the money toward purchases and investments that have the greatest multiplier effect on the economies of the home country. Remittances have been criticized as adding to income inequality between those who receive the payments and those who do not. Catholic social teaching could respond to this and other concerns by reminding remittance recipients of their duty to use remittances in ways that will best promote the common good of the larger community.

could encourage STEP OUT migrants to create or expand networks for knowledge exchange with their home countries, which would benefit all participants, just as it now encourages the participation of migrants in established local associations in receiving countries.[13] Indeed, the Church itself, as one of the largest transnational institutions in the world, is also in a position to participate in such knowledge transfers. With churches and facilities in many countries around the world, members of the universal Catholic Church can actually deliver messages and spread ideas throughout its network and the world. For example, the Church can circulate information about efforts by communities to take advantage of the diaspora living abroad.

Relevant Research and Development and Other Initiatives

STEP OUT migrants in particular could be encouraged to use their knowledge of their home countries to devise creative ways to assist in the home countries' development. For example, researchers of various kinds could be encouraged to pursue research agendas that may particularly benefit those back home. Many STEP OUT migrants are positioned to assist their home countries in ways that would not be pursued by outsiders. The Church can encourage these migrants to contribute in ways that optimize their unique backgrounds to help people of their home countries.

In discussing this opportunity, it would be helpful to recognize contributions of a non-scientific nature as well as scientific efforts, in order to maximize the potential for action. For example, non-scientist STEP OUT migrants could be inspired by the work of Blaise Judja-Sato. A former STEP OUT migrant who received an M.B.A. at Wharton and worked for Andersen Consulting, Judja-Sato had moved back to his native Mozambique and was working for the Seattle-based satellite communications firm, Teledesic, when he decided to form an organization called VillageReach. Making use of his contacts in the United States, Judja-Sato received some assistance from Teledesic and a large contribution from the Bill and Melinda Gates Foundation "to attack the problem of delivering vaccines."[14] Judja-Sato's approach was to build an infrastructure and logistical capability in Mozambique sufficient to prevent the huge problem of vaccines spoiling due to a lack of refrigeration, electrical power, and transportation. VillageReach has achieved much success since it started, and is now seeking to expand to other countries where the need is just as great.[15]

Philanthropy and Fundraising

Current or past philanthropic effort should be recognized as fulfilling a duty to one's country of origin, and STEP OUT migrants and others also should be encouraged to use whatever positions or abilities they have to pursue future philanthropic endeavors that would benefit their native countries. Philanthropy "provides significant resources for community development at the local level."[16] It can take many forms, including fund-raising, pooling resources to provide needed social services, or organizing trade missions. It sometimes can lead to a more active engagement; for example, when a group of Afghani professionals living in the United States formed an organization ("Afghans4Tomorrow") devoted to the reconstruction of their native country, many members of the group ended up returning to Afghanistan to help rebuild their country.[17]

One growing form of philanthropy that should be particularly encouraged is the formation of "hometown associations." These groups consist of individuals who migrated from a particular town or village to the United States and who have pooled their resources together to fund development projects, such as roads, water and sanitation systems, schools, and health clinics, in their hometowns.[18] Hometown associations by communities of Mexicans, Salvadorans, and other Latin American migrants in the United States are models for similar programs that could be started around the world.[19] These efforts can have significant and lasting impact at the macroeconomic level.[20]

Indeed, because of the economic importance of hometown associations, they are currently the subject of much study, as well as outside financing. The Multilateral Investment Fund of the Inter-American Development Bank, for instance, has initiated several projects studying how the contributions of hometown associations might best be leveraged for maximum impact.[21] If possible, one additional service the Church could provide, perhaps on a national level, is to track the opportunities available to hometown associations from outside sources, and make the information available to the hometown associations for their review.

Tourism

STEP OUT migrants, who are likely to have greater means than other migrants, can also be encouraged to support their home countries through tourism and commerce. In truth, with regard to tourism, this will be largely a case of preaching to the converted, as tourism "from immigrant communities to the 'old country' is a major earner for countries from Ireland to Vietnam."[22] Indeed, some of the statistics are stunning; for example, over 40 percent of persons flying to El Salvador are Salvadorans residing abroad, and statistics for other countries are similar.[23] Even those who need no prodding to visit the home country, however, may be prodded by the Church to make an additional contribution in a related way, perhaps by talking to other persons at an individual level about the migrant's country and culture, as a way of encouraging others to visit. Local churches might also facilitate encouragement of such tourism by migrants by occasionally featuring migrants as speakers at events designed to showcase one or more cultures.

Trade

Finally, STEP OUT and other migrants can help to create markets for products from their home countries both through their personal consumption and through the promotion of their culture in the receiving communities. Churches can assist in this development of the sending communities' economies as follows: (1) by publicly recognizing the importance of it, and (2) through the discrete sale of imported products. At a recent Mass we attended in Lambertville, New Jersey, for example, Guatemalan coffee was mentioned as being available for sale after the Mass—the coffee was, by the way, delicious.

5. URGE IMPROVEMENTS TO
LOWER THE COST OF REMITTANCES

The Church should encourage governments and their banking institutions to work to reduce the commission and transaction costs of remittances. Improvements in this area effectively create incentives that will cause migrants to remit both more often and in greater amounts, all to the furtherance of the common good in the receiving nations. Increasing incentives for STEP OUT migrants is especially important because migrants with higher levels of education "are more likely to remit for asset accumulation."[24]

The mechanisms currently available for sending remittance payments abroad are often costly and, in some case, inconvenient.[25] In some countries, transferring money to one's native community can cost as much as 25 percent of the transmitted amount,[26] although the percentage cost has been falling in recent years. For example, in Latin America and the Caribbean, for the average remittance amount of $200, the remittance fee has fallen from 15 percent of the amount to 7.9 percent since 2000.[27]

The high cost traditionally was due substantially to financial institutions' general lack of "interest in serving the 'remittance population.'"[28] The period of disinterest is ending, however, as the remittances market continues to expand, and the revenues become large enough to attract even large companies[29]—for example, Mexicans spent one billion dollars on remittance commissions alone in 2001.[30] And, as noted, as companies have become more interested, increased competition (and the use of technology) has caused the cost of remittances to fall.[31]

However, more can still be done. For example, competition is "less robust" or even "'controlled'" in some countries—Jamaica, the Dominican Republic, and Cuba, for example—and, not surprisingly, these countries have remittance transfer costs 33 to more than 50 percent higher than their regional average.[32] These outlier averages constitute a substantial and unnecessary drain on the resources of the poor of those countries; an obvious, though in some instances perhaps politically unfeasible, recommendation is that parties in these nations work to introduce more competition into their systems. Of course, this is a goal other nations may productively continue to work towards as well, though the exact details of what should be done may be quite particular to each nation. Mexico, for example, recently introduced increased competition into its system by changing the laws prohibiting rural credit unions from receiving remittances, and by promoting price awareness through the publication of cost information.[33]

Other recommendations may be of more general applicability. To take one example, remittances can be transmitted more cheaply from the United States if the Federal Reserve Board's Automated Clearinghouse (FedACH) system extends to the receiving country. Mexico has recently been brought within this system, but no other country in Latin America is, nor are many other countries throughout the world.[34] Broadening the Automated Clearinghouse system is a goal interested parties within and without the United States might productively work towards in order to, among other things, reduce the transmission costs of remittances.

Changes at the retail level can also be important. Mexico again provides a good example. In one new program, the "employer sends some of the [employee's] salary by direct deposit to an automated clearinghouse" and a relative at home can withdraw the funds using an automated teller card, all at a substantially reduced transaction fee, usually only a few dollars.[35]

All these changes would be worth advocating in at least some countries because, by making it easier and less costly to send remittances, the changes get more resources into the hands of the intended beneficiaries; they create additional incentives for remitters to use their assets to aid their native communities' development; and they may entice those who are not currently active in the remittance process to take part.

6. URGE DEVELOPED NATIONS TO SUPPORT THE EFFORTS OF STEP OUT MIGRANTS

Developed nations benefit from STEP OUT migration; as a matter of reciprocity and solidarity, the Church should encourage particular beneficiaries to make it easier for STEP OUT migrants to fulfill their duties to their homelands. Such reciprocity can manifest itself in many ways. For example, corporations might allow research scientists to spend a certain percentage of their work time pursuing individual interests, and encourage STEP OUT migrants to use that time to focus on problems especially acute in their homelands. By freeing researchers to this extent from the research agenda of the developed world, one could expect an increase in advances of particular benefit to underdeveloped nations.

Governments can assist in this process. One way the Church could urge them to do so would be by supporting a global orphan drug agreement. In the United States, the Orphan Drug Act provides tax incentives and enhanced patent protection for pharmaceutical companies that develop drugs for rare diseases, as such drugs otherwise could not be expected to pay for themselves. The result has been a ten-fold increase in drugs for rare diseases. A global orphan drug agreement could be similarly beneficial, by "provid[ing] a much needed push for research on tropical diseases, which also represent small commercial markets—not because they are rare but because they afflict poor people."[36]

The Church also should encourage large healthcare providers in the developed world to look for ways to facilitate the efforts of immigrant medical professionals to contribute to their homelands. The providers might, for instance, allow STEP OUT migrants flexibility in taking vacation or leave time in order to allow them to travel back home to provide care. Healthcare providers could organize such trips themselves. They also might develop programs that allow STEP OUT migrants to make use of modern technology to remotely serve patients in the homeland. The programs need not require cutting-edge medical equipment in order to be useful. On the remote island of Ginnack, for example, "nurses use a digital camera to record patients' symptoms. The pictures are sent electronically to a nearby town to be diagnosed by a local doctor, or sent to the United Kingdom if a specialist's opinion is required."[37] Replication of programs such as this would provide tremendous opportunities for STEP OUT migrants to contribute to their homelands.

7. ENCOURAGE STUDY OF PROPOSALS TO INCREASE THE BENEFITS OF STEP OUT MIGRATION TO SENDING COUNTRIES

Although there is ample evidence that STEP OUT migration provides significant benefits to sending nations, that does not mean that the status quo represents the best of all possible worlds. Recognizing this, the Church should urge analysts in government, academia, think tanks, and elsewhere to investigate ways to increase the benefits received by sending countries. Below we note some possible avenues of study. The particular ideas mentioned may be more or less necessary for different nations, and thus any decision to go beyond the statement of general exhortations to study and actually endorse a specific idea would probably best be left to individual national churches, based upon the unique circumstances of each society. In every nation receiving or sending a substantial number of STEP OUT migrants, however, it seems to us that the Church might reasonably insist at least that attention be paid to the general issue of finding new ways to help the performance of

STEP OUT migration for underdeveloped nations match the promise, with the specifics left to the devising of each nation's political branches.

As for possible subjects of study, one area that is appropriate for further analysis is tax policy. One might look, for example, at ways the tax system might be used to encourage "brain return," such as by having the receiving country refund social security taxes upon a STEP OUT migrant's departure. Perhaps the biggest issue involves the wisdom and feasibility of requiring STEP OUT migrants to pay taxes to their home country. While in some cases even a small tax would generate relatively significant revenues for the sending country, numerous questions of fairness and practicality remain open for exploration. Is it fair, for example, to tax all STEP OUT migrants from a given country? At first the answer might seem yes, but what of the person who left because people of her faith or ethnicity or gender were (and still are) discriminated against or even persecuted in her homeland? Should STEP OUT migrants of every nation be taxed? Wouldn't that reward corrupt governments who drove people away, while doing little to help the people who remained? Perhaps the revenues should be distributed by international agencies—which one or ones? How would the tax be collected? Should sending countries, in order to promote enforcement, follow the lead of Eritrea, which imposes a 2 percent income tax on expatriates, and which conditions the right to buy land in Eritrea and the right of passport renewal on payment of the tax?[38] Or do policies such as Eritrea's simply work to distance STEP OUT migrants from their homeland? Further thought is needed on all these questions and others—such as the appropriateness of requiring STEP OUT migrants to pay for their education upon departure—and the Church might rightly identify them as questions worthy of serious study.

Study of possible reforms to the immigration laws also might be urged by the Church. Particular attention might be paid to reforms that would allow freer movement of skilled persons on a temporary basis, which might enable many of those who otherwise would become STEP OUT migrants never to leave the home country except for short trips of certain duration.[39]

Finally, in addition to advocating for changes that would lower the transmission costs of remittances—an unqualified good, it seems to us—the Church also could advocate study of reforms that could create additional incentives to remit and that could remove some of the inconveniences of remitting. For example, in some nations, policies have been adopted that increase the monetary incentives associated with sending remittances. The Portuguese government, for instance, has attracted additional remittances by permitting its national banks to offer special benefits to overseas customers, including lower taxes and premium interest rates, as well as programs to "attract emigrants to take out loans to build or buy homes in Portugal."[40] The Indian government also has introduced mechanisms that encourage emigrant nationals to invest in the home country.[41] Indian state and national banks offer emigrants incentives, including higher interest rates on deposits and tax exemptions, to place and keep their money in the Indian banking system. Other available incentives are the option to have an account denominated in foreign currency and the ability to designate beneficiaries who are residing within India.[42] In addition, banks in Egypt and Turkey both offer premium exchange rates on certain investments by emigrants.[43]

As for reduction of the inconveniences associated with remitting, one difficulty that migrants often face when sending remittances is that they lose control over the funds once they are sent. The Moroccan state-owned bank responded to this concern by establishing joint checking accounts that are accessible by both the overseas national and her relatives who remain in Morocco. By using these accounts, overseas nationals can remit money to their family members at no cost by making a bank deposit and having the relative withdraw the money in Morocco.[44] The overseas nationals also retain control over the account in the event they need access to the funds. Similarly, other countries have created "foreign currency accounts with domestic banks," which allow expatriates to deposit funds in banks headquartered in their native countries with assurances that they can withdraw the funds at their discretion.[45] These accounts sometimes even offer a premium interest rate to individuals living abroad as an incentive for them to invest in domestic banks. For example, recognizing that its nationals remit $600 to $750 a month on average to relatives in Pakistan, the Pakistani government has created a device, known as the Foreign Exchange Bearer Certificate, that is issued in exchange for foreign currency payments.[46]

As noted earlier, whether the Church in any nation would advocate any or all of these specific proposals is a judgment call based on the particular circumstances of that nation's society. But the issue of maximizing the benefits of STEP OUT migration for sending countries is important enough that a general policy of encouraging additional research into the matter clearly is warranted.

8. URGE FACILITATION OF CONTACTS BETWEEN STEP OUT MIGRANTS AND THEIR HOMELANDS

When governments of underdeveloped nations decide to try to establish technology centers in their countries, they call upon their diasporas for assistance.[47] When the Commission for Africa researched its 450-page report in 2005, it "made a particular effort to engage with the African diaspora."[48] The United Nations Development Programme, the United Nations Development Fund for Women, and the Information Communications Technology Task Force of the United Nations have all supported programs to connect Africa digitally to its diaspora in order to promote development.[49] The consensus is broad: reaching out to and connecting with diaspora communities is vitally important to successful development efforts.

The Church should commend such outreach where it exists, and call for improvement where it does not. Private groups, national governments, and regional and international organizations all have contributions to make. Each is fully capable of utilizing "communication technology and virtual networks [which] are ideally suited to a talented diaspora that wants to make a positive contribution."[50] Contributions of this sort can be direct or indirect. Direct contributions enabled by the Internet include programs such as the "reverse brain drain project" initiated by Thailand "that is designed to identify and attract experienced Thai professionals in the diaspora to participate in mission-related projects without requiring them to uproot and return home."[51] Indirect contributions could be as simple as giving notice of or providing links to other Internet sites dedicated to fostering communication between particular STEP OUT migrants and their homeland.

Of course, real (as opposed to virtual) world contacts should be fostered as well. Particularly valuable are contacts tailored to the sending countries' greatest needs. The Ethiopian diaspora, to take one typical example, provides several instances of groups working to establish such contacts. The existence of these groups—such as the Ethiopian North American Health Professionals Association, which is dedicated to supplying medical personnel and equipment to Ethiopia, and the Association for Higher Education and Development, which has a similar focus but centered more on the needs of Ethiopian medical school students and faculty—highlights the wisdom of countries remaining open to potential contributions by their STEP OUT migrants.

9. PROMOTE EFFORTS TO INCREASE PROFESSIONAL SATISFACTION IN SENDING COUNTRIES, PARTICULARLY IN UNIVERSITIES

Frustration with working conditions due to a lack of equipment, books, and a critical mass of professional colleagues has long been recognized not only as a cause of STEP OUT migration, but also as a reason STEP OUT migrants choose not to return to sending countries. In such cases, the promise of one of the chief benefits of STEP OUT migration, brain return, remains unfulfilled.

Professional frustration of the type noted above can be endemic in a society. When it is, the only cure is successful development. But merely to urge successful development is a hope, not a plan. Underdeveloped nations need plans, and workable plans need to start somewhere particular, not everywhere at once.

Our view is that the best way to address *directly* the professional dissatisfaction that is a cause of brain drain and an impediment to brain return is to focus on a discrete area that has a relatively high chance of success, especially if the benefits of success will reach throughout society and not be isolated. The field of higher education best satisfies these criteria.

Accordingly, the Church should urge those capable of improving the working environment in universities in developing countries to do so. Universities in the developed world are well situated to aid in this process, and perhaps the Church could particularly urge Catholic universities to help address the problem.

An intellectually stimulating environment supportive of the search for new knowledge is the ideal environment for a university. Universities in the developed world can take a number of actions to help to create this environment in underdeveloped nations. They can, for example, encourage their own faculty members to consider teaching temporarily in underdeveloped nations. A twist on this contribution would be to establish a regular program of faculty exchange, so that as a scholar from the developed world was adding to the diversity of and learning at the university she was visiting, a scholar from an underdeveloped nation would have a chance to interact with new colleagues and gain increased exposure to the latest developments in his own field of study. The developed world's universities and university faculty members also can work to decrease the isolation of those who work at some under-funded and under-equipped universities in the underdeveloped world by increasing efforts to collaborate on papers or projects; by seeking the increased participation of scholars from underdeveloped nations on international committees or working groups; and by dismantling barriers that keep such scholars from fully enjoying the international flow of ideas—academic conference fees, for example, which can sometimes be substantial, could be waived or reduced.

Another way universities can work to increase the professional satisfaction of their colleagues in underdeveloped nations is to promote and volunteer to provide distance learning and interactive classes. A study on STEP OUT migration from Fiji concluded that making use of the Internet in this way could help to curb STEP OUT migration.[52] Distance learning and interactive classes can improve the academic environment at under-funded schools by, among other things, expanding the range of courses offered; providing a different perspective on some subjects; allowing local professors to teach a more varied and perhaps more advanced selection of courses; and offering students some opportunity for interaction with those in the developed world. These benefits could be multiplied via a partnership with a multi-university organization such as African Virtual University, which currently offers degrees in nineteen African countries.

Internet courses, of course, require Internet capability, and this and other resources are often in short supply. Universities in developed nations can provide some assistance here as well, but the need is beyond their ability to meet on their own. To the extent job dissatisfaction among academics in underdeveloped countries is attributable to a lack of equipment, books, Internet access, and so forth, businesses, governments and multi-national organizations must also provide resources if these shortcomings are to be remedied. The Church should make clear the importance of meeting this challenge to all persons and organizations in a position to help.

The first benefits of improving the working environment at the universities of underdeveloped nations will be a strengthening of the universities themselves. As the universities become more attractive places to work, it is reasonable to expect that an increase in "brain return" will partly be the cause of the improvement. This development will help ensure that the benefits of improving the universities will not end at the universities' borders, but will redound to the benefit of the universities' wider societies. There is much work to be done, and much of it needs to be done locally, such as research into the problems of local farmers.[53] The Church should emphasize that even small contributions can help in this effort and can have large consequences. Citizens of underdeveloped nations, after all, have used cell phones and pre-paid phone cards to overcome problems caused by the absence of electricity, refrigeration, and efficient banks.[54] They can do a lot with a little, if only given the chance.

10. WORK TO IMPROVE DATA COLLECTION ON STEP OUT MIGRATION

Finally, the Church should encourage—indeed, look for ways to initiate or participate in—improved data collection efforts. No one doubts the need; what one scholar has said with reference to a specific country—"[s]tatistical information on the Ethiopian brain drain tends to be anecdotal, confusing and sometimes conflicting . . . [with] no reliable, long-term macro statistics for documenting the problem"[55]—many others have said generally.[56]

Several scholars have proposed a "World Migration Organization" or "WMO" to monitor immigration policies of countries and to establish acceptable norms of behavior.[57] The more ambitious the proposed agenda for the WMO, the more dubious we are about its likely effectiveness. To the extent that such an organization focuses on conducting and standardizing the collection of statistical data on immigration, however, with a tightly defined charge so as to avoid the temptation of mission creep, it could prove extremely useful. The Church might consider lending its support to a WMO of this more circumscribed type.

The Church also might look for ways to actually initiate or participate in data collection efforts. In a previous article on the feasibility of a more detailed social teaching, we noted that

the Church's international reach and the Church's status as the world's largest non-governmental provider of social services provides an ideal vantage point from which it could generate rigorous analyses of many social issues, that is, immigration. Such work not only might be non-duplicative of any prior work, it might be non-duplicable by any other party.[58]

We might have added explicitly what we then only implied—that the Church also was in an ideal position to generate the raw material of rigorous analysis, that is, good data.

After the publication of that article, the Church initiated in 2005 a census of Maronite Christians living outside of Lebanon, where the Maronite Church originated. (Maronite Christians, among other things, recognize the universal authority of the Pope, but maintain their own hierarchy and allow priests to be married. They also use some Aramaic, the language of Jesus, in their liturgy.) The purpose of the census—which has been noted at announcements during Mass and in Church newspapers and bulletins—is pastoral, not scholarly, and "stems from years of religious persecution in Lebanon and the fleeing of Christians to other countries searching for a better life."[59] Nonetheless, despite its non-scholarly purpose and genesis, the census is likely to generate information useful to scholars; it asks, for example, for occupation and place of birth, and thus, upon analysis, could yield some insights about STEP OUT migration. The Church would provide a valuable service by conducting or supporting similar surveys among other groups and then releasing the data, at least in summary or redacted form, for scholars and others to assess. The eventual result would be improved immigration policy, for good data is essential to effective policymaking.

NOTES

1. Pontifical Council for the Pastoral Care of Migrants and Itinerant People, *Erga migrantes caritas Christi (The Love of Christ toward Migrants* (Vatican City: 2004), at Juridical Pastoral Regulations, Art. 21, available at http://www.vatican.va.

2. Pontifical Council for the Pastoral Care of Migrants and Itinerant People, *Erga migrantes caritas Christi*, at Juridicial Pastoral Regulations Art. 21.

3. Pope John Paul II, *Sollicitudo Rei Socialis* (1987), sec. 15.

4. One startling demonstration of the sensitivity of STEP OUT migration to changes in the human rights environment is found in the negative example of Ethiopia:

> [P]rior to the 1974 revolution virtually all Ethiopians who attended university in the country remained at the completion of their work and the vast majority of those who studied overseas returned to Ethiopia. . . . The environment created during the Derg government as a result of political persecution and the Red Terror was a major turning point. It caused a significant emigration of highly skilled Ethiopians that continues to the present day. . . .

David H. Shinn, "Reversing the Brain Drain in Ethiopia," November 23, 2002, at http://chora.virtualave.net/brain-drain8.htm

5. "Our Common Interest: Report of the Commission for Africa" (2005), 99.

6. "Our Common Interest: Report of the Commission for Africa," 142.

7. "Our Common Interest: Report of the Commission for Africa," 107.

8. World Bank, "World Development Report 2000/2001: Attacking Poverty: Opportunities, Empowerment, and Security" (2000), 101.

9. David Banisar, "The Freedominfo.org Global Survey: Freedom of Information and Access to Government Record Laws Around the World" (2004), 2–7, at http://www.freedominfo.org/survey.htm.

10. "Our Common Interest: Report of the Commission for Africa," 33.

11. Manjeet Kripalani, "The Digital Village," Business Week Online, June 28, 2004, available at http://businessweek.com/magazine/content/04_26/b3889003.htm; "Our Common Interest: Report of the Commission for Africa," 133. Indeed, not only has the digitization of India's land records virtually wiped out land fraud committed against poor farmers, it also has sharply reduced the costs of securing the records. Manjeet Kripalani, available at http://businessweek.com/magazine/content/04_26/b3889003.htm.

12. Pope John Paul II, *Laborem Exercens* (1981), sec. 23.

13. Pontifical Council for the Pastoral Care of Migrants and Itinerant People, *Erga migrantes caritas Christi*, Juridical Pastoral Regulations, Art. 3, sec. 3.

14. Kerry A. Dolan, "The Last Mile," *Forbes*, September 6, 2004, 86, 87.

15. Dolan, "The Last Mile," 87.

16. Kathleen Newland, "Migration as a Factor in Development and Poverty Reduction," *Migration Information Source* (Washington, D.C.: Migration Policy Institute, June 1, 2003), at http://www.migrationinformation.org/Feature/display.cfm?ID=136.

17. Peter Loftus, "For Native Afghan, Bearing Point Job Is a Homecoming," *Wall Street Journal*, April 1, 2003, B12; Jennifer M. Brinkerhoff, "Digital Diasporas and International Development: Afghan-Americans and the Reconstructions of Afghanistan" *Occasional Paper Series, No. CSGOP-03-23* (2003), 9–12, at http://gwcsg.gwu.edu/OPS/CSGOP-03-23.pdf. For more information about Afghans4Tomorrow, see http://afghans4tomorrow.com/.

18. Susan Martin, "Remittance Flows and Impact, Remarks at Remittances as a Development Tool: A Regional Conference Organized by the Multilateral Investment Fund," Inter-American Development Bank, May 17, 2001, at http://www.iadb.org/mif/v2/files%5Csusanmartin.doc.

19. See Manuel Orozco, "Latino Hometown Associations as Agents of Development in Latin America," *Sending Money Home: Hispanic Remittances and Community Development*, eds. Rodolfo O. de la Garza and Briant Lindsay Lowell (Lanham: Rowman & Littlefield, 2002): 85, 93–96 (describing characteristics of hometown associations). One Salvadoran association collected enough money over time to construct a Red Cross clinic, buy an ambulance, build a school, and build a septic tank for its village in El Salvador. Susan Martin, at http://www.iadb.org/mif/v2/files%5Csusanmartin.doc. Similar projects are being funded in sending countries by their emigrants, including in Turkey, Italy, the Dominican Republic, Mexico, and Slovenia. Deborah Waller Meyers, "Migrant Remittances to Latin America: Reviewing the Literature," *Sending Money Home* (2002): 53, 72–73.

20. Meyers, "Migrant Remittances to Latin America," 73.

21. Inter-American Development Bank, Multilateral Investment Fund, "Sending Money Home: Remittance to Latin America and the Caribbean" (2004), 27–28.

22. Newland, "Migration as a Factor in Development and Poverty Reduction," at http://www.migrationinformation.org/Feature/display.cfm?ID=136.

23. Inter-American Development Bank, Multilateral Investment Fund, 15 (mentioning the Dominican Republic, Mexico, and Nicaragua as also being beneficiaries of much tourism by former residents living abroad).

24. Manuel Orozco, "Remittances, the Rural Sector, and Policy Options in Latin America," *Migration Information Source* (Washington, D.C.: Migration Policy Institute, June 1, 2003), at http://www.migrationinformation.org/Feature/display.cfm?ID=128. See Mark R. Rosenzweig, *Copenhagen Opposition Paper on Population and Migration* (2004), 10 (noting that "the data do show that higher skill immigrants send a greater amount of remittances").

25. Immigrants use several different mechanisms to send remittances to their families and communities, including money transfer companies (such as Western Union), banks, postal services, and hand delivery through a third party or a courier. Western Union has the broadest presence worldwide in this industry, capturing one-quarter of the worldwide market in money transfers. Manuel Orozco, *Worker Remittances in an International Scope* (Multilateral Investment Fund of the Inter-Amer. Devel. Bank, Working Paper 2003), 5–6. The fees charged by Western Union can be substantial, amounting to as much as $17 to send $50 overseas. Robert Suro et al., *Billions in Motion: Latino Immigrants, Remittances and Banking* (Pew Hispanic Center & the Multilateral Investment Fund, 2002), 9; Roger Böhning, "Copenhagen Consensus: Migration Opponent's Paper," 6 n. 5 (noting that, in France, Western Union "lops off 21% from migrants' small remittances"). The U.S. Post Office recently entered the business with its own system called Dinero Seguro. Orozco, *Worker Remittances in an International Scope*, 6.

26. Meyers, "Migrant Remittances to Latin America," 56. See also "Binational Study on Migration between Mexico and the United States" (U.S. Commission on Immigration Reform and Mexican Department of External Relations 1997), 37, available at http://www.utexas.edu/lbj/uscir/binational.html (noting that the cost of remittances can be as high as 25 percent in some cases). There are two sets of charges incurred in remittance transfers. The first includes fees for the service. The second is the commission charged to convert the remittance into local currency. Of all the transfer mechanisms, money transfer companies typically charge the most, while banks usually offer the least expensive alternative. Orozco, *Worker Remittances in an International Scope*, 7.

27. Inter-American Development Bank, Multilateral Investment Fund, 12–13.

28. Inter-American Development Bank, Multilateral Investment Fund, 17.

29. Inter-American Development Bank, Multilateral Investment Fund, 20 (noting "[s]everal major U.S. banks entered the market in the past two years with new remittance transfer products").

30. John Authers and Gary Silverman, "Banks Eyeing Green, Green Cash of Home," *Financial Times*, June 5, 2003, 13.

31. Inter-American Development Bank, Multilateral Investment Fund, 13.

32. Inter-American Development Bank, Multilateral Investment Fund, 13.

33. Inter-American Development Bank, Multilateral Investment Fund, 16; World Bank, *Global Economic Prospects 2006: Economic Implications of Remittances and Migration* (Washington, D.C.: World Bank, 2006), 148.

34. Inter-American Development Bank, Multilateral Investment Fund, 14. Approximately 23,000 payments are sent from the United States to Mexico each month through the FedACH system; this number would increase if some technical weaknesses in the system, such as insufficient coding flexibility, were remedied. World Bank, *Global Economic Prospects* 2006, 148 at Box 6.4.

35. Tim Weiner, "Mexico Seeks Lower Fees on Funds Sent from U.S.," *New York Times*, March 3, 2001, A1. The fee for using this system is $3.50 plus 1 percent of the transaction. Mexicans using credit unions to remit funds are charged a $10 fee plus 3.5 percent of the transaction. Weiner, "Mexico Seeks Lower Fees," A1. See also Alexander O'Neill, "Note, Emigrant Remittances: Policies to Increase Inflows and Maximize Benefits," *Indiana Journal of Global Legal Studies* 9 (2001): 345, 354–55 (explaining that the South Korean government works closely with Korean companies abroad to create incentives for individuals to send remittances back home).

36. United Nations Development Programme, "Human Development Report, 2001: Making New Technologies Work for Human Development" (2001), 100.

37. United Nations Development Programme, "Human Development Report, 2001," 33.

38. Philip Martin, "Copenhagen Consensus: Challenge Paper on Population and Migration" (2004), 21.

39. See Martin, "Copenhagen Consensus," 25–27.

40. Orozco, *Worker Remittances in an International Scope*, 8. The results of this program are impressive. During the 1990s, deposits from emigrants amounted to close to 20 percent of total deposits in the banking system of Portugal.

41. Like Paskistanis, reports show that Indians remit an average of between $600–750 a month. Orozco, *Worker Remittances in an International Scope*, 9.

42. Orozco, *Worker Remittances in an International Scope*, 8. These bank accounts, which are offered through Indian state and national banks, can be opened by Indian citizens residing outside of India. Also, in conjunction with the State Bank of India, the Indian government allows foreign banks to sell "Resurgent India Bonds" to non-resident Indians, thereby "encouraging Indians living in the United States and elsewhere to invest in their home country." Orozco, *Worker Remittances in an International Scope*, 8. As of 2000, reports show that 15 percent of remittances produced and sent worldwide were sent to India. Orozco, *Worker Remittances in an International Scope*, 3.

43. Meyers, "Migrant Remittances to Latin America," 70. The Philippines, Bangladesh, and Sri Lanka "have also put in place measures to increase remittance inflows, creating special departments within central banks or ministries for diaspora-related issues, implementing special schemes (low-interest housing loans, insurance), facilitating local and foreign-currency deposits, and even granting dual nationality. World Bank, Development Prospects Group, Migration and Remittances Team, "Migration and Development Brief 2: Remittance Trends 2006" (2006), 2.

44. Orozco, *Worker Remittances in an International Scope*, 9. The state bank, Groupe Banques Populaires, also "provides subsidized credit for real estate and entrepreneurial investments in Morocco." Orozco, *Worker Remittances in an International Scope*, 9.

45. O'Neill, "Note," 355 (explaining the development of foreign currency accounts in domestic banks). See also Meyers, "Migrant Remittances to Latin America," 70 (noting that "Sri Lanka, Bangladesh, Pakistan, and India all have foreign currency accounts that pay above-market interest rates and convert into local currencies at premium rates").

46. Orozco, *Worker Remittances in an International Scope*, 9.

47. See, e.g., chapter 14, at text accompanying notes 39–42.

48. "Our Common Interest: Report of the Commission for Africa," 1.

49. Shinn, "Reversing the Brain Drain in Ethiopia," at http://chora.virtualave.net/brain-drain8.htm.

50. Shinn, "Reversing the Brain Drain in Ethiopia."

51. Shinn, "Reversing the Brain Drain in Ethiopia."

52. Reserve Bank of Fiji, *RBF Quarterly Review*, December 2002, 40, 45.

53. "Our Common Interest: Report of the Commission for Africa,"46.

54. "Our Common Interest: Report of the Commission for Africa," 28, 117. For example, in order to avoid the spoiling of meat that they could not refrigerate, butchers in Africa would conservatively estimate demand, and therefore would often run out of meat. The proliferation of cell phones in nations whose landline telephone systems are inadequate enables butchers to ask customers to call orders in; butchers can thus confidently increase their production without unduly risking financial loss. "Our Common Interest: Report of the Commission for Africa," 28. The productivity of customers also is increased by this development, as they can call in to check supplies rather than traveling to the butcher only to find he has run out of meat to sell. As for the importance of pre-paid phone cards, these cards are being sent from migrants,"via cellphones, to . . . relatives back home, who can then sell the cards to others. Thus the cards have become a form of currency by which money can be sent from the rich world . . . without incurring the commission charged on more conventional ways of remitting money." "Our Common Interest: Report of the Commission for Africa," 28.

55. Shinn, "Reversing the Brain Drain in Ethiopia," http://chora.virtualave.net/brain-drain8.htm.

56. See chapter 10, notes 38–41 and accompanying text.

57. See, e.g., Jagdish Bhagwati, "A Champion for Migrating Peoples," *A Stream of Windows: Unsettling Reflections on Trade, Immigration, and Democracy* (Cambridge: MIT Press, 1998): 315; Bimal Ghosh, "New International Regime for Orderly Movements of People: What Will It Look Like?," *Managing Migration: Time for a New International Regime?*, ed. Bimal Ghosh (New York: Oxford University Press, 2000): 220, 227; Roger Böhning, "Copenhagen Consensus, Population: Migration Opponent's Paper" (2004), 7–10.

58. Michele R. Pistone, "The Devil in the Details: How Specific Should Catholic Social Teaching Be?," *Journal of Catholic Social Thought* 1 (2004): 507, 532.

59. See Bishop Robert J. Shaheen, D.D., Letter at Maronite Census Official Website, at http://www.maronitecensus.net/Shaheen_letter.htm.

Chapter Eighteen

Conclusion

The Brain Drain, a book of essays published in 1968, notes on its first page that "[t]he drain from Asian nations, particularly Taiwan and [South] Korea, is most serious."[1] In the years immediately before 1968, Taiwan and South Korea had already begun a long period of outstanding economic performance. For example, despite the "serious" drain both countries suffered in 1968 and before, in the typical year of 1968 the economies of South Korea and Taiwan grew at a rate well more than double the long-term growth rate for the United States, the chief destination for elite immigrants. After 1968, growth in South Korea and Taiwan accelerated, despite the continued emigration of many educated citizens.[2] The cumulative effect of such growth is mind-boggling. Real Gross Domestic Product in Taiwan, for example, grew *fifty* times, from approximately $6 billion a year in the 1950s to $300 billion a year in the 1990s.[3] And South Korea's gains were similar, as it emerged as the "fastest growing economy in the world."[4] Once poorer than its neighbor to the north, by 2002 South Korea's per capita income was *twenty times* that of North Korea.

For the entire forty-year period of 1960 to 2000, these "Asian Tigers" of South Korea and Taiwan—identified in the 1960s as twin victims of the world's "most serious" cases of the suspected economic plague known as "brain drain"—were among the best growing economies in the world.[5] The rate of their economic growth is particularly remarkable given that in the 1960s, "South Korea was no richer than the Sudan, and Taiwan was about as poor as [the Congo]"[6]—the two African states, having stagnated or worse over the same time period, being still among the poorest in the world.[7]

This record of incredible success in two countries that all along suffered from what are certainly two of the world's most dangerous geopolitical situations, should—at the very least—give pause to any advocate of restricting STEP OUT migration. The numerous aspects of STEP OUT migration that positively affect sending countries—the knowledge transfers, the remittances, the technological optimization, and so on—likewise should give pause, as should the increasing globalization of the world economy and the resulting increased utility of skills uniquely possessed by STEP OUT migrants. Similar pause should be given by the many technological changes that have occurred in the last four decades, many of which allow migrants an unprecedented opportunity to assist their home countries, and by the increased awareness of how dependent economic growth is on the existence of supportive governmental policies. Finally, for Roman Catholics, Catholic social teaching's increased emphasis on the importance of the right of economic initiative and increased awareness of how it can be stifled also should, in light of all these developments, create an opportunity for reflection on the appropriateness of maintaining a policy of opposition to STEP OUT migration.

In our view, at the end of all this reflection, the appropriate action for the Church would be to abandon its policy of opposition to STEP OUT migration. That policy represents a prudential judgment based on a specific factual understanding that time has rendered obsolete; no one has ever contended that opposition to STEP OUT migration represents a fundamental principle of the Church. As Catholic social teaching recognizes, all such prudential judgments are contingent on specific circumstances, and are appropriately subject to reassessment when those circumstances or the interpretation of them changes. At one time, it was "clear" that STEP OUT migrants could not contribute to their home countries and that "brain drain" damaged the common good; at present, due largely though not exclusively to a variety of new developments, this clarity is lacking. Catholic social teaching's position on STEP OUT migration must reconcile itself to these new developments. In so doing, it will in turn have an opportunity to reconcile itself with the deeper pro-immigrant strains of Church tradition and teaching.

It is our hope that making this change will spur the Church to articulate and proclaim with even more confidence and vigor those principles and policies that will maximize the benefits of STEP OUT migration. Perhaps, then, in forty years a new book will be written; perhaps it will be called "STEP OUT Migration," using a well-known acronym of the time to describe a phenomenon that the young people are surprised to hear once was called "brain drain." The book may note that migrants from Sudan and the Congo are now returning to their home countries, as their Korean and Taiwanese counterparts had begun to do more than fifty years before.[8] The book may discuss what the Congo's fifty-fold GDP increase has meant in practical terms—that, as previously happened in South Korea, expected lifespan increased 50 percent, widespread hunger became unthinkable, and education became the birthright of all. Perhaps the book might even discuss how the Congo's vastly improved medical infrastructure and increased wealth allow it to take advantage of the latest medical innovations, such as the AIDS vaccine invented by the first Sudanese Nobel laureate, a biologist who migrated to the United States during the first decade of the third millennium, on the very day that the Church modified its policy toward migrants like her.

In truth, for the Congo, for Sudan, and for many countries like them, the road from the present to this imagined future will be a long and hard one. Amending the Church's position on STEP OUT migration will not immediately make the road any easier. We all recall the saying of the Chinese sage who said, "A journey of a thousand miles begins with a single step." Less well known is the remark of the sage's sarcastic brother, who responded, "Sure, as long as you're facing in the right direction." In too many places, despite many determined and courageous individual efforts, the thousand-mile journey the grandfather set forth on in 1960 is now the grandson's two-thousand-mile journey—"conditions have become *notably worse*."[9] The heart recoils at the implications. Clearly, on the road to development, too many countries started in the wrong direction. Catholic social teaching's opposition to STEP OUT migration was born in another era and echoes the development policies of the past. It is time to face this fact forthrightly, and turn the social teaching on this specific issue in a new direction. STEP OUT migration need not be endorsed by the Church, but—on the current evidence and in light of new developments—it should not be disfavored, either. Revising the current policy is the right step.

NOTES

1. Walter Adams, "Introduction," in *The Brain Drain* 1, ed. Walter Adams (New York: Macmillan Company, 1968): 1.

2. B. R. Mitchell, *International Historical Statistics: Africa, Asia & Oceania, 1750–1993*, 3rd ed. (London: Macmillan Reference, 1998): 1,032, 1,037.

3. Lawrence J. Lau, *Taiwan as a Model for Economic Development* (Oakland; ICS Press, 2002), 4, available at http://www.stanford.edu/%7Eljlau/Presentations/Presentations/021004.PDF.

4. Jong-Wha Lee, *Economic Growth and Human Development in the Republic of Korea, 1945–1992*, Occasional Paper 24, available at http://hdr.undp.org/docs/publications/ocational_papers/oc24aa.htm.

5. See World Bank Group, *The East Asian Miracle: Economic Growth and Public Policy* (New York: Oxford University Press, 1993), 27–29 (noting post-1960 economic growth records of South Korea and Taiwan are exemplary even judged against other successful East Asian economies); see also Shahid Yusuf, "The East Asian Miracle at the Millenium," in *Rethinking the East Asian Miracle*, eds. Joseph E. Stiglitz and Shahid Yusuf (Washington, D.C.: World Bank, 2001): 1, 2–3 (indicating that, from 1973 to 1996, South Korea's annual growth rate of real gross domestic product per capita was, at 6.8 percent, more than four times that of the United States, and that the growth rate of South Korea and Taiwan exceeded that of the United States even from 1996–2001, when the U.S. experienced a period of unusually high growth and the Asian countries suffered, in the late 1990s, from a deep regional financial crisis).

216   *Chapter Eighteen*

6. "Remarks of Ambassador Alfonso T. Yuchengco before the Columbia University Graduate School of Business, Silfen Leadership Series," printed in American Business Competitiveness, *BusinessWorld*, July 2, 2002. In the quotation in the text above, the reference to the Congo is bracketed because the Ambassador actually referred to Zaire, which is now known as the Democratic Republic of the Congo.

7. International Bank for Reconstruction and Development, *World Development Indicators* (Washington, D.C.: World Bank, 2000), at Table 1.4 (showing a *negative* per capita growth rate of 3.8 percent for the Democratic Republic of the Congo and negative 0.2 percent for Sudan for the years 1965–1998). Many other nations could have been selected, with similar effect, to make the unfortunate comparison with Taiwan and South Korea. For example, "[f]orty years ago, Ghana and the Republic of Korea had virtually the same income per capita. By the early 1990s Korea's income per capita was six times higher than Ghana's." World Bank, *World Development Report: Knowledge for Development* (Washington, D.C.: World Bank, 1998–1999), 1. In fact, "the sad reality is that Ghana is about as poor today as it was forty-three years ago at independence." William Easterly, *The Elusive Quest for Growth: Economists' Adventures and Misadventures in the Tropics* (Cambridge: The MIT Press, 2001), 44. Indeed, in the whole of sub-Saharan Africa, "most people are as poor today as they were three decades ago." Jan Hogendorn and Robert Christiansen, "Perspectives on the Economic Experience of Two Countries of Sub-Saharan Africa: Ghana and Malawi from the 1960s to the 1980s," in *The Wealth of Nations in the Twentieth Century: The Policies and Institutional Determinants of Economic Development*, ed. Ramon H. Myers (Stanford: Hoover Institution Press, 1996): 230, 230. See Benjamin M. Friedman, *The Moral Consequences of Economic Growth* (New York: Alfred A. Knopf, 2005), 299 (noting that because of its economic growth, "life expectancy [in South Korea] is now seventy-two years for men and seventy-nine years for women," while in much of economically unsuccessful Africa life expectancy is less than fifty years).

8. Anne Marie Gaillard and Jacques Gaillard, *International Migration of the Highly Qualified: A Bibliographic and Conceptual Itinerary* (Staten Island: Center for Migration Studies, 1998), 27 (noting that Korea and Taiwan are among "the champions of the 'brain return'" that began in earnest by the 1980s).

9. Pope John Paul II, *Sollicitudo Rei Socialis* (1987), sec. 16 (emphasis in original); see also id. at sec. 13 (stating that the "situation has noticeably worsened" for "many millions" found "in many parts of the world"). Indeed, economists agree that many countries today are about as poor or poorer than they were when the U.N.'s first "Development Decade" was inaugurated more than forty years ago. See Easterly, *The Elusive Quest for Growth*, 60–61, 64 (stating that, even excluding the worst cases, which tend to be omitted from statistical surveys because their economic performance is so poor that they cannot "keep statistical offices running," as a whole "[t]he poorest three-fifths of countries have had nearly zero or slightly negative growth of income per person since 1981," and that "[f]or the whole period 1960 to 1999, the poorest countries did significantly worse than the rich countries, with the poorest two-fifths barely mastering positive growth"; moreover, in poor countries, the minimum per capita income was actually "lower in 1998 than in 1950"); World Bank, *Can Africa Claim the 21st Century?* (Washington, D.C.: World Bank, 2000) (noting that many African countries are economically weaker than they were when they gained independence in the 1960s).

Appendix A

Catholic Social Teaching
and Political Discourse

The foundational principles of Catholic social teaching include "human dignity," "the common good," "solidarity," and "subsidiarity." All of these terms or the concepts they embody are increasingly being used in political speech, sometimes in ways that make the allusion to Catholic social teaching evident. President George W. Bush, in particular, employs Catholic social teaching terms quite regularly. Mark J. Rozell, "'The Catholic Vote?' No Such Thing," *Pittsburgh Post-Gazette*, August 8, 2004, J1 (stating that President "Bush's speeches are frequently laced with language that is commonly used in Catholic discourse."). His speeches, for example, often "make explicit references to subsidiarity, solidarity and human dignity." Peter O'Driscoll, "Catholic Social Teaching and 'Mindful Makers': The Case for Corporate Accountability," *America*, January 7, 2002, 12. The use of subsidiarity—"a uniquely Catholic principle," Robert K. Vischer, "Subsidiarity as a Principle of Governance: Beyond Devolution," *Indiana Law Review* 35, 2002, 103, 108. See Thomas Massaro, *Living Justice: Catholic Social Teaching in Action* (Franklin: Sheed & Ward, 2000): 128 (stating that the term "was coined by Pope Pius XI . . . in the 1931 encyclical *Quadragesimo Anno*"); *U.S. Bishops' Committee on Migration, One Family Under God*, 23 n.2 (U.S. Catholic Conference, 1995) (tracing doctrine of subsidiarity "back to the teachings of Thomas Aquinas")—is particularly telling. In Catholic social teaching, "[t]he principle of subsidiarity calls for the establishment of *intermediary groups* between individuals and the state, and means that the higher level (the state) should never intervene when economic and political realities can be handled adequately on the local level." Marvin L. Krier Mich, *Catholic Social Teaching and Movements* (Mystic: Twenty-Third Publications, 1998): 82. The word is well known in Europe; see, e.g., Magnus Linklater, "I Side with the Yanks: My Beautiful Friendship with Europe Has Been Marred," *Times of London*,

July 17, 2003, Features 18 (establishing his European credentials, the author states that he is "just about capable of holding my own on subsidiarity"), but much less so in the United States—indeed, the popular word processing program we are using to type this book insists "subsidiarity" does not exist, as do many dictionaries (especially those published more than ten years ago). Yet, "the Catholic concept of subsidiarity" was one of the primary tools of George W. Bush's 2000 presidential campaign. Franklin Foer, "Spin Doctrine," the *New Republic*, June 5, 2000, 18. Indeed, his "faith-based initiative," under which care of the poor and needy is delegated to grassroots faith-based organizations, is grounded on the principle. Adam Clymer, "Bush Aggressively Courts Catholic Voters for 2004," *New York Times*, June 1, 2001, A14 (noting that during the 2000 presidential campaign President George W. Bush's message of "compassionate conservatism" was compared to Catholic social teachings); Fred Barnes, "George W. Bush's Catholic Problem," the *Weekly Standard*, March 13, 2000, 15 (commenting that George W. Bush understood that his policy of "compassionate conservatism" was fundamentally in line with Catholic social teaching and the principle of subsidiarity). See also Vischer, "Subsidiarity as a Principle of Governance," 105 (collecting uses of "subsidiarity" by other politicians).

President Bush also often employs the cornerstone term of Catholic social teaching, "human dignity"—see, e.g., George W. Bush, "George W. Bush Delivers Remarks to Urban Leaders," (FDCH Political Transcripts, July 16, 2003); George W. Bush, "George W. Bush and President Mogae of Botswana Deliver Remarks," (FDCH Political Transcripts, July 10, 2003); George W. Bush, "George W. Bush Delivers Remarks on Early Childhood Development," (FDCH Political Transcripts, July 7, 2003); George W. Bush, "George W. Bush Delivers Weekly Radio Address," (FDCH Political Transcripts, July 5, 2003); Jeffrey Sachs, "Weapons of Mass Salvation," the *Economist*, October 24, 2002, Special Report 2—sometimes more often than the much more common "human rights." Samantha Powers, "Force Full," the *New Republic*, March 3, 2003, 28–29 (noting that the Bush Administration's National Security Strategy employed "human dignity" more often than it used "human rights"). In a State of the Union Address, President Bush has even invoked "human dignity," as a foundational principle, exactly the way it is utilized by the Catholic Church. See President George Bush, "2002 State of the Union Address," (Washington, D.C., January 29, 2002), available at http://www.whitehouse.gov/news/releases/2002/01/20020129-11.html (stating that the "nonnegotiable demands of human dignity [include] the rule of law; limits on the power of the state; respect for women; private property; free speech; equal justice; and religious tolerance"). "Human dignity" also is often used in bioethics debates. See, e.g., *Human Cloning and Human Dignity: The Report of the President's Council on Bioethics* (2002).

President Bill Clinton also often employed Catholic social teaching principles. As the spokesman for the U.S. Conference of Catholic Bishops explained, the language President Bill Clinton used is "very clearly the language
of Catholic social teaching." Gustav Niebuhr, "Presidential Pulpit Has Ecu-
menical Echo," *Washington Post*, March 10, 1994, A1 (noting in particular
President Clinton's use of the principle of the "common good"). Additionally,
the language of Catholic social teaching is used internationally, especially in
Europe, where "[i]t has had considerable impact on policy and practice
mainly because of the influence of Christian Democratic parties." *The Oxford
Companion to Christian Thought*, eds. Adrian Hastings et al. (Oxford: Oxford
University Press, 2000), 675, 676. The Treaty of Maastricht, for example, ex-
pressly makes "subsidiarity" an organizing principle of the European Union.
"Treaty Establishing the European Community," February 7, 1992, art. 3b,
Common Market Law Review 63 (1992) 573, 590. Similarly, the draft of the
European Union's currently moribund constitution includes mentions of "hu-
man dignity" and "solidarity" as foundational values, and "subsidiarity" as a
fundamental principle. See *Draft Treaty Establishing Constitution for Europe,
Title I, Art. I-2; Title III, Art. I-9(1), (3)*.

Appendix B

A Short History of the American Catholic Church's Programmatic Support for Immigrant Communities

The American Catholic Church's social network for immigrants—"a sweeping program of immigrant uplift," (Charles R. Morris, *American Catholic: The Saints and Sinners Who Built America's Most Powerful Church* (New York: Times Books, 1997): 110) has its roots in the mid-nineteenth century, when large groups of Catholic immigrants first began to enter the United States. The network grew so that, by the 1920s, representatives from various Catholic Church dioceses were regularly meeting ships as immigrants arrived at U.S. ports, with the representatives holding signs in various languages. Morris, *American Catholic*, 132. The network provided "[s]ame-language workers [who] would assist Catholic immigrants through processing, help with housing and job referrals, and see that children were enrolled in parochial schools." Morris, *American Catholic*, 132.

The tradition of providing support to immigrants continues today, and is evidenced by the Church's allocation of significant resources to support the pastoral care and rights of migrants directly and through advocacy. Cardinal Anthony Bevilacgua, "Ministry to the World's Uprooted People," *Origins* 14 (1985) 517, 519–22. The Church is organized on all levels to accomplish this task. On the local level, the bishops require parishes to engage in "active pastoral outreach." National Conference of Catholic Bishops, *Together A New People: Pastoral Statement on Migrants and Refugees* (U.S. Catholic Conference, 1987) 14 (approved November 8, 1986). In doing so, local churches and diocesan offices assist migrants to meet their basic needs, including spiritual needs, food, shelter, education and related services. It also is recommended that parishes appoint immigrants to the parish council and "provide scholarships to poor immigrant children." National Conference of Catholic Bishops, *Together A New People*, 15–16. Attempts to communicate with immigrants in their own language are highly recommended. National Conference of

Catholic Bishops, *Welcoming the Stranger Among Us: Unity in Diversity* (U.S. Catholic Conference, 2000) 36 (noting that "[s]pecial efforts to acquire the languages of the new immigrants by all church ministers constitute an essential, concrete step towards a full and effective welcome"); National Conference of Catholic Bishops, *Together a New People*, 15–16 (explaining that clergy are encouraged to learn the languages of their parishioners and integrate those languages into "prayers and hymns for special liturgies"). For example, in the numerous parishes of the Los Angeles archdiocese, "Mass is said in more than fifty different languages [and] some fifty-five national groups are served by priests from their own countries of origin." National Conference of Catholic Bishops, *Welcoming the Stranger Among Us*, 13. This emphasis on language reflects a longstanding policy of the Church in the United States. In the 1800s and early 1900s the policy was often effectuated through the establishment of "national" parishes, in which Germans were free to pray in German at St. Boniface's, Italians could pray in Italian at St. Anthony's, and the Irish at St. Patrick's, speaking American, could use however heavy a brogue as they desired. See Morris, *American Catholic*, 89; National Conference of Catholic Bishops, *Welcoming the Stranger Among Us*, 7; U.S. Bishops' Committee on Migration, *One Family Under God* (U.S. Catholic Conference 1995), 8.

In addition to activities of local parishes, dioceses are also encouraged to meet special needs of ethnic and cultural groups in their communities. Thus, parishes are expected to provide—and do provide—"funds to support special projects to meet the needs of various ethnic groups: [such as] refugee resettlement, family reunification services for refugees and immigrants, legal services for those in need of assistance with immigration laws, [and] assistance on naturalization." National Conference of Catholic Bishops, *Together a New People*, 17. In the Archdiocese of Philadelphia, for example, these various responsibilities are performed by, among other groups, Catholic Charities–Catholic Social Services of the Archdiocese of Philadelphia, the Office for Pastoral Care for Migrants and Refugees, and the St. Vincent de Paul Society. The mission of the Office for Pastoral Care of Migrants and Refugees is to facilitate "full participation of immigrants, refugees and migrants in the Church through identifying current needs and resources and collaborating with parishes and regions to develop strategies to assist in the process of welcoming and integration." Philadelphia also has thirteen immigrant-focused apostolates serving communities of newcomers. See http://www.archdiocese-phl.org/offices/opcmr.htm. In addition, in dioceses across the country with large numbers of immigrants, special apostolates have been created to work on behalf of many immigrant groups, including those from Albania, Cambodia, China, Croatia, Cuba, the Czech Republic,

Ethiopia, the Phillipines, Germany, Haiti, Latin America, Laos, Hungary, India, Italy, Japan, Korea, Latvia, Lithuania, Poland, Portugal, Russia, and Vietnam. United States Catholic Conference, *Directory of Pastoral Care of Migrants, Refugees, and People on the Move* (U.S. Catholic Conference, 1987): 9–187. The Diocese of Honolulu alone has "ministries to Chinese, Filipino, Hispanic, Japanese, Korean, Samoan, Tongan and Vietnamese Catholics." National Conference of Catholic Bishops, *Welcoming the Stranger Among Us,* 13.

On a national level, an organization created by the United States Conference of Catholic Bishops—Migration and Refugee Services ("MRS")—is charged with carrying out the church's pastoral and social policy on immigration issues. Within MRS, the Office for the Pastoral Care of Migrants and Refugees responds to the spiritual needs of migrants and refugees; the Office of Migration and Refugee Policy advocates for fair and just public policy towards immigrants; and the Office for Refugee Programs administers programs of welcome and service to refugees resettled in the United States by the Church. *See* http://www.usccb.org/mrs/. In addition to MRS, the Catholic bishops also established the Catholic Legal Immigration Network, which trains lawyers around the country to assist immigrants with their legal needs, provides direct legal representation to immigrants who are held in the custody of the U.S. immigration authorities, and advocates for fair immigration policies. *See* http://www.cliniclegal.org/.

Index

About the Authors

Michele Pistone is a professor of Law and Director of the Clinical Program at Villanova University School of Law. She also directs and teaches the Clinic for Asylum, Refugee and Emigrant Services (CARES). In 2006 Professor Pistone received a Fulbright scholarship to help create a refugee law clinic at the University of Malta, and to study refugee law and international migration in Europe and the Mediterranean region. She has published widely in the areas of international migration, refugee and immigration law, and Catholic social teaching. Before teaching at Villanova, Professor Pistone taught in the asylum clinic at the Georgetown University Law Center and served as the Acting Legal Director for a human rights lawyers' group, Human Rights First. Her husband and co-author, **John J. Hoeffner**, is an attorney and a former editor-in-chief of *The Catholic Lawyer*. He has taught appellate litigation at Georgetown University Law Center and practiced at several leading law firms. He also prosecuted civil rights cases while working for the U.S. Department of Justice. Recent publications by him include articles in the *Georgetown Immigration Law Journal*, the *Mediterranean Journal of Human Rights*, and the *Journal of Catholic Social Thought*. The authors maintain a website on skilled migration and other topics at www.stepoutmigration.com. They live in Villanova, Pennsylvania, with their three-year old daughter.